THE ROAD FROM LA STORTA

THE
ROAD
FROM
LA STORTA

PETER-HANS
KOLVENBACH, S.J.,
ON
IGNATIAN
SPIRITUALITY

THE INSTITUTE OF JESUIT SOURCES
SAINT LOUIS

Number 17 in Series II: Modern Scholarly Studies
about the Jesuits in English Translation

Edited by Carl F. Starkloff, S.J.

©2000 The Institute of Jesuit Sources
3601 Lindell Blvd.
St. Louis, MO 63108
Tel.: 314-977-7257
Fax: 314-977-7263
e-mail: IJS@SLU.EDU

Library of Congress Catalogue Card Number 00-135914
ISBN 1-880810-40-9

CONTENTS

SECOND PART
"TO GAIN SOME UNDERSTANDING": ANALYSIS

THIRD PART
CONTEMPLATION IN ACTION: "PRAXIS"

SOURCES OF ESSAYS CONTAINED
IN THIS VOLUME

INTRODUCTION: THE VISION AT LA STORTA

Taken from *CIS*, Vol. XIX, 57, No. 1, 1988, pp. 9-13, with adaptations. A homily in the Church of St. Ignatius, Rome, on the occasion of the anniversary of the vision of La Storta, November 21, 1987.

DO NOT HIDE THE HIDDEN LIFE OF CHRIST

Taken from *CIS*, Vol. XXIV, No. 3, 74, 1993, pp. 11-25, with adaptations.

IGNATIUS OF LOYOLA: EXPERIENCE OF CHRIST

Taken from *CIS*, Vol. XXVIII, 1997, No. 86, pp. 25-37. Originally a conference held in the chapel of the University *La Sapienza* in Rome, 18 December 1996.

THE EASTER EXPERIENCE OF OUR LADY

Taken from *CIS*, Vol. XIX, 58-59, nn. 2-3, pp. 145-163. Originally a talk addressed to the participants of the ninth Ignatian Course, Rome, January 29, 1988.

OUR LADY IN THE SPIRITUAL EXERCISES OF ST. IGNATIUS

Taken from *CIS*, Vol. XVI, 48, No. 1, pp. 11-24. This was a talk addressed to the participants of the eighth Ignatian Course organized in Rome by the Ignatian Centre of Spirituality, February 1, 1985.

THE PASSION ACCORDING TO ST. IGNATIUS

Taken from *CIS*, Vol. XX, 63-64, nn. 1-2. 1990, pp. 63-73.

"CHRIST . . . DESCENDED INTO HELL"

Taken from *CIS*, Vol. XXII, 68, No. 3, 1993, pp. 11-24.

FOOLS FOR CHRIST'S SAKE

Taken from *CIS*, Vol. XX, 63-64, nn. 1-2, pp. 74-91.

A LINGUISTIC INTERPRETATION OF THE SPIRITUAL EXERCISES OF ST. IGNATIUS

Taken from the volume *Fous pour le Christ: sagesse de Maître Ignace*, Bruxelles, Editions Lessius, 1998, pp. 45-61. Original essay: "Le message spirituel á travers les particularités linguistiques des "Exercices Spirituels" de Saint Ignace" (Editor's translation). Originally a conference given at the Pontifical Gregorian University, Rome, March 6, 1997.

LANGUAGE AND ANTHROPOLOGY: THE SPIRITUAL DIARY OF ST. IGNATIUS

Taken from *CIS*, Vol. XXII, 67, No. 2, pp. 9-19. Originally published in French in *Gregorianum*, Vol. 72, fasc. 1, 1991, pp. 211-221.

IMAGES AND IMAGINATION IN THE SPIRITUAL EXERCISES

Taken from *CIS*, Vol. XVIII, 54, No. 1, 1987, pp. 11-32. Originally a talk given to participants of the ninth Ignatian Conference, Rome, June 30, 1986.

THE WORD: A WAY TO GOD ACCORDING TO MASTER IGNATIUS

Taken from *CIS*, Vol. XXV, 77, No. 3, pp. 5 - 24.

THE LETTERS OF ST. IGNATIUS: THEIR CONCLUSION

Taken from *CIS*, Vol. XXIII, 70, No. 2, 1992, pp. 75 - 89, with adaptations.

ON THE EFFECTIVENESS OF THE SPIRITUAL EXERCISES

Taken from *Fous pour le Christ: sagesse de Maître Ignace*, pp. 144-156. Original essay: L' efficacité des "'Exercices Spirituels'" (Editor's translation). Originally published in *Cahiers de spiritualité ignatienne*, Vol. 68, 1993, pp. 221-231.

A CERTAIN PATHWAY TO GOD ("VIA QUAEDAM AD DEUM")

Taken from *CIS*, Vol. XXII, 68, No. 3, 1991, pp. 25-45.

ST. IGNATIUS'S NORMS ON SCRUPLES

Taken from *CIS*, Vol. XXVII, 86, No. 2, 1996, pp. 7-18. An address to the annual Ignatian Course at the Jesuit Curia, Rome, February, 1996.

SOCIAL JUSTICE AND THE SPIRITUAL EXERCISES OF ST. IGNATIUS OF LOYOLA

An address delivered at Our Lady of Lourdes Church, Toronto, November 1, 1998. First published by the Jesuit Centre for Social Faith and Justice, Ottawa, July, 1999.

THE SPIRITUAL EXERCISES AND PREFERENTIAL LOVE FOR THE POOR

Taken from *CIS*, Vol. XV, 45, No. 1, pp. 77-90. An address given to the participants of the seventh Ignatian Course, Rome, February 7, 1984.

THE VOCATION AND MISSION OF THE BROTHER IN THE SOCIETY OF JESUS

Taken from *CIS,* Vol. XXVI, 78, No. 1, pp. 8-18. Adapted from a talk given at Loyola, June 12, 1994 to a commission established to study the vocation of the brothers, in preparation for General Congregation 34.

LAYMEN AND LAYWOMEN IN THE CHURCH OF THE MILLENIUM

Taken from *CIS*, Vol. XXX, 91, No. 2, pp. 23-30. An address given to colleagues in Merida, Venezuela.

CONTEMPORARY EDUCATION IN THE SPIRIT OF ST. IGNATIUS

Taken from *Fous pour le Christ: sagesse de Maître Ignace*, pp. 267-280. Original essay: "Eduquer des hommes et des femmes aujourd'hui dans l'esprit de Saint Ignace" (Editor's translation). A conference given to teachers in Toulouse-Purpan, France, November 26, 1996.

ABBREVIATIONS

AR . . . . *Acta Romana*

Autob. . . . . *The Autobiography of St. Ignatius*

CIS . . . . *Center for Ignatian Spirituality*

Const. . . . . *Constitutions of the Society of Jesus*

Diary . . . . *Spiritual Diary of St. Ignatius*

Dir. . . . . *Directory of the Spiritual Exercises of 1599*

Gen. Ex. . . . . *General Examen*

MI . . . . *Monumenta Ignatiana*

Ratio . . . . *Ratio Studiorum*

The *Spiritual Exercises of St. Ignatius* will always be indicated
throughout the book by the text number in brackets, e.g., [1]. When
the actual text is intended, the name will be in italics, while the
process (e.g., "making the Exercises") will be in ordinary type.

EDITOR'S PREFACE

Among the daunting qualities demanded of the superior general of the Society of Jesus in the *Constitutions*, one reads no requirement that he be an "expert on Ignatian spirituality." Fittingly enough in this light, Father Kolvenbach makes such a disclaimer for himself in the course of the following essays—many of them presented originally as lectures on various occasions. Nonetheless, regardless of any disclaimers, this anthology bears the marks of one deeply steeped in a knowledge and practice of the Spiritual Exercises, in an expertise on the *Constitutions*, and in a striking grasp of the history of the Society of Jesus. Beyond these skills, Father Kolvenbach brings the talents of a linguist and a linguistic philosopher to bear upon several aspects of Ignatian spirituality and on the apostolate of Jesuits.

In assembling the present collection, we found that these writings can be categorized under three headings having deep significance for both Ignatian spirituality and the ministry of the Society of Jesus: prayer and contemplation, analysis of and reflection on Ignatian spirituality, and the "praxis" of "contemplation in action." The essays differ in content, ranging in style from "spiritual" to heavily analytical to practical and pastoral. Thus, readers may wish to choose the sections that they find more congenial: thus, Part One contains more directly "spiritual" discussions, Part Two consists of heavily analytical essays, and Part Three is devoted to articles focusing on pastoral and social issues.

It should be added at once that such an organization is that of the editor of this volume, and not systematically intended by Father Kolvenbach. But it remains our hope that all of the articles express the spiritual and intellectual leadership through which this present superior general of the Society of Jesus exercises his mandate.

The selections have been drawn from several sources, as is indicated at the beginning of each essay. All but four of them have been taken from existing translations, with adjustments intended to suit a North American readership. One of them—"Justice in the Spiritual Exercises"—was delivered in English, and three others have been translated from the French by the editor.

INTRODUCTION:

THE VISION AT LA STORTA

Though we ourselves do not know the exact date of the La Storta experience, St. Ignatius never forgot it. Seven years after that autumn of the year 1537, he writes in his *Spiritual Diary* that he recalls the moment when the Father placed him with his Son bearing the cross.[1] Something of the spiritual confirmation which the Church celebrates today under the image of the Presentation in the Temple of the *Theotokos*, the all-holy woman received in the Holy of Holies, something of such a confirmation in the Spirit is accomplished in the little chapel of La Storta.

On the road to the Eternal City St. Ignatius experiences all the burden of the tensions accumulated in the course of his pilgrimage towards the core of the mystery of God. Interiorly he is still geared towards the Holy Land, but it is Rome which increasingly looms large as the concrete place where the Lord wishes to be favourable to him. For some months now Ignatius is already priest of the Lord, but he has in fact not yet, as priest, celebrated the Eucharist: everything within him urges him on to a priesthood of "apostolate," a priesthood of "gratuity," a priesthood of "radical availability" for whatever mission with which the Vicar of Christ on earth would choose to entrust him. With his "friends in the Lord," Ignatius has already formed a genuine "company" or companionship, although not named for himself. In the ancient monastery of San Pietro in Vivarolo outside Vicenza, the companions had chosen the name "Company of Jesus," so that the Incarnate Word could make use of this apostolic body to carry on his paschal journey through human history. This desire to present "a body for the Spirit" made Ignatius face a whole lot of questions and challenges in the concrete. Through them all he keeps begging of our Lady the grace to be placed by the Divine Majesty, the

---

[1] Part I, no. 22, 23 February 1544.

1

all-powerful Father, with his Son carrying the cross, as a sign of the Spirit's confirmation of his plans and undertakings in the service of the Lord's Church.

St. Ignatius's primary concern at this time is not the Society: he already has a glimpse of its concrete features that will be so different from the religious life of the monks and of the mendicants. Neither are the tensions he brings with him even unto the portals of Rome his major concern; no, not even the conflicts and misunderstandings that await him in the city of the Popes. His only concern, his one passion, remains that of being able to be acceptable to God's Divine Majesty through his constant striving after becoming like Christ, his Son and our Lord, and bearing the cross with him so that the world may have life to the full. "And so," writes Ribadeneira, "those who in response to a divine call join this religious family should understand that they are called not to the Order of Ignatius, but to the Society and service of the Son of God, Jesus Christ our Lord, and . . . should follow *his* standard, take up with joy *his* cross and fix their gaze on Jesus, the one leader. . . ."[2]

On the Via Cassia, in the village called La Storta, St. Ignatius receives for himself and his companions, through the intercession of our Lady, the spiritual confirmation of his longing in love and of his discerning prayer when God the Father places him with his Son bearing the cross, so that he may serve him in his Church. This is not a call, not a vocation: it is a mission, in which is fulfilled the prayer of Christ himself to his Father: "Father, they belonged to you, and you gave them to me" (Jn 17:6). In the spiritual event of La Storta, with its utterly simple divine word of "being placed *with* the Son," echoes anew the mystery of the Covenant—God is *with* his people; and the paschal promise, "I shall be *with* you till the end of the ages," is revealed in its fullness. But La Storta confirms above all the Eucharistic spirituality of St. Ignatius, for it is within the Eucharistic prayer *sereno et propitio vultu respicere digneris* (. . . look kindly and with favor on this our offering . . .) that is given the divine assurance: *Ego ero vobis Romae propitius* (I shall be favourable to you in Rome). This spiritual confirmation of being placed with the Son and of being sent by the Father to serve becomes part and parcel of

---

[2] P. Ribadaneira, *Vita Ignatii Loyolae*: *MI*, Font. Narr, IV, p. 273.

all Ignatius's activity, of his plans and his directives, of his style of service and his way of proceeding. The grace of La Storta is bestowed at the moment of those crucial decisions that will mark the Roman sojourn of Ignatius—that is, at the moment in which all the inner drive of the Spiritual Exercises with its "offerings of greater value and of more importance" [97] must be transformed eucharistically into the concrete "this" of specific choices, the "here and now" of the task to be actually accomplished. But St. Ignatius goes ahead of the whole Society and of every Jesuit, with the Son bearing the Cross, in this gift of the Spirit of making life decisions and concrete choices such as the Lord himself made—of making them in him, with him and through him in the here-and-now of today, plunging ourselves into the work that must be done in the measure of our strength and of our possibilities. But in making these concrete choices we must never forget the event of La Storta that is their source of inspiration.

The vision of La Storta has not been given to us so that we might stop to gaze at it. No, it is the light in which the Jesuit regards the whole world. This vision which opens out on to the very mystery of the Trinity in its work of love for the salvation of mankind—indeed, on to the mystery of the Divine Majesty that nothing can constrain or impede—places us, in virtue of this ineffable mystery, with the Incarnate Word who took the form of servant and slave in the well-defined and limited reality of our history. To be open to reality in all its extension, and at the same time to be committed to what is most concrete and limited, is the divine mystery of the Christ of La Storta. With this kind of Christ has the Father placed St. Ignatius and every one of us to share existentially in the Incarnation primarily by being rooted in the Church; this ecclesial rootedness was always for Ignatius the mark of fidelity to the Lord of La Storta.

It is well known that Fr. Arrupe, whose task it was to discern the will of God's Divine Majesty for the Society in a period of upheaval, had a great devotion to St. Ignatius's mystical experience at La Storta. He stated frequently with insistence that, if the Society—indeed, every Jesuit—wishes today to receive fruitfully the gift of this experience for the good of the Church and of the world, it must make it a point to place itself courageously in the third class of men with a freedom with respect to everything, to its works and its enterprises, to its prestige and its number of members, to its priorities and even to its very apostolic drive and thrust. Too often the Society lingers on in the second class of persons, [cf. 149-157] whereas it is only through that freedom in love (of the third class), which must be constantly renewed and won afresh, that God's Divine Majesty can make use of the Society by placing it with his Son for the paschal redemption of the world. In his spiritual testament Fr. Arrupe prays, with trust in the graces of which the memory is cherished at La Storta, to the Virgin Mother of God, as did Ignatius, that all of us may be placed with her Son in a concerted effort at spiritual and apostolic renewal so that the greater glory of God may be all in all (1 Cor 15:28).

PART ONE

"SEEING THE PERSONS":

CONTEMPLATION

ONE

DO NOT HIDE THE HIDDEN LIFE OF CHRIST

Introduction: The Importance of the Childhood
Meditations in the Spiritual Exercises

We all know that Ignatius's great visions included in the Spiritual Exercises for prayer during the second week are accompanied by scenes from what we call the gospel of the infancy of Jesus. The contemplation Ignatius proposes for the first day focuses in fact on the incarnation [101] and embraces the whole course of the annunciation to Our Lady [102]. For this same day he also proposes the history of the nativity [110] from the journey from Nazareth to Bethlehem [111] to what happened in the cave of the nativity [112]. For the second day he proposes two mysteries of the infancy gospel which are an extension of the contemplation of the nativity: the presentation in the temple and the flight into Egypt [132]. The object of the prayer of the third day is the Lord's hidden life: "The obedience of the Child Jesus to his parents" in Nazareth and "The finding of the Child Jesus in the temple" [134]. The introduction to the fourth day and the meditation on the Two Standards clearly indicate that the subject Ignatius proposes for contemplation has a definite orientation [135-136]. The Lord lived in the service of his Father in the obedience of a home, a family—this is the first state—and "in the exclusive service of his eternal Father" [135] he renounced this home, this family; this is the second state. The point now is to pursue the project "of seeking to serve God, which is the end" [169] and only after having done this, of discerning in what state of life, in what specific conditions we should do this. "To choose that which is better" [149]: for the fourth day Ignatius proposes the meditation on the Two Standards [136] and the one on the Three Classes [149]. But the prayer still dwells in the environment of the gospel of the childhood. It is only on the fifth day that Christ our Lord's departure from

Nazareth for the river Jordan and his baptism are proposed [158]. Ignatius specifies that the question of choices is treated only "from the contemplation on the fifth day" [163] and he lists a whole series of scenes from the childhood gospel—the visitation of Our Lady to Saint Elizabeth, the shepherds, the circumcision of the Child Jesus, the three kings "and also others" [162]—in case one may wish to extend this prayer.

This link between the great Ignatian meditations of the second week and the gospel of the childhood appears quite normal and even inevitable. Father Karl Rahner stresses the felicitous association of the contemplation of the Incarnation with that of the Annunciation. Separating the truth of the incarnation of the Word of God from the story of the annunciation means falling fatally into the danger of diminishing this truth, and turning it into a purely metaphysical abstract speculation. Thanks to this close association, the contemplation of the Incarnation of God retains its existential nature and encourages us to truly progress in the concrete knowledge of this mystery.

Two Reasons for Omitting the Childhood Meditations

This insistence on the mysteries of the childhood gospel is not shared by all those who give the Spiritual Exercises. One quite frequently comes across commentaries on Ignatius's work which reduce the stories about the child Jesus to a minimum or do not mention them at all. There are two reasons in particular for this phenomenon.

1. In the first place the apostle Peter situates the beginning of the mystery of Christ after his baptism by John (Ac 10:37-38). Those who are with the Lord "from the outset" (Jn 15:27) are not his childhood companions but apostles who participate in Christ's mission. Luke takes the same stand in the prologues to the gospel and the Acts. Consequently [these commentators] pass over the Lord's hidden years in silence out of a sense of fidelity to the scriptures and start directly with his public life. That is, they associate his incarnation with his baptism and the Two Standards with the temptations in the desert.

2. The second and most important reason is that the childhood gospel cannot be considered "history" in the same way as the story of the Lord's passion and resurrection. After all that modern exegesis tells us about the

Magi's visit, is it still right to propose it for contemplation on a par, for example, with the story of the last supper? Undoubtedly the popular piety of both believers and non-believers is better acquainted with the manger than with the well of Sychar. But if, as Ignatius wished, we are to acquire "an intimate knowledge of Our Lord, who has become man for me" [104], ought we not set aside the beginnings of Luke's and Matthew's gospels in order to pray the prologue of John's gospel? Since Ignatius himself keeps rigorously to evangelical history, barely admitting the ass and the maid [111] which come from other sources—Jacobo da Voragine's *Flos Sanctorum*—are we not following his spirit if we omit from the gospel account what we now know to be imagery and imagination? To sum up, we must not give equal value to the stories of Jesus' childhood and all the other parts of the gospel. For the author of the Spiritual Exercises, as for the men of his time, the childhood gospel was made of the same stuff as what follows. If today we can no longer uphold or defend this presupposition we must renounce these texts with their apocryphal auras and replace them with the history of the mysteries of the Lord's public life, which simply means returning to the original kerygma of the apostles. Thus, we meditate on such texts as: "Jesus . . . a man commended to you by God by the miracles and portents and signs that God worked through Him . . . You killed Him . . . God raised Him to life . . . ." (Ac 2:22 ff.). To obtain "the knowledge of the true life exemplified in the sovereign and true Commander" [139], we must listen to the testimony of these men who knew the Lord "from the time when John was baptising until the day when he was taken up from us" (Ac 1:22). At all events the data given on the thirty "hidden years" are scarce and, at the beginning, inconsistent. There is a clear break between the early Jesus and Jesus on his mission. With Mark and John, let us leave the Lord's hidden years in the shadows and base the second week, according to Ignatius's own expression, on "the solid foundation of facts" to find in it "greater spiritual relish and fruit" [2].

> To conclude this *"status quaestionis,"* let us allow a modern author to speak on the subject of the use of the gospel in the Spiritual Exercises. Modern research on the history of the gospels' tradition and redaction suggests that we follow only one of the four gospels . . . . The third gospel seems to fit best in a first approach to the second Ignatian week, for Luke is the gospel of Jesus' journey and

the way of the following of Jesus. A continuous reading of the
gospel from its beginning—Lk 1:1 ff., or better Lk 3:1 ff.—(that
means without the birth narratives) seems to be much more
effective than a premature choice of texts or themes fixed in
advance by the retreat-giver.[1]

The difficulty of this orientation does not lie in the suppression of almost
half of the "mysteries" Ignatius chose for the second week, nor is the problem
one of a certain freedom concerning the letter of the Exercises, especially
since Ignatius himself anticipates the need to shorten or lengthen them [4]. The
question is whether one can acquire "the knowledge of the true life exemplified
in the sovereign and true Commander" [139], without meditating on the
history of Jesus' childhood.

A Lacuna in the Knowledge of Christ
Without the Childhood Meditations

The author of the Exercises did not present the problem in these terms.
For him—as for us—no life begins at the age of thirty. Ignatius simply
followed the complete sequence of the mysteries of Christ in the 181 chapters
composed by Ludolph the Carthusian (1350) for his *Vita Iesu Christi*, which
Ignatius was given to read by his sister-in-law when he was convalescing in
the castle of Loyola and the reading of which determined his conversion. The
originality of the author of the Exercises lies in his selections from the
Carthusian's abundant material. Ignatius leads those following the Exercises
from the point of contemplating the mysteries to the point of the decision to
appropriate Christ's choices, revealed in his mysteries. Ignatius carefully
chooses the mysteries which are likely to lead to this election.
    Although the third and fourth weeks must necessarily contemplate the
paschal mystery in its entirety since no further choice is possible and the
election needs to be confirmed in Christ crucified and risen again, the

---

[1] Francesco Rossi de Gasperis, "*Lectio divina* in the Exercises," in *The Word of God in
the Spiritual Exercises*, Centrum Ignatianum Spiritualitatis, Rome, 1979, p. 90.

selection of the second week mysteries implies a certain freedom and is made in function of this election. Ignatius distinguishes two categories of persons who have quite different elections to make. Some people are already engrossed in the cares and obligations of their condition in life [19]; they can learn from certain mysteries of the life of Christ how "to amend and reform" [189] their state of life. But there also are people who can still truly elect a state of life [20]. For these people Ignatius himself takes the liberty of reversing the gospel order: he first has them contemplate the obedient Jesus obeying within his family, and then Jesus exclusively obeying his Father in the temple [134], thus preparing for the considerations on the states of life on the fourth day [135]. This is only one example of the freedom Ignatius advocates when choosing the mysteries of the life of Christ, which should be selected in such a way that one may "profit more greatly from them" [209]. But this freedom of choice only works within the mysteries of Jesus' childhood [162], within the mysteries of his public life (162), and within the paschal mystery [209]. Nothing in the Spiritual Exercises seems to favor the contemplation of the mysteries of Christ's public life alone in function of the choice or renewal of a religious or lay apostolic life. On the contrary, Ignatius develops the presentation of the mysteries of Jesus' childhood so personally that our knowledge of Christ would be incomplete without these contemplations which occupy the days preceding the election. What would be lacking?

The Childhood and the Hidden Life of Christ
in the Spiritual Exercises.
The Child in the History of Spirituality

First of all, the child Jesus, *el niño*, would be lacking. The child in the manger has moved people from the origins of Christianity and, even in our century of secularization and de-mythologizing, Christmas still charms them. One can leave out everything concerning the mystery of the incarnation except for the guileless image of the baby Jesus between the ox and the ass. It doesn't matter whether this story is true; it deserves to be invented. And yet this wonder-filled atmosphere throws shadows over faith in the incarnation instead of opening it up to discovery, and the learned are put off by this faith in "God become a child." Marcion, in his time, already eliminated the tales of Jesus' childhood in order to deny the disconcerting and indeed scandalous reality of Christ's flesh. Later, certain apocryphal books deprived the child Jesus of his childhood, presenting him as a baby who accomplished miracles or who already taught like a master. The French school stressed the "four lowlinesses" of a child: bodily smallness, indigence and dependence on others, subjection, and uselessness.[2] To sum up, according to Bérulle childhood is "the vilest and most abject state of human nature, after that of death."[3] Bérulle so stresses both the child's shameful impotence and the extreme destitution of his childhood "in which the Holy Spirit is silent," "in which Jesus is hidden and captive within us, and the living Adam reigns" that he invites us to "rejoice with the angels and saints in the presence of God" when finally, having reached the age of reason, "Jesus and his spirit are freed."[4] Not that Bérulle refuses to smile in front of the manger, but the direction in which this mystery leads is an austere one: it teaches the annihilation of self, the total loss of the use of one's spirit and implies no longer belonging to oneself. Is not this observation of the French school paramount to the wish to be considered "in-sane" [167] for Christ, who was the first to be considered such, rather than that of being wise and prudent in this world? Is this how Ignatius makes us find the child in the crib? It is not easy to guess Ignatius's vision concerning Jesus' childhood. Nothing is explicit, as it would be in a treatise; everything is suggested through clues which have to be discovered under words and expressions.

The Child in the Spirituality of the Spiritual Exercises

a. The Christological Attributions

If we start from the Christological attributions, it is easy to see that the title "Christ Our Lord" dominates the whole of the Exercises. In the text itself

---

[2] Charles de Condren, "Considérations," pp. 58-62, cit. in Henri Bremond, *Histoire littéraire du sentiment religieux en France*, t. III, Paris, 1925, p. 520.

[3] Pierre de Bérulle, "Œuvres," in H. Brémond, *op.cit.*, p. 525.

[4] Pierre de Bérulle, "Lettres," in H. Brémond, *op.cit.*, p. 519.

forty-nine out of sixty-eight attributions of Christ belong to the group "Christ our Lord," "Christ" and "Our Lord." The same is true of the "mysteries of the life of Christ" [261 ff.]: here, because of biblical references, Ignatius is not as free in his choice of Christ's titles. Forty-one out of fifty-seven attributions belong to the group "Christ our Lord," "Christ" and "our Lord." Consequently the fact that we read in the "mysteries" [262 ff.], "the birth of Christ our Lord" [264, 265], "the conception of Christ our Lord" [262], "how Christ our Lord returned from Egypt" [270], "the life of Christ Our Lord from the age of twelve to the age of thirty" [271] and "Christ goes up to the temple at the age of twelve" [272] is not surprising. For Ignatius Christ is always "the eternal Word" [130], this "eternal Word Incarnate" [109], "the Second Person" [102]. Jesus is never dissociated from the fullness of his Trinitarian being which sends him into our world for our salvation. Of course it is through the historical Jesus that we reach Christ Our Lord, but it is always Christ in his glory who is contemplated through the gestures and words of the historical Christ. Consequently the attribution of "the Child Jesus" is limited. In the "mysteries" we find "the babe lying in the manger" [265], "They circumcised the child Jesus" [266], "They returned the child to his mother" [266], "They take the child Jesus to the temple" [268] for "the presentation of the child Jesus" [268], but then "Herod wished to kill the child Jesus" [269] so "the child had to be taken" [269] and "brought back" [270] to save him. In the text Ignatius invites us to "see" "the child Jesus after his birth" [114] and to contemplate "the obedience of the Child Jesus to his parents in Nazareth" [134].

Christ's presence is entirely passive in all the texts which explicitly mention the child Jesus. Everything changes after Jesus remains in the temple in Jerusalem. To begin with, at the moment of the "presentation," the child Jesus is brought to the temple to be presented to the Lord, as first-born [268]. Later, that is, when he is twelve years old, it is Christ our Lord who goes up from Nazareth to Jerusalem and it is Christ our Lord who remains in Jerusalem [272]. With this Christological attribution Ignatius indirectly indicates the end of Jesus' childhood. Just as "Our Lady" dominates the childhood scenes as "Mary" [262], "the handmaid of the Lord" [262] "woman and wife" [264], "his Mother" [266], so the title of "Christ our Lord" dominates the stories of Jesus' childhood as "a son" [262], "the fruit of your womb" [263], "her first-born son" [264], "the Saviour of the world" [265], "the babe" [265], "Jesus" [266], "carpenter" [271]. Ignatius obviously does not consider "Jesus the child" an isolated state; he does not pledge allegiance to one or another evangelical perspective. He adheres to the entirety of the Majesty of the one who is the Lord, the eternal King [91]. The attribution and reality of the child Jesus stress only one particular aspect of Him who is always the crucified and risen Lord.

b. The Selection of the Mysteries

Can we learn anything from Ignatius's *selection* of these eleven mysteries of the child Jesus of which eight come from Luke's gospel and three from Matthew's? Since we are dealing here with the mysteries of the life of Christ [261], Ignatius first of all eliminates everything concerning "the conception of Saint John the Baptist" [262]. Even what directly concerns Our Lady's life, for example, Mary's dialogue with Gabriel or Simeon's predictions concerning Mary, has no place in the statements of the author of the Exercises. Neither the Magi's efforts in Jerusalem to find the manger nor the shepherds' discussions are mentioned. What goes on in Joseph's troubled spirit and what our Lady kept in her heart are set aside to concentrate entirely on the eternal Lord "who has become man for me so that I may love Him more and follow him more closely" (104).

Christ Our Lord and the Childhood Meditations

In organizing the Gospel material proposed for contemplation, Ignatius views the mysteries of the life of the Lord as a movement. The first preamble of the contemplation on the King invites us to fix our eyes upon a Lord who preaches, "going into the synagogues, villages, and towns" [91]. In this movement we meet the call "to come with me" [95] or "to follow" [275]. This movement of Christ attempts to counteract the movement of humanity toward inescapable death: "to go to Hell" [108], "to go down into Hell" [106]. These two movements—that of Jesus and that of humankind—merge in the third week, where the mysteries are arranged along a route on which Pilate and Herod "send" Jesus [294] and "send him back" [295], until, finally, "the blessed soul (of Christ) descends into hell" [219].

Now it is important to note that, in choosing his mysteries in the infancy gospels, Ignatius explicitly calls attention to this movement which the child Jesus already grasped before "Christ our Lord, at the age of twelve years, goes from Nazareth up to Jerusalem" [272]. For this reason, the road from Nazareth to Bethlehem should be studied by the imagination even in detail [112]. It is on this journey that the mystery of the Nativity will take place [264]. The angels arrive [264], the shepherds come and go [265]. The same is true for the kings [267]. Jesus is brought to the temple and crosses paths with Simeon who comes to the temple, and then with Anna who comes [268]. The flight into Egypt is presented as a fatal going-and-coming [269-270]. Finally, it is Christ himself who takes the route to go to the temple to cause his worried parents to discover that all of this movement falls within the plan of his Father [272]. All of this movement finds its explanation and dynamism in a mission from the Father [102] and Christ, as sent, "sends people into the whole world to spread" [145] his mission. By including the mysteries of the childhood in this movement of being missioned by the Father, Ignatius would like to emphasize that, before any possibility for activity, *el niño* is already at the pure service of his Father (135). This is true because of his total abandonment to the accomplishment of "the holy incarnation" [108]. There is then no surprise that Ignatius personally intervenes by proposing for contemplation the mysteries of the annunciation and nativity. In truth, despite current translations of the Exercises which are readily adapted to fit current translations of the Gospels, the author of the Exercises does not write that the angel Gabriel "announces" the conception of Christ our Lord [262]. Ignatius would have used the word *anunciar* as he does in 301 "to announce to the disciples the resurrection of the Lord." However, for the Annunciation he prefers the verb *significar*, as he uses this verb in 271 to say "as St. Mark shows." The holy angel Gabriel then informs Our Lady of the eternal decision of the Holy Trinity that "the second person should become man to save the human race" (102). As a confirmation of this decision, the angel "informs"—again *significar*—Our Lady of the conception of St. John the Baptist. Our Lady has no choice: the decision has been made and she is part of it. It is not for her "to be deaf to this call, but rather prompt and diligent in accomplishing his most holy will" [91].

It is only in comparing this detail with the treatment of the annunciation in other schools of spirituality that one can assess this mystique of pure service

concerning the mission which the word of the angel communicates. In the
history of spirituality, there is no lack of treatises which insist upon the
dialogue between the angel and Our Lady, or even upon a truly deliberate
choice made by our Lady, on which the life and death of humanity will
depend. However, this is more a question of "nuances" than of substantial
differences between spiritualities. Into the text of the gospel, Ignatius directly
intervenes to stress the fact that the birth of the Child Jesus takes place in a
situation of obedience. In effect, he writes: "Joseph goes up from Galilee to
Bethlehem to obey Caesar, accompanied by his wife who is already pregnant."
This response of obedience to Caesar could have been inspired by a
consideration from Ludolph the Carthusian: "Although the Blessed Virgin
Mary had already conceived the King of heaven and earth, she wished, like
her husband, Joseph, to obey the imperial decree."[5]

At any rate, this humiliating circumstance of the birth of the "eternal
King and Lord of all" [97] moves Ignatius to change the order of the Gospel
account. The celestial army should have sung the genuine "Glory" in the
passage which narrates the announcement to the shepherds [265], but the
author of the Exercises locates the praise by the angels directly after the birth
in the crib [264]. Truly, the composite of the infancy mysteries is
criss-crossed by a kind of alternation in the recognition of the infant God. We
are dealing with the "Second Person" [102], the Word who mysteriously does
not speak (in-fans), except by being. There is no lack of places where Ignatius
reinforces the gospel text to place in high relief this reality of the infant Jesus.
In removing from the story of the three Magi kings [267] all of their search
in the holy city, and in centering their story on their adoration (four times in
the first two points), Ignatius again shows that his interest runs toward the
practice of Christology and less toward the contemplation of a Christological
theology. Small details, like the addition "of the world" to the title of
"Savior" in the announcement to the shepherds [265] or the sentir of John
upon the manifestation "of the fruit" of the womb of our Lady [263], bring
into strong light this Ignatian concern to know fully "Christ our Lord" "who
for me has been made man" [104]. The other aspect of the alternation is, not
only a human nature, but a human nature "in the greatest poverty" [116]. On

---

[5] Ludolph the Carthusian, Vita, I, ch. IX, 2.

this point, Ignatius explicitly intervenes in the contemplation on the circumcision [266], which manifests a passivity with which the child Jesus had to undergo these rites at unknown hands: through his naming, his mission to save the world has been laid out in advance; by his circumcision, his solidarity with that world already demands his immaculate blood. Our Lady is witness to this, and she "felt compassion for the blood which flowed from her Son."

Even from the Nativity, Ignatius is at pains to show the crucified condition of Christ our Lord. The theme of the journey and of movement is not forgotten; on the contrary, the Nativity manifests the beginning of a way of the cross "to travel and suffer so that the Lord be born in the greatest poverty and, at the end of so many trials, after hunger, thirst, heat, and cold, desecrations and insults, he should die on a cross" [116]. The two contemplations given over to the "flight into exile toward Egypt" [132] and the perilous return (269-270) show how Ignatius drew from the gospel accounts their prophetic richness—in this case, the quotations from the prophets—retaining only the fact of the criminal plan of Herod and of his son and its consequences for the child Jesus. Thus, the complex of the mysteries of the childhood of Jesus becomes an apt illustration of the call of "the eternal King" [97]: "whoever would come after me ought to suffer with me so that, following me in pain, he may follow me also in glory" [95].

Conclusion

With greater clarity we now see the specific interest of Ignatius in the infancy mysteries. It is less a question of devotion to the child Jesus than to Christ our Lord who manifests himself forever in the mysteries of his childhood. Thus, the lovely expressions of Bérulle, like "an incapability capable of divinity" or even "need filled with sublime life," do not characterize Ignatian adoration of the God-child. This Jesus, "our Lord, thus newly made flesh" [109], is the manifestation of the One who was sent by the Father because he eternally proceeds from the Father and is, at the same time, on mission as a man close to and in the midst of people. Ignatius strongly believes that the cross is the place where, so to speak, one believes in this procession from the Father and in this incarnate mission of solidarity with humanity under affliction. The mysteries of the passion and resurrection sing of the glory of the cross, the mysteries of the public life of the Lord proclaim it, but, in the Ignatian concept, the infancy mysteries make it known that the mystery of salvation through the cross constitutes the essence of the being of Christ. In this infant, who can neither act nor speak and, in his helplessness, seems to be only the plaything of the Caesars and the Herods, so many people—shepherds and magi, Elizabeth and her son John, Simeon and Anna, Joseph and our Lady—recognize and adore the "eternal Word made flesh" [109].

Ignatius does not stop with their emotions and with what is going on in their hearts. These people seem to be present only in order to accomplish their part in the mission of Christ. It is not then by chance that, from their words, Ignatius keeps only those which refer directly to the Lord. This focus on the child-Word explains why, in the contemplation on the nativity, Ignatius asks for some reaction to the mystery which goes beyond mere availability to be a servant or slave. To serve the Lord on his mission means undertaking this service in the situation of a little one who has no strength or power: "making myself like a poor little person and a small unworthy slave" [114] "with all possible respect and reverence" [114]. The two notes which characterize the infancy mysteries come to meet: the characteristics of the Christ of the Kingdom, triumphant, majestic, firmly committed and responsible for his mission, and the characteristics of the Christ of the Two Standards, one who is sent in the most abject poverty and humility. To this power of God who reveals himself in weakness (1 Cor 1:27 ff.), each one is invited to unite himself in the person of the servant as *un pobrecito y esclavito indigno* [114]. One could hardly imagine that Ignatius would make his own the expression of St. Bernard: *magnus Dominus et laudabilis nimis; parvus Dominus et amabilis nimis*. This is so because the author of the Exercises is less interested in contemplating the child, his gentle tiny form, or his complete subjection, than in praying on the journey which this infant Savior is already starting to pursue as an integral part of his mission. With the French school, Ignatius would prefer to say that in this context one needs indeed to adore the scandal of the Cross, but also to venerate the scandal of the manger.

Precisely because we are already dealing with the very being of Christ, there is nothing astounding in that every Gospel event will keep some element of this "extravagant" infancy which is lived out in poverty and abuse [167], the last shout of which will be that of an abandonment which is lived out but entrusted into the hands of his Father [297]. It is the eternal wisdom reduced to infancy, to the divine madness of the childhood of Christ. It is in following closely, in participating in this mission of Christ, in retracing his infancy, that his call could arouse in each of us a personal, specific response in espousing the cause of the God-child. The only one to know Christ is the one who follows him, tracing out, in the integrity of his way of life and in his choice of genuine values, the direction proper to one created to praise, reverence, and serve God our Lord [23]. Thus Ignatius sets out the infancy mysteries, like all the other mysteries of the Gospel, to lead us to an election. There, with the unlimited potential of a free and generous child, we take upon ourselves the limitation intrinsic to any concrete, true service which, if it is to be fruitful, must pass through "the suffering" of the cross which signalized the infancy of Jesus. The sublimity of the mission thus takes on the spirit of the child Jesus, without whom the mission will be vain.

TWO

IGNATIUS OF LOYOLA:
EXPERIENCE OF CHRIST

One day, near Caesarea Philippi in Palestine, Jesus asked a question of a group of twelve men: "Who do you say that I am?" (Mt 16:15). It is a clear and precise question that we still ask today. To tell the truth, at first Jesus had asked something more simple: What did the people think of him? The Twelve could have limited themselves to giving the routine responses. But hearsay or slogans were of no interest to Jesus, nor were the crafted formulas of professional theologians. He desires and insists on receiving from us an authentic response that comes from deep within ourselves. This response should not be merely the chance to say or to repeat some truth heard from others or recounted in books. The issue is to speak the honest truth: "And you, what do you say?"

Leafing through the book of two thousand years of Christianity, we find an uncountable number of personal responses, new and unsettling. Occasionally it has been noted that, while each of the thousands of images and statues that illustrate the figure of Buddha rigidly maintains the same characteristics, the most extraordinary diversity runs through the attempts at depicting the countenance of Christ. To start with, a Michelangelo, a Dalí, the painter of an icon, and the sculptor of a medieval cathedral appear to have nothing in common when they try to depict the countenance of the Word Incarnate. But then, turning to personal experiences of encounters with Jesus, holy men and women have communicated markedly personal and individual ways of responding to Jesus's question: "And you, what do you say?"

Of course, "Only one is your Master, Christ" (Mt 23:10). But his person is so rich and his personality so inexhaustible that it is impossible to reduce his face to a single expression. It is possible, on the other hand, to be caught up in one or other of the unique characteristics in the treasury of the Good

News that is Christ. He can be the Poor Man for Francis of Assisi, the
Omnipotent Lord for the Byzantine of the East, the Beloved Groom for the
school of Carmel, or the Suffering Servant for a base community in Latin
America. We are dealing each time with a new response to the same question
posed by the Person of Christ. Ignatius of Loyola's Christ is located in this
spiritual context.

Jesus Christ, the God to Serve

In the first period of his life, Iñigo Lopez de Loyola, born in 1491, was
content with being a refined and joyous young man, who loved fine clothing and
the good life. A solid Basque, however, he was strongly attached to a faith that
made him repeat what was said of Jesus. To elicit from him a personal response,
Jesus makes use of what happens around May 24, 1521, in Pamplona. The
Spanish city is awakened that day by the sound of a French horn to the proposal
of an honorable capitulation. The French soldiers are many and the Spanish
garrison, unpaid for eighteen months, not very confident. But Don Iñigo de
Loyola prevails, for a Spanish garrison ought never surrender without resisting
the French invaders. During the murderous duel of artillery around the city of
Pamplona, Iñigo stations himself in the most exposed spot to regulate and
correct the firing ranges. Then the moment comes when a canon ball ricochets
off a wall and strikes his right leg under the knee.

The wounded man insists on returning to the manor house in Loyola,
where recovery is long and painful. He asks for some books to read in order to
distract himself. Accustomed to immersing himself in novels patterned on
themes of chivalry, he discovers with deep chagrin that the library offers him
only the *Life of Christ* and a book in Spanish on the lives of saints. Attracted in
spite of everything by the golden legends of the holy knighthood of this gentle
captain, the Eternal Prince Jesus, Iñigo begins to discover the call of another
King. And he pauses to reflect.

One is not converted by a book; one is converted by what a book makes
one discover. So the reading that excites Ignatius's imagination while recover-
ing—and makes him dream for two, three, and four hours without realizing
it—achieves something. On the one hand it proposes all that he must do in
service of a certain lady of noble rank; on the other, it incites him to put himself
at the service of Jesus to do the "great deeds" which characterize St. Francis of

Assisi and St. Dominic de Guzmán. The worldly dreams fascinate him but leave a taste of vanity, sadness, and hollowness. The seductive alternative of being at the service of Jesus leaves him happy and contented, as if his life has finally found there its true fulfillment.

Within these conflicting trains of thought that agitate him and the growing recognition of the service to be rendered, Ignatius progressively discovers Jesus Christ whole and entire as his God. In fact, it is precisely in the experience of meaninglessness, of disgust with life, and of the joy of living to serve Jesus that the encounter with Christ occurs. The new thing for Ignatius will not be confessing his Christian faith—which will be simply the Church's faith—but a vision of Jesus that cannot be separated from serving him in the concreteness of daily life, oriented now apostolically, and which in itself evidences a response to the question asked by the Lord. This response is transfomed into a triple scrutiny which should lead to the service of Jesus' mission: What have I done for Christ? What am I doing for Christ? What ought I do for Christ? For Christ—who from Creator became a man, and who passed from life to death on the cross, for my sins.

Ignatius's initial experience is then enriched by immersion in life with Christ, by being a companion in a real sense in a "pure service of the Father" guided in everything by the Spirit. If we try to distinguish in this experience the features of Christ that Ignatius saw and lived, what strikes us above all else is that Christ is one of the Trinity. From the beginning of his experience with God, Ignatius discovers the Triune God—no doubt influenced by the *Life of Christ* written by Ludolph the Carthusian (who died in Strasbourg around 1377). His great devotion to the Holy Trinity is characterized by a growing familiarity into which is interjected a spirit of reverence in the presence of the Divine Majesty. This Trinitarian attraction will not be, as in the monastic tradition, a repose in abandonment to the mystery of the contemplation of glory; for Ignatius, it transforms itself into a contemplation of all created things, starting in their Creator who is the Trinity.

Probably, Ignatius was the first person in the history of Christian spirituality to perceive the Trinity as God at work—as the God who continues to work, always filling up the universe and actively awakening the divine life in all things for the salvation of humanity. If the inspired monk contemplates, the inspired Ignatius works—adhering with all his heart to the designs of the Trinity, offering himself to act in synergy with the Trinity so that his work is for the Trinity's glory. In that way, the Trinitarian attraction in Ignatius's devotion tends to embrace the whole of humankind. His devotion seeks only God, not, however, only for himself, but rather for all his brothers and sisters. Thus might all created things, not evil in themselves but often averted by humankind from their source and origin, return with humanity to true meaning in God.

In this Trinitarian prospective, Christ comes as God. It is sufficient to examine Ignatius's semantics to note that his Christological titles revolve around *Christ our Lord, the Christ, the Lord, the Eternal Word,* much more rarely *Jesus,* and it follows from this that Ignatius refuses to see Jesus in any way other than in his majesty as Lord, One of the Trinity. In this way, the glory that surrounds Christ with splendor is not only the glittering renown of an extraordinary ruler or the halo of an outstanding spiritual leader, but the glory of the Eternal Lord of all things. This will never be disconnected or disassociated from the fullness of the divine being which reunites him to God the Father. It does not really matter that this divinity is hidden in the manger or on the cross; it does not really matter that it shines through his words or at the right hand of the Father: for Ignatius, Jesus is the Lord, the Eternal King, because he is the Word of God.

As a consequence, Ignatius does not recognize the distinction made between the historical Jesus and the Christ of faith. This does not involve, however, any depreciation of the intense passion that Ignatius feels for the historical Jesus—his words and gestures, his lifestyle and the place where he lives—all of which help in reaching him whom Ignatius never stops loving and praising in his majesty as Eternal Lord. It does mean that Jesus can never be what some people today claim: one voice among the many voices of spiritual teachers, of the wise, and of prophets. His is rather *the* voice, *the* light, *the* truth, because Jesus has the status that none of the others have, One of the Trinity.

One of the Trinity Always with the Spirit

Since Ignatius's Christ is One of the Trinity, he is always with the Spirit. What exists in modern Western culture today already existed in the sixteenth century: the temptation to liberate the Spirit from Christological mooring, which is trammeled in Paul's conviction that the Lord is the Spirit (2 Cor. 3:17). In this area, Ignatius proves cautious. He cannot forget the painful experience he went through in 1527 in Salamanca, where he was arrested and imprisoned as an enlightened one (*alumbrado*), one of those who believed themselves directly instructed by the Spirit alone. "You, Ignatius, talk about your experience with God. Now one cannot do that unless he is qualified either by theological learning or by the Spirit. You do not speak out of theological learning; therefore you speak by the Spirit" (see *Autob.* 65). Ignatius says nothing; should he claim to be enlightened by the Spirit he would move onto dangerous ground, risking an encounter with the pyres fired by the Inquisition to still the voices of those *enlightened* by the Spirit.

Ignatius intends to live under the Spirit, though he is aware how often it is troublesome to discern what the Spirit is inspiring, and how one can let himself be confounded by theories or in religious beliefs, above all when trust in the Spirit leads to marginalizing Christology and with it ecclesiology. Extremely sensitive to the mystery of the One of the Trinity who made himself incarnate, Ignatius finds the Spirit, now not as pure spirit acting in illimitable space, but from the annunciation made to Mary, always as the Spirit who reaches out to the person of Christ, and in the same spiritual reach, to the body of Christ that is the Church. In this way, Ignatius's spiritual experience moves intricately into the dialectic between the Spirit and the body of Christ—the Spirit that forms and continues to form the body of Christ, inspiring in the concreteness of our lives here and now the options and the orientations that were those of Christ, in order to make us like Christ.

Ignatius discovers in his experience of faith that, between what the Spirit tells me in the depths of my own self and what the Gospel and the Church tell me from outside, there can be intense conflict. But that conflict can be only temporary and apparent, because in the final analysis it is the same Spirit who utters its word within me—enlightening, unique, irrevocable—and who in the selfsame movement guides and enlightens the Church. Companion of Jesus in his Spirit, Ignatius knows that he must never be absolutely rational, a calculating person who reduces everything to the reasonable. Rather, he must remain open to the impetuosity of a Spirit who breathes where it will, completing the work of Christ: open to the enthusiasm, to the gracious and the fresh that the Spirit does not cease to stir up in the body of Christ that is the Church, incessantly making all things new.

From this, it follows that Ignatius moves in a Christology of the visible. If the Spirit moves me, it is the visible aspect of Christ's earthly life that allows me to verify the authenticity of this motion of the Spirit. To this Christology of the visible belongs also the body of Christ which is the Church. Ignatius cannot conceive a division of, or envision any opposition between, the charismatic Church and the institutional Church: the Church whole and entire is where the breath of the Spirit creates the body of Christ, the Bride—with its own hierarchy and authority, with its grace and its laws, its Easter joy and its cross, its charismatic enthusiasm and its institutional structures, its Christ and its Vicar of Christ: it is the same Spirit who inspires and leads to the truth, whole and entire. This approach was called by the Fathers of the Church "a sober drunkenness," and by Ignatius, "a spiritual sense," the human reason searching for Christ, enlightened by the light of faith in the Spirit.

But what is true for the Spirit is also true for the Father, with whom Christ is united in the Trinity. Again, in his spiritual experience, Ignatius cannot conceive a Jesus detached from his Father. Ignatius finds access to the Father in the actions and gestures of Jesus, in each of which (following the tradition of the *devotio moderna*) he discovers so many theophanies, believing that all the scenes of Jesus's life are also mysteries that speak and reveal the very mystery of God.

Christ on His Way to the Cross

It is the concrete particular that expresses what God is, Jesus's Father and our Father; and the concrete particular is the only way to know the universal. How can we reduce to a neat sentence this Ignatian vision? In a book published in 1640, an author set himself the task and created this maxim: *Non coerceri a maximo, contineri tamen a minimo, hoc divinum est.* Translating that is not very easy, but the sense is this: "To be unconstrained by the greatest, to be contained even so in the slightest—this is divine."

To put that into our perspectives: to live in the dimension of the universal, yet to labor on the concrete particular, this is the divine. This is the mystery of Christ, because he who is the "greatest"—above and beyond every conceivable frontier border, the unconstrainable Majesty of God, the Divine Majesty that nothing can force or impede, he is found in the "least"—in the flesh and heart of the Incarnate Word, in a precise place in the Roman empire, in a precise time during human history. In this vision of Christ's mystery, Ignatius adopts a line of conduct: following Christ, to immerse oneself in concrete work according to one's opportunities and one's abilities, but singleheartedly straining towards the infinity of God, who presents in the here-and-now the wide horizons of his plan of salvation.

In selecting the readings that will reveal the universal of him who is One of the Trinity, Ignatius has clear preferences. So, starting from the call he has heard, he chooses those parts of the Gospels that fit best with the perspective he has adopted. They form, to put it this way, a Gospel according to Ignatius. Looking closely at the selection Ignatius made, one notices immediately that his Christ is always on the move. He is in a *paschal* state: that is, according to the etymology of the term, he is constantly on *passover*, passing over from city to city, from village to village, until the fulfillment of the great Passover-- Easter in which for our sakes he *passes over* from a cruel and debasing death to the joy of everlasting life. Contemplating the Lord, One of the Trinity, in movement and on the way, is a summons to us to start on a way along which he will be our companion.

As a consequence, understanding Ignatius's Christology requires entering personally into the movement which it depicts. Even when Ignatius invites us to contemplate in simplicity of heart the mysteries of Jesus' childhood, his contemplative gaze finds everything in action: Mary and Joseph travel without stopping with and for the sake of the child; angels, wise men, and shepherds come and go in order to greet him who is sent by God his Father, and who for thirty years continues to advance and progress in order to fulfill the mission on which he was sent. And it is in his role of announcing the Good News of the coming Kingdom of God, of his Father and of the Father of all humankind, that Christ makes his ascent to Jerusalem.

The sixteen mysteries chosen by Ignatius to mark this journey bring us to encounter the Lord fully active. On this journey, sufferings seem not to exist; the cross is never mentioned here. Only in the last mystery does Ignatius observe that "there was no one to receive him in Jerusalem" [288].

It is the icon of the *Pantocrator* that determines the selection of passages proposed by Ignatius: five passages of the Gospels that reveal his glory as Son of God, five others that put in high relief his divine actions in performing miracles, two that similarly reveal his power over sin, two that call attention to his speaking with divine authority, and finally two passages that tell how the apostles were sent out to continue along all the roads on earth the mission of the Lord. Then, suddenly, the *Pantocrator* disappears and its icon darkens. As always, there is a way that must be traveled; and on this path, too, intense activity rules. But the Lord finds himself condemned to a passivity to be painfully endured, which deprives him of everyone and of everything. Even at the level of language, Ignatius distinguishes this *kenotic* change with a distinctive linguistic mark: he no longer uses the Name, but designates the Lord simply as "he." He, One of the Trinity, who until now exhibited incessant activity in words and works is changed into the grammatical subject of a passive verb: "He is dragged before Annas." Even more often, he is the grammatical object of an active verb: "He led him out" [291, 295].

The Eternal Lord Compassionate in Powerlessness

It is no longer the Lord who lays out his route; now others drag him along a route of "labors, fatigue, and sufferings" from one place to another, and the divine omnipotence is revealed now in human powerlessness (116). The point here is the choice that Ignatius made, attracted by this unsettling mystery. The Evangelists themselves reveal to us a more active Christ who does not cease, in what he says and by his silences, to condemn the injustice inflicted upon him. The Ignatian perspective in contemplating this way of the cross clearly focuses on what Jesus suffers and not on what he does: his not responding during the trial; his not reacting to the provocations and ill-treatment. It is true that Jesus carries the cross; but Ignatius immediately adds, "but he could not carry it" [296]. He does not hesitate to see the proclamation of this powerlessness already present in the *kenosis* which the Gospels announce beginning with the time of the infancy: the Word as *infans,* the one who does not speak. This time, in the mysteries of the passion, the powerlessness is freely accepted: "journeying and toiling, in order that the Lord may be born in greatest poverty; and that after so many hardships . . . injuries and insults, he may die on the cross!" [116].

Ignatius is not looking for a kind of compression of feelings to the one feeling of attachment to Christ, and he does not even raise the problem of human suffering and death. His entire attention is focused on the total abasement of Christ who suffers, of this One of the Trinity, Creator and Savior, who submits to the shame of the cross and to the hatred of his own people. The divinity hides, but not in a sort of pure negation. There is a purpose and motive, which Ignatius discloses in a series of "fors" that explain the meaning of the path the Lord has chosen. One of the Trinity has suffered *for* us, *for* me, *for* my sins, *for* filling human pain with his divine presence, for saving the human race, and all this *for* love.

Christ has not ceased to fight against suffering, which he always considered an infamy and which he felt in himself with such anguish that in the olive grove "his clothes were already full of blood" [290]. No word of the evangelists renders the disgrace sacred; rather, it is the compassion of Christ who suffers with us and for us that sanctifies the suffering. Bound to this passage for love of us, Christ does not abandon his mission, he does not retreat or retrace his steps, as he must defeat suffering through suffering. The radicality of the way in which Ignatius proposes to us this God who suffers and dies lies less in the sorrow and suffering themselves than in the disconcerting choice that God has made for love of us. Because of his experience with Christ, Ignatius knows our instinctive resistance to it, our almost visceral refusal. "All of Christ is my God," he will write later in his spiritual diary, well aware of our tendency to make up a Christ to fit our own standards, one who legitimizes our refusal to accompany him on his passage, wherever he may go, knowing that his ways are not our ways *(Diary, 87)*.

In a certain sense, we have to accept this on the evidence: in the beginning, Christ deluded Ignatius. From the One who has every power in the heavens and on earth and who is the King of the Universe forever, Ignatius—extraordinarily sensitive to all that is great and honorable—would have looked forward to an evangelical enterprise of resounding success for the sake of this same God. Instead of that, he encounters in the Son of God the one through whom scandal comes. Christ certainly has what it takes to create enthusiasm in crowds or to mobilize an elite; he can handle the hard labor and dangers of engaging in brilliant combat that ends with a magnificent victory. What is more, Ignatius aspires to the remarkable and the spectacular—of course purely for the greater glory of God. But this is not the way Christ chose. He will announce the coming of the Kingdom "in poverty, in humiliation, and on the cross."

Ignatius, unlike other masters of the spiritual life, does not seem to be interested in what went on in Christ's spirit, in his prayers and his feelings. What matters to him is what Christ chooses as his way, as his paschal journey. This is entirely traced out in a freely chosen dynamic development toward a hazardous and outcast human state. This choice is particularly surprising since Jesus belonged to a class of society that, neither well-off nor wretched, enjoyed a lifestyle that was modest but quite secure. Nonetheless, the Son of God truly and freely chose to go down to the last place, going against the impulse that drives every one of us to go up higher and to put distance between ourselves and the marginated and rejected, the stranger, and the poor of every kind. The cross is the result of this choice. It is the reason why Ignatius, who writes often about the Lord's passion, can maintain a gravely sober tone—nothing lyrical, no flights. For in the end the cross is not about death; it is, rather, the symbol of the role that the One of the Trinity has chosen. It is this choice that Ignatius privileges first among all the real events on Calvary—the choice full of the love of God. Then he talks about the crucified Creator and Lord.

Ignatius Imitator of Christ for God's Glory

On November 15, 1537, on the Via Cassia in an area north of Rome still called "La Storta," Ignatius has a vision of his Christ. He carries the cross; and Ignatius obtains the reassurance that Father God places him with his Son—he carries the cross—as companion on his paschal journey. Then he gladly sees Christ in the middle, in a sense: in the *last place,* which he has chosen, and in the *first of all places* on high, which is his own place. It was not Jesus who fabricated that last place, it was humankind following after Cain who devised it for the successors of Abel. This last place is at the frontier of the inhuman, on the border of the human. Ignatius cared about this social insertion of Christ among those who are condemned to misery, who are dispossessed and bereft of real freedom. Yet in this *last place* the face of Jesus intimates his mystery and allows his divinity to show through. Ignatius always deals with the Word Incarnate in the fullness of his sovereignty. In this unsettling paschal context, Ignatius dares to advance the choice that Christ made, fully aware from his own personal experience that the last place, despised and repulsive, disgusts us absolutely.

If the foolish love that the Lord has for humanity has made him choose the foolishness and the scandal of the last place, which disgraces and crucifies, then Jesus' companion can only present himself as a fool for Christ, should the service of God's glory deign to designate him for that.

In order to imitate Christ our Lord better and to be more like him here and now, I desire and choose poverty with Christ poor rather than wealth; contempt with Christ laden with it rather than honors. Even further, I desire to be regarded as a useless fool for Christ, who before me was regarded as such, rather than as a wise or prudent person in this world. [167]

To choose what Christ has chosen: but as Christ made this choice out of love, to complete the mission given to him by God his Father, so Ignatius wants to make the choice not on his own initiative, but only if Christ calls him to choose the last place to serve better the praise of him who holds in everything the highest place, his Divine Majesty. The initiative belongs to the Lord who is at work here and now, in his Church, in his people, and in all the things that happen in the world.

The companion of Jesus wants union with the Christ who wears himself out in order to bring every man and woman to the Father—to bring everything created to its fullness, accomplishing again and again, anew, the choice which the Christ has made, and so to collaborate with him for the salvation of the world. In and through this election, the companion of Jesus is invited to place himself actively in this *middle* which is, for Ignatius, Christ reaching the universal of the Trinity who dwell there and refining everything authentically Christian in himself. In his personal encounter with Christ, Ignatius yielded to the evidence in the end: announcing the Good News of the glory of the Trinity to a people who give quite a contrary meaning to *glory* requires following the One of the Trinity and appropriating the Gospel of the cross. This is not in the first instance a question of desiring to suffer and die; rather, in the first instance it is to live dying wholly to self for the sake of putting oneself at the service of Christ in everything—even at the risk of being considered, as he was, a madman—so that in the end the glory of the Trinity radiates in the life of our brothers and sisters, and illuminates history, which is already filled with the Spirit of Christ who is working in it. This paschal glory will impart a characteristic Ignatian optimism to a vast variety of vocations and missions, through which men and women, made fools for Christ, will participate in the revelation of the foolish love of God, incarnate in the person and in the choices of Christ, the One of the Trinity, crucified.

This is how Ignatius responds to Jesus' question: "And you, who do you say I am?" Once he has gazed on and lived through all of the mysteries of the life of Christ our Lord, the joyous light of the Incarnate Word shining out in him who was crucified and rose, Ignatius responds with a little phrase that he wrote in his spiritual diary: *ser todo mi Dios*: you, whole and entire, you be my God.

CHAPTER THREE

OUR LADY IN THE SPIRITUAL EXERCISES
OF ST. IGNATIUS

This modest contribution by one who is not a specialist in Ignatian Spirituality, coming as it does at the close of that part of the Ignatian Course that deals with the Bible and the Exercises, has one simple intent. It intends very simply to evoke the presence of a figure eminently and thoroughly biblical—Mary of Nazareth—at the very heart of the *Spiritual Exercises* of Master Ignatius.

Is it at all necessary to recall this presence? Is it not self-evident? Frankly, not seldom does one come across excellent commentaries on the *Exercises* today with no reference whatever to Our Lady, or at best a quick mention in passing. How are we to explain this phenomenon?

First of all, it is so attractive for the mind to study the *Spiritual Exercises* as a systematic and progressive pedagogy leading to the fulness of personal freedom or to the total formation of man that the role of Christ as mediator, and consequently of Mary as mediatrix, is easily obscured.

Then again, it is tempting to set aside the sequence of the "mysteries of Christ" as found in the *Spiritual Exercises*, to replace it, thanks to the findings of modern exegesis, with the path followed by the disciples in their discovery of the mystery of Christ—moving, that is, from the paschal mystery to the Lord's baptism, and from the Lord's baptism to the infancy gospel. Thus reversing the path traced out by the itinerary of the *Spiritual Exercises*, the Contemplation to Attain Love coincides with the contemplation of the incarnation, so that the delicate narrative section concerning the Child Jesus with his Mother, so much insisted on by Ignatius, is relegated to the museum of Christian piety.

Finally it is enticing with Pierre Teilhard de Chardin—even though the name of Mary figures in practically every one of his retreats—to push back into the shadows, or be completely oblivious of, the "little" history of Mary in order to develop at length, beyond all personalization, the "great" idea of the "mystery of the feminine" symbolized by Our Lady in her association with the "cosmic Christ."

True, we can no longer describe the Virgin Mary as Fr. M. Meschler could still do in his day in his commentary on the *Spiritual Exercises* and their meditations:

> When Mary lifts the corner of her veil, we see her beautiful oval face, of a pure colour, slightly pale, with big blue eyes and pink perfectly shaped lips, giving to her mouth an expression of ineffable tenderness and kindliness. The Holy Virgin has flowing hair, bright blond hair, falling on her shoulders.[1]

Yet, after all, would not the pilgrim Ignatius, who gladly gave free rein to his great devotion to Mary—Mary, so deeply loved in Spain and venerated at all the shrines that dotted his pilgrimage—would he not feel more at ease with Meschler's commentary in his *Spiritual Exercises* than with the learned ones of our days? He well might: Fr. Hugo Rahner remarked how Ignatius in the course of the *Exercises* strikes a balance between the appearances and the absences of Our Lady with a certain exquisite dogmatic tact. Fr. Peter Schineller for his part is convinced that Ignatius would have availed himself of "the views and insights of modern biblical scholarship and systematic theology" had this been within his power.

Basing himself on the text of the *Spiritual Exercises*, the reader will not fail to notice the constant presence of Our Lady, signified either by her titles or by her name: twenty-seven times the title "Our Lady," thirteen times the designation of "Mother," five times the name "Mary," and once each "Virgin" and "Handmaid of the Lord." More important than this is the distribution of these titles and this name over two very different kinds or categories of texts. First set forth in 1954 by Fr. Maurice Giuliani in a classic article entitled "Le mystère de Notre Dame dans les Exercices,"[2] this division

---

[1] See French edition, Paris, 1913, p. 371.

[2] In *Christus*, 3, 1954, pp. 32-49.

has been partially taken up very recently by Fr. R. La Fontaine.[3] Linguistics will readily designate these two categories of texts as *narrative* and *functional*. The *narrative* texts would be those that make us contemplate Mary's part in the actual unfolding of the history of salvation; the *functional* texts would be those that make Mary take an active part in the new history that the Exercises set in motion between the Divine Majesty and the retreatant. The very existence of such a division makes it clear that Mary is not only an object of contemplation, but an agent within the contemplation itself.

The analysis of the *narrative* texts should evoke for us that type of icon of the Virgin that Ignatius depicts through his particular handling of the biblical material. The Retreat Master is to "narrate accurately the facts of the contemplation or meditation," so that the retreatant can "take the solid foundation of facts," as the second annotation prescribes [2]. But, that the re-treatant may arrive at a "better understanding (or experience—*sentir*) of the facts" [2], the *Spiritual Exercises* present a mode of reading or interpretation of the biblical material which leads to what I have called Ignatius's icon of "Our Lady." Which are these hermeneutical approaches?

A first interpretation key, semantic in character, is provided by the predominant use of the title "Our Lady." As such, this designation has nothing extraordinary about it. Spain being the Marian fief it was, the expression was commonly in use to honor the Lady par excellence. However, within the Exercises this title appears to compete with two other designations: "Mother" and "Mary." The name "Mary" is not just freely used: it is connected with biblical quotations (4 times: 262, 263, 264, 265), with the beginning of the prayer "Hail Mary" (9 times) and with the expression "the Virgin Mary," used only once in the *Spiritual Exercises* [299].

Neither is the word "Mother" employed haphazardly. Its use is not only linked to commonly current expressions such as "the Child and his Mother" [266, 269, 270] or "the Mother and the Son" [199, 276]; but it is strictly connected with a selective usage of possessive adjectives. Ordinarily there is question of "his Mother" [135, 219, 266, 269, 270, 273, 297, 298], only once of "your Mother" [98]. The use of "our Mother" refers exclusively to the

---

[3] "Nuestra Señora en los *Ejercicios Espirituales,*" *Manresa,* Vol. 56, No. 220, pp. 205-217.

Church [353, 363, 365; cf. 170]. If the possessives in the singular show Our
Lady as closely associated with her Son and the possessive in the plural
indicates the Church, the absence of any possessive places her as Mother
between her Son and "us." Beneath the cross "his Mother" becomes "the
Mother," as Ignatius notes with amazing precision [297]. It is the same at
Cana: "The Mother draws the attention of the Son" to our needs [276]. Hence
the use of "the Mother" twice when suggesting the colloquies: "He may use
three colloquies: one with the Mother, one with the Son, and one with the
Father" [199]; again, the colloquies proposed at the end of the contemplation
of the incarnation suggest the following equation: "The Mother," namely "Our
Lady" [109]. The refusal to use the expression "our Mother" to designate
Mary underlines the primacy of her divine motherhood—"your Mother," "his
Mother"—which cannot be put on the same level as a very real yet spiritual
motherhood—"the Mother"—in regard to us. The familiarity implied in the
term "our Mother" yields to the transcendence of the mystery of the
Theotokos. The refusal to call her "our Mother" fits in most naturally with
that "all possible homage and reverence" with which the mystery of the
Nativity is to be contemplated [114]. Fr. Charles O'Neill has already called
attention to the deep meaning of the term *acatamiento* or "homage": "In
Ignatius *acatamiento* is a happy consciousness of divine presence, an awe
suffused with warm attractiveness and resulting in love."[4] The use of the word
"Mother," therefore, seems to be governed by that "greater reverence" which
Ignatius says is required when "we address God our Lord or his saints" [3].

The usage of the title "Our Lady," dominant in the Exercises and free of
other qualifications, corresponds to the attitude of reverence inspired by the
mystery of the *Theotokos*. It suffices to compare the Autograph text with that
of the Vulgate to realize that, but for some five exceptions—if the count is
correct—the Vulgate replaces the Autograph's *nuestra Señora* with "Virgin
Mary," or "Mary," or "holy Mother." This adaptation—for it is not really a
translation—alters the perspective altogether. The Vulgate creates an
atmosphere of intimacy changing "to see the house and room of Our Lady"
into "the little house of the Virgin Mary" [103]. The annunciation of "the

---

[4] "*Acatamiento*: Ignatian Reverence in History and in Contemporary Culture," *Studies
in the Spirituality of Jesuits*, Vol. VIII (January, 1976), No. 1, p. 3.

conception of the Divine Word" to "the blessed Virgin," as the Vulgate puts it, has different connotations from the Autograph text's annunciation of "the conception of Christ Our Lord (*nuestro Señor*)" to "Our Lady" (*nuestra Señora*) [262]. The same holds true of the first apparition of the Risen Lord. The Autograph text's lapidary "Our Lord" appearing to "Our Lady" becomes in the Vulgate "the Lord Jesus appeared to his holy Mother," thus breaking up the close association of Christ and Mary in the work of our salvation [218]. It is significant that in order to elicit "greater reverence" in the contemplation of the Nativity, the Vulgate reinforces its usual substitute for the Autograph's "Our Lady," viz. "the Virgin," by adding "Mother of God" [114]. The figure of the Virgin Mary, such as it emerges from the Vulgate, remains basically very biographical by its use of the name of Mary apart from biblical quotations; it also remains very elementary—a mystery that barely begins to open out—by its use of the title Virgin, which the Autograph text avoids, except once. On the contrary, the figure of the Virgin Mary evoked by the discerning use of Marian titles in the Autograph is that of the one uniquely associated ("Our Lord," "Our Lady") in the work of our salvation. Ignatius contemplates this work of our salvation in its fulfillment—that is, in the perfect creature Mary/Our Lady—while he prays for the grace of being associated with this plan of salvation for the aid and perfection of "souls."

The accomplishment of grace has been realized not only in the Son of the Father coming from on high, but also in a daughter by the name of Mary, who comes like us "from below." It is not only "Our Lord"" but also Mary who has entered forever "into the glory of my Father." The pilgrim, who together with "Our Lord" sets out on his journey towards "Glory," makes his commitment through the Kingdom oblation "in the presence of your glorious Mother" [98]; in Mary the pilgrim or companion can contemplate that accomplishment of the work of our salvation which every Christian hopes for by God's grace in her own life as pilgrim. From the start the creature Mary is not just a character whose doings are recalled by the retreatant as belonging to a dead and buried past; rather, she is "Our Lady," the creature perfected by grace, and as such she who remains for us an ever actual "today." It is in this "eternal now" that Ignatius has us contemplate the mystery of "Our Lord, who has just become man for me"—*ansi nuevamente encarnado*—and "Our Lady" who forever humbles herself and offers thanks to the Divine Majesty" [108].

A second interpretation key completes the Ignatian icon of "Our Lady." At least during the second week, Ignatius makes it a point to bring together certain mysteries that emphasize those features of a "glorious Mother" [98] which bear the marks of a "sorrowful Mother" [298], just as her Son, the Risen Lord, bears the wounds of his passion even in his "glory" today. There is a stark contrast between the richness of the Trinitarian plan contemplated in the incarnation [101-109] and the "extreme poverty" of the Birth of the Lord [110-117]. Ignoring, it would seem, both Luke's perspectives and Matthew's orientations, Ignatius offers for the second day of the Second Week a description of the presentation in the temple that breathes life, peace, and salvation [268 a, b, c], to contrast it then with a picture of the flight into Egypt which clearly spells death, escape and exile [269 a, b, c]. The contrast is carried over to the third day, when "Our Lady" experiences both the obedience [271] and the disobedience [272] of her Son, both the peaceful atmosphere of a family life of work [271] and the rupture caused by the work for the Kingdom [272].

It is this alternation of suffering and joy—the paschal journey of the Kingdom [95]—that in the dialectics of the Spiritual Exercises calls for the apparition of the Risen Lord "to his blessed Mother" [219] after all her experience as a "sorrowful Mother" [298]. All through this alternation the sorrowful Mother remains inseparably associated with the passion of her Son. Ignatius explicitly highlights her "compassion because of the blood her Son shed" [266] at the circumcision. However, though deeply devoted to the Mother of Sorrows (so say the historians), Ignatius does not impose this devotion of his in the *Exercises*. He offers no meditation on Mary's personal and interior suffering: no mention of the sword that will pierce her heart, or of the doubts and misunderstandings; indeed, nothing at all of her suffering at the foot of the cross. Her sufferings are invariably associated with those of her Son: "He was taken down from the cross... in the presence of his sorrowful Mother [298]." Her sufferings are unfailingly placed within the context of the glory of her Son, as in the case of that "farewell to his blessed Mother" [273] that issues in the manifestation of his true sonship at the baptism: "This is my beloved son" [273]. The very same house—which Ignatius saw with his own eyes in Jerusalem, if we are to believe the pilgrim guides of that era—witnessed "the solitude of Our Lady, her great sorrow and weariness" when she "retired" to it "after the burial of her Son" [208 f and e] as well as her "intense gladness and joy because of the great joy and glory" of the Risen Lord when he visited "the house of Our Lady" in his role as Consoler [219, 220, 221 and 224]. Most closely associated with the paschal mystery of her Son, Our Lady lives in the ever-present fulfillment of the glory resulting from her sufferings. The icon of Our Lady depicted by Ignatius sums up perfectly the basic features that the Spiritual Exercises aim at forming in the retreatant, namely, the features of the Kingdom.

Yet another key of interpretation allows us to penetrate even more deeply into the mystery of Mary as sketched by Ignatius. The obvious selection of the biblical material in the "points" does not merely set forth the contemplation of a mystery; it gives it a clear orientation. The "points" constitute a veritable code of interpretation; but it is a delicate matter to read an interpretation into what clearly appears as no haphazard division into "points." At any rate, it leads to not a few surprises, the first of which is certainly the absence of any meditation on the inner feelings of Our Lady, on her interior life. Mary is not the daughter of Sion eagerly awaiting the Savior; neither is she in adoration before the crib, nor the one who "keeps all these words in her heart"; she is not presented as the model of any particular virtue nor shown in prayer in the midst of the infant Church. All this passed over in silence reduces the story of Mary, such as we have it in the Bible and even more amply in medieval devotion, to the very essentials of her role in the work of our salvation. Such a reduction is particularly noticeable in the "points" for the mystery of the Lord's presentation in the temple. Once the "purification of Our Lady" is announced in the title, the three "points" do not mention her at all. Our Lady disappears behind her ministry of taking Jesus: "They take the Child Jesus to the temple" [268]; after that, Simeon and Anna are concerned only with him. Despite the mention of Mary in the Lucan text, Ignatius's "points" encompass the "mother" (Lk 2:48) within the ministry of the parents [272]; what is highlighted is the true parenthood, that of the Father. A similar absence occurs in the "points" for the mystery of the "three kings, the magi." Matthew mentions the Mother; Ignatius does not [267]; all attention is focused on the adoration of the Child and on not returning to Herod. All these traits point to the meaning of true motherhood, which consists in welcoming and accepting the unfathomable designs of the Divine Majesty. Mary is the one who, with her absolutely total and unconditional assent of faith, undertook and fulfilled in her own living her unique mission in the work of our salvation. Or, in

Ignatius's own words, "making the journey and labouring that Our Lord might be born in extreme poverty, and that after many labours . . . he might die on the cross, and all this for me" [116]. Just as her Son must leave "his Mother according to the flesh to devote himself exclusively to the service of his eternal Father" [135], so too Our Lady, in her pilgrimage of faith, transcending the mere bonds of flesh and blood, joins herself intimately to her Son's service for the sake of the Kingdom, devoted "exclusively to the service of the eternal Father" [135]. It is this "devotion" alone that Our Lady is wholly given to.

No wonder, then, that the Spiritual Exercises go beyond the mere *narrative* section of texts to focus on Our Lady's action in this experience, thus highlighting an entire *functional* section of texts. A venerable tradition—though one rather doubtful: *traditio sat incerta*—as the *Monumenta Ignatiana* warns us[5]—would even have it that Our Lady dictated to Ignatius the Spiritual Exercises from beginning to end. Even though this tradition be nothing more than a pious hyperbole, a symbolic metaphor to emphasize Mary's undeniable mediation in the composition of the Exercises, as supported by the *Autobiography* (cf. nn. 28-29), yet the entire functional section of the text of the Exercises demonstrates that Our Lady is taken to be its co-author. Roland Barthes has sought to draw on a literary analysis of the book of the Exercises to discover in it not just a multiple text, but principally the existence of four authors who really make the Exercises. Ignatius relates his own experience, but wants the one for whom he is writing (the retreat director) to have enough freedom to give "his own exercises." Speaking from long experience Fr. François Varillon testifies: "While there is a basis common to all, there is a very personal way of grasping it. . . in passing through me [the spirituality of the Exercises] takes on a particular tint. But I must beware lest this tint or hue become so vivid as to be wholly Varillon's and cease to be Ignatius's."[6] The authority of the one who gives the Exercises consists in converting the retreatant into a true "author." Made personally responsible [2 and 6], he is to respond through his prayers and supplications, his offerings and colloquies. The contemplation of the incarnation concludes with an

---

5 *Exercitia Spiritualia*, Rome, Vol. 100, p. 62.

6 *Beauté du monde et souffrance des hommes*, 1980, p. 188.

invitation to "think over what I ought to say to the Three Divine Persons or to the eternal Word Incarnate or to his Mother, Our Lady" [109]. The retreatant becomes the author of a new text, his own Exercises. In the last analysis, however, the retreatant's text is only a beginning, because the author par excellence of the Exercises, the one before whom the other authors—Ignatius, the director, the retreatant—recede into the background, is "the Creator and Lord himself" [15]. The retreatant, it is true, starts the sentence, but it will have no meaning unless the Creator completes it—"offer him all . . . that his Divine Majesty may dispose . . . ." [5]. Taking the "colloquy" seriously, the real communication between author and Author [15] is "speaking exactly as one friend speaks to another, or as a servant speaks to his master" [54]. But even Our Lady—right from the first week, in fact—is involved in the colloquies and belongs fully to the functional domain of the Exercises. By means of the triple colloquy Our Lady, too, becomes a co-author of the Exercises we make, sensitizing the expression of our desires and refining our reflection on the work of salvation and on ourselves. In his beautiful prayer to "the Virgin Mary at noon," Paul Claudel prays: "I have nothing to offer and nothing to ask for; I come, Mother, just to gaze at you. . ." But this is only one aspect of the praying activity. In his *Spiritual Exercises*, Karl Rahner sheds light on the specific aspect of the Exercises.

> We should try to speak, in all simplicity and with all the tenderness of our heart, with the Woman of the new and eternal covenant; speak to her of her Son, Our Lord Jesus Christ; speak to her about herself, the one full of grace, who became all service and love; and speak to her about ourselves who so desire with her to follow Christ.[7]

Not only do these words of Rahner capture that icon of Our Lady that the *narrative* section depicts; it also defines her role—her ministry—in the *functional* section as *nuestra Señora*.

While the *narrative* part does not begin until the second week, the

---

[7] Karl Rahner, S.J., *Spiritual Exercises*, trans. Kenneth Baker, S.J. (New York: Herder and Herder, 1965), p. 142.

functional part covers the entire sweep of the Exercises, right from the first week. Our Lady will be present throughout the process of the election. Indeed, she need no longer be mentioned explicitly: Ignatius is satisfied with inviting the retreatant to make the colloquies [156, 168], in which Our Lady occupies a preferential [148], though by no means a necessary, place: "he may engage in only one colloquy with Christ our Lord" [199].

The triple colloquy, which constitutes the essential element of the *functional* part in regard to Our Lady, was a practice disputed and challenged in Ignatius's own time. In a sermon he preached in 1546, Doctor Martin Luther illustrated the danger of the triple colloquy with an example borrowed from a sermon of Bernard of Clairvaux: ". . . I wish to call on Mary, who will pray to her Son for me; the Son will pray to his Father, and the Father will listen to the Son. All this amounts to a picture that represents God in anger (needing to be placated), with Christ showing his wounds to him, while Mary presents her breasts to Christ. . . ." (*Oeuvres* IX, p. 346). This kind of criticism will issue in an insistence of the exclusiveness of the one Mediator (1 Tim 2:5), or, as present-day Protestantism would have it, in the belief that Christ is sufficiently close to us for one to understand for oneself what is so poorly expressed in the hearts of sinners such as we are. That is, we rely on the belief that he loves us dearly enough to intervene directly in response to our prayers and present them to the Father without any other intermediaries. Ignatius does not exclude at all the direct recourse to the Son [199]; but, in the context of the above-mentioned controversy, the prayer of the triple colloquy becomes a confession of faith in an economy of salvation to which the Divine Majesty has chosen to associate Mary in a privileged manner, just as it chooses to have need now of our association and collaboration. This mediation of Mary is not added on to the unique mediation of Christ. The triple colloquy is not a sort of compulsory chain of mediations; it does not function after the fashion of a series of entreaties one must work through because immediate access to God has been barred. Beyond all theological controversies, Ignatius puts the finishing touches to his icon of the Blessed Virgin Mary by means of the triple colloquy. While the *narrative* part of the text of the Exercises depicts her as "Lady"—*Señora*—the *functional* part highlights soberly, yet distinctly, the full significance of the fact that she is "Our Lady"—*Nuestra Señora*.

This stands out clearly at the very first intervention of Our Lady in the Exercises, namely in the third exercise of the first week [63]. Here, then, the *functional* part exists before any introduction of the *narrative* part. By her action Our Lady leads us into the mystery of her Son, which in turn will illumine her own icon. Ignatius's introduction is, as usual, sober and concise: "To Our Lady, that she may obtain grace for me from her Son and Lord for three favours. . ." [63]. Our Lady is the mediatrix of a grace because she is, all at once, pure grace of God in herself ("grace . . . from her Lord") and associated with the work of this grace for us ("grace from her Son").

Since this intervention is situated at the very heart of the first week of the Exercises, and since the grace asked for is interior knowledge of my sins, it is understandable that some authors see in this intervention of Our Lady the appearance of the "Immaculate one, whose purity lights up for us the way to forgiveness,"[8] or the appearance of the "Immaculate Virgin who sums up all the perfection of the universe redeemed and restored to its original beauty." More in keeping with the analyses we have so far presented of the title "Our Lady" is the suggestion made by Fr. La Fontaine.[9] Seeing that the graces we beg for in this colloquy through the intercession of Our Lady take up the three sins of the first Exercise [45], but in reverse order, Our Lady in fact makes us pass from the history of sin—cf. the genealogy Angel - Adam - Man—to the history of our salvation: cf. Mary—the Son—the Father. In this activity—the *functional* part—the Lady comes to the fore as "Our" Lady, not only because she belongs to our race, because she is our "yes" to the salvation offered by the Father through his Son. This "our" is a point we must insist upon.

Using highly concentrated cosmic language, Ignatius proposes as a prelude to the Exercises, in his "Principle and Foundation" [23], that no person can genuinely seek after God without being integrated within the human community, and conversely that no committed involvement in the human community is possible unless it flow from a discovery of "God-with-us." Just as the sin of the prodigal son leads to degrading isolation, so too the first week emphasizes how sin causes isolation from the human community. Suffice it here to quote some well known passages: "cast out in

---

[8] Cf. François Courel, *Exercices Spirituels*, Desclée de Brouwer (*Christus* 5) Paris, 1960, p. 51.

[9] Cf. "Notre-Dame dans les *Exercices spirituels* d'Ignace de Loyola," in *Marianum*, 46, pp. 301-316.

exile here on earth, to live among brute beasts" [47]; "I alone, what can I be?" [58]; "pass in review all creatures: how is it that they have permitted me to live?" [60]. Mankind is condemned to the solitude of blindness [106] and to the isolation brought on by pride [142]. Mary leads "the human race" as redeemed by the Divine Majesty [107] into that universe of grace where men and women are "chosen" [145] to be "mediators" to "conquer the whole world" "with me," the Son of Mary [95]. In this way the world becomes the universe re-created by "the love that comes from above," which is described in the contemplation to attain love [230, ff.], and is the very antithesis of what the first week makes us "weigh" and "ponder" as the infernal reality of sin [57 and 234].

All are "mediators" for all: some are hell for others; yet some there are who sustain others in mutual solidarity on the road to salvation. In this world of mediators, the mediation of Mary is privileged on behalf of all others. The contemplation of the incarnation shows her as chosen from among all men for the salvation of all. Her "yes," humble and grateful (108), pronounced on behalf of us, is not treasured as a thing of the past; but as an event of a graced personal history, her "yes" can be repeated "for the aid of souls," for the ongoing salvation of the world together "with us." In the trial of "solitude" [208 ff.] that along with suffering our solidarity in sin brought to Our Lady, Mary experienced what was demanded of her as mediatrix in the area of interior knowledge of sin as abhorrence for the disorder of the world and its worldly values [63]: in a word, all the consequences of saying "no." God willed to obtain Mary's "yes" for his Son, and so there is no grace for us except through the "yes" of Our Lady. Ignatius is so convinced of this that, despite his "modernizing" tendency of not encumbering his devotion to Our Lady with legends [as in 310] or with pious meditations [111], he makes us have access to the grace of Easter through the mediation of a first apparition of the Risen Lord to Our Lady [219]. For if grace comes down to us through Our Lady's "yes," our ascent to the Easter joy poured out on us is also accomplished through Our Lady's mediation. In this way the *narrative* section confirms and completes that icon of Mary that Ignatius has depicted for us in the *functional* section by means of the characteristic traits of Our Lady.

This rapid survey of ours stands in need of revision and completion. It has been an attempt to illustrate the title of "Our Lady" given to Mary in the Exercises. A prayer by Ignatius sums it all up beautifully by emphasizing how

Our Lady makes us change from weak persons (first week) into strong ones (second week), from sad (third week) into joyful ones (fourth week), through our mediation (that is, our work and efforts) and thanks to her unique mediation "with her Son and Lord" [63] for the praise of God. "May it please Our Lady to intercede for us sinners with her Son and Lord, and to obtain for us the grace that, with the cooperation of our work and efforts, she may change our weak and sorry spirits into strong and joyful ones to the praise and glory of God" *(MI, Epp.,* I, 72).

FOUR

THE EASTER EXPERIENCE OF OUR LADY

Introduction

We owe it to the Ignatian Spiritual Exercises that the first apparition of Christ Our Risen Lord to Our Lady [218 and 299] remains alive in the Christian consciousness. It is fitting to recall this Ignatian contribution to Marian devotion in the current Marian year.

This first apparition continues to be a subject of discussion. The theologian Francisco Suárez sums up the faith of the 17th century in these words: "And yet, without any doubt, one should believe that after his resurrection Christ appeared first of all to his mother."[1] In our own days a theologian of repute like Hans Urs von Balthasar confirms the certainty of Suarez and of his age: "It is to her (Mary), as seed of the Church, that without a shadow of doubt the Son first appeared."[2]

Nevertheless, Father Yves Congar notes that on strictly biblical grounds a very first apparition to the Blessed Virgin Mary stands no chance at all. It is too clearly in literal opposition to the text of St. Mark (16:9), which states that the Lord appeared first to Mary Magdalen.[3] On the other hand Congar places the relationship between the Lord and his mother on so deep a level of faith and charity that an apparition to her of the Risen Lord, such as is geared to strengthen the confidence of the disciples and to found the Church, just seems to make no sense. And yet, even while acknowledging the difficulty

---

[1] F. Suarez, *De mysteriis vitae Christi*, disp. 49, sect. I, n. 2 (*Opera*, XIX, p. 876).

[2] Hans Urs von Balthasar, *Triple couronne: Le salut du monde dans la prière mariale*, Paris, 1978, p. 96.

[3] Yves Congar, "Incidence ecclésiologique d'un thème de dévotion mariale", in *Mélange de Sciences Religieuses*, 7 (1950) 291.

based on Scripture, Ignatius plainly affirms: "He appeared to the Virgin Mary. Though this is not mentioned explicitly in the Scripture, it must be considered as stated when Scripture says that he appeared to many others. For Scripture supposes that we have understanding, as it is written, 'Are you also without understanding?'" (Mt 15:16; Mk 7:18) (299). The polemical tone of this statement, quite exceptional in the Spiritual Exercises, leads us to believe that Ignatius expresses in this "mystery" an incontrovertible reality of salvation history.

The scriptural difficulties, which this first apparition to Our Lady meets with, are not the only ones to explain why, in presenting the fourth week of the Spiritual Exercises in their writings, some authors pass over this "mystery" in silence. How is one to pray on this mystery, and how present this meeting between the Risen Lord and his mother? Father Congar himself has spoken of the real danger, whatever the stance taken with regard to this first apparition, of transforming the mystery of the resurrection, which is the very centre of our faith, into an expression of affectionate "consolation." Indeed, in presenting this mystery, there is the great temptation of recommending to the exercitant to contemplate a most intimate conversation between the Lord and his mother, or to contemplate a meeting between the two whose only purpose is that of consoling Our Lady in her "solitude with great sorrow and weariness" [208].

It would not be difficult to mention hundreds of examples in which the retreat director gives in to the temptation to describe elaborately "the joys and delights of this most intimate meeting." May I be permitted to quote the concluding passage of the book *Marie, mère de Jesus* (Mary, Mother of Jesus) of Shalom Asch, a Jewish writer? It is quite surprising to read in this Jewish author's work on Myriam, the Jewish girl from Galilee, his attempt to describe the first apparition of her son Yeshuah:

"Suddenly a shiver ran through the body of Myriam. They [the Christian community] saw her eyes fixed on a point in space, her lips open and speechless . . . they saw her smile, her eyes filling with tears. Her hands were held out, trembling, and from her smiling lips came forth the familiar words filled with sweet tenderness: 'tinoki, tinoki' (my child, my child). . . the disciples heard the voice they knew so well: 'Shalom alei'hem' (peace be with you)." This literary passage of a Jewish writer proves at once the lasting nature of a tradition and the sensitivity required to grasp and contemplate the "history" of this apparition to Our Lady.

The Tradition Inherited by St. Ignatius

St. Ignatius gives witness in his Spiritual Exercises of being the recipient of a longstanding tradition. Most certainly it was not just the *Life of Christ* of the Carthusian, Ludolph of Saxony, that acquainted Ignatius with this first apparition of the Risen Lord to his mother. The visit to "the chapel of the Blessed Virgin Mary where he [Jesus] first appeared to her after rising from the dead, as is piously believed" formed an integral part of every pilgrimage to Jerusalem: the pilgrim guidebooks of . . . the 15th and the pilgrim accounts of the 16th century bear witness to this. The Roman liturgy celebrated the Easter Pontifical Mass in the Basilica of St Mary Major in remembrance of the first apparition of the risen Lord—so we are told by the writers of the time.[4] In Spain the popular ceremony of "the meeting" is preserved up to our own days: it consists of two processions—one of the Risen Lord, and the other of Our Lady—which meet in front of the church. All these external manifestations, well known to St Ignatius, were just witnesses to an ancient tradition which bears recalling, not precisely to draw up a list by means of an exhaustive enquiry of the rather complex texts referring to this debated and debatable subject, but to grasp more deeply the theological foundations of this "mystery" which St Ignatius continues to have us contemplate as the basis of the fourth week of his Exercises.

A first witness of the apparition of the Risen Lord to his mother goes back to the 4th century—the commentary on the *Diatessaron* of Tatian, preserved in classical Armenian. Its author, the deacon Ephrem[5], has no need to regret the silence of the gospels on the matter, as St.Ignatius will have to. Thanks to an error in the biblical manuscript at his disposal, the first apparition of the Risen Lord concerns Mary, not Mary Magdalen. Strangely

---

[4] Ubertinus de Casali, *Arbor vitae crucifixae Jesu*, Venetiis 1485, 1, IV, c. XXIX, f. 174d.

[5] *Evangelii concordantis expositio.*

critical with respect to the Lord's mother Mary, St. Ephrem is not astonished at Our Lady's believing she was encountering a gardener; he is convinced of her doubts.[6] With the same excessive earnestness for which St. Ephrem reproaches her at the time of the miracle of Cana[7], Mary wishes to touch her Risen Son; but once again the Lord puts her off: "After the resurrection, too, he prevented her from again drawing near to him because, said he, 'From now on John is your son. . . .'" Thus when his mother saw him after his victory over the powers of death, she wanted to caress him maternally. But Mary, who had followed him even unto the cross, had on that day been entrusted to John."[8] "However, as Mary was present at the first miracle, she also received the first-fruits of his return from the dead. So, even though she did not touch him, she was comforted."[9]

St. Ephrem's exegesis is doubtless completely devoid of any foundation. As for his reproaches towards the Blessed Virgin Mary, they express his concern for presenting her as a woman "from among us"; else, as other Oriental writers will affirm, she would not be in truth the *Theotokos*. However, despite his critical stance in regard to Our Lady and notwithstanding his faulty exegesis, St. Ephrem presupposes and takes for granted a meeting between the Risen Lord and his mother because of their unique and intimate collaboration in the work of our salvation. Hence it is not a mistaken reading of the gospel—Mary in place of Mary Magdalen-that accounts for St. Ephrem's conviction that Our Lady received "the first-fruits of his return from the dead." It is his "understanding," to take up the Ignatian expression, his understanding of faith which looks in the gospel for a historical foundation, a proof.

Led by the same understanding of faith, St. John Chrysostom, still in the fourth century, looks for a gospel confirmation of his conviction in the mention of "the other Mary," whom the evangelist Matthew presents "seated in front of the sepulchre" with Magdalen, and who is blessed with the first

---

[6] *Ibid.*, II, 17.

[7] *Ibid.*, V, 1.

[8] *Ibid.*, V, 5.

[9] *Ibid.*, XXI, 27.

apparition of the Risen Lord (Mt 27:61; 28:1,9)[10]. In the 6th century Severus, Patriarch of Antioch, develops the theological reasoning to which Chysostom's understanding of faith had opened the way: "The other Mary: it is fitting to believe that this is the Mother of God, because she was not far removed from the passion, but had remained close to the cross, as John has related; to her it was rightly fitting that the joyous news be announced as well, since she was the cause of joy. . . ." The part played by Our Lady in the mystery of our salvation thus receives its specific quality in the understanding of paschal faith: those who share in the sufferings of Christ will share in his Easter consolation (2 Cor 1:3-8). This is the paschal promise and assurance that St. Ignatius receives from the eternal King: "that by following me in suffering, he may follow me in glory" [95].

Even while keeping to this understanding of paschal faith, the Eastern Christian writers are aware that their scriptural proof cannot be accepted. To remove Our Lady from the gospel framework of the apparitions in which she has no explicit place, these writers begin by keeping her from leaving the sepulchre so that she will in this way be the first to meet the Risen Jesus, and they finish by not letting her go back to the tomb. Rather, she remains in her house so that she can there, in the assurance of her faith, await the first apparition of her Risen Lord.

Interpreting the "Mystery"

St. Ignatius invites the retreatant to see on the one hand "the arrangement of the holy sepulchre," and, on the other the place or house of Our Lady, noting its different parts, and also her room, her oratory, etc" [220] Ignatius knows that the gospel says nothing about a first apparition of the Lord to his mother. While acknowledging this explicit silence, he invites us to an *intus legere*, a "reading from within" which compasses all that Scripture says implicitly—"he [Christ Our Lord], appeared to many others [299] (a probable reference to 1 Cor 15:6 mentioned in 308)—and which draws on an in-depth

---

[10] Ciro Gianelli, "Témoignages patristiques grecs en faveur d'une apparition du Christ ressuscité á la Vierge Marie," in *Revue des Etudes Byzantines*, XI (1953), p. 109.

reading of the history and economy of our salvation such as the Risen Lord does for the disciples on the road to Emmaus: "How foolish you are, how slow you are to believe everything the prophets said! Was it not necessary for Christ to suffer these things and enter his glory?" (Lk 24:25; cf. [303]). Referring to the Lord's words in Mk 8:17: "Do you not know or understand yet? Are your minds so dull?" St Ignatius considers the denial of the apparition of our risen Lord to Our Lady a lack of faith (cf. Mt 16:8) in the love of the Lord for his mother. The silence of the gospels, lived in the understanding of faith, speaks more eloquently of the "mystery" than the simple description of the event could ever have done.

How to Pray this Mystery

In a Coptic fragment of the *Gospel of Bartholomew*, belonging to the fourth century, which seems to be the most ancient witness that we possess,[11] the apparition is spelt out in the form of a colloquy. Our Lady proclaims her faith in her Risen Son, and the Lord greets his mother: "Peace be to you who have borne the life of the world . . . Mary, my mother, the one who loves you loves life." Another witness, probably of the same period, is the Ethiopian fragment of the *Gospel of Gamaliel*.[12] The Risen Lord exercises his role as consoler, saying to Our Lady: "Mary, you have shed enough of tears until now. He who was crucified is alive. He who brings you consolation is the one you are asking about . . . He has burst open the brazen gates and freed the prisoners from Sheol." It is always the word of God that nourishes the contemplation of the "mystery"; the development is once again theological, thus preparing the icon of the resurrection that is proper to the Byzantine tradition.

A century later—we are in the fifth century—St. Romanus Melodus has no hesitation in placing this meeting between the Risen Jesus and his mother beneath the cross in the hope of the resurrection. Our Lady, called the "sheep

---

[11] E. Cothenet, *Marie dans les apocryphes de la passion et de la résurrecton*, in *Maria* (Etudes. . . sous la direction du P. Hubert du Manoir, S.J.), Tome VI, c. II, section III, p.109.

[12] *Ibid.*, p.112.

without blemish" (as is usual in the Oriental liturgy), questions "the Lamb," her Lord, on the meaning of the passion: "Rest assured, Mother," replies the Son, "you will be the first to see me when I come forth from the grave. I shall come to show you at the cost of what suffering I have ransomed Adam and what sweat I have poured out for him. To my friends I shall manifest the marks of these sufferings which I shall show in my hands. And then mother, you will contemplate Eve alive as before, and you will cry out with joy: 'He has saved my parents, my Son and my God. . . .'" The Blessed Virgin Mary is here in very truth the mother of the living.

The influence of St. Romanus Melodus on the Byzantine liturgy is well known. This oriental prayer does not look on the apparition of the Risen Christ to his mother as in isolated fact, but as an integral part of the Lord's passion and his mother's compassion within the totality of the paschal mystery. When St. Ignatius proposes the apparition of the Risen Lord to Our Lady for contemplation [n.218], it is whole of the *triduum sacrum* that is in fact recalled.[13] This apparition draws its meaning not from some need for justification in the sense of apologetics, nor from some need felt in the Church, but from the understanding of paschal faith. By giving it a special place in the text of his Exercises St. Ignatius highlights the altogether unique character of this first apparition.

From all that has so far been said it is clear that this "mystery" finds its place within a long tradition of faith, even if the Church's magisterium never attributes to it more than the qualification of *verosimiliter* (probably), expressed by Innocent III in the thirteenth century. It is not without significance to note that it is precisely this qualification of *verosimiliter* which we find in the addition made by the Latin "Vulgate" version of the Spiritual Exercises to its n. 219.[14] Undoubtedly St. Ignatius was not acquainted with the

---

[13] Cf. Edouard Hamel, "Marie et 'Eucharistie à propos d'un texte de saint Ignace", in *Cahiers de spiritualité ignatienne*, 17 (1981) pp. 1-13. It refers to n. 14 of the first part of the *Spiritual Diary* (15 February, 1544), in which Our Lady is called *part* and *portal* of the Eucharist which is "the living, life-giving, unifying presence of Christ, and of Christ alone; but it is also at the same time the *whole* Christ, head and members, dead and risen in his glory, accessible in fellowship through the Holy Spirit" (p.12).

[14] Cf. Jean-Claude Guy, "L'apparition à Notre Dame, Exercices n. 219, 299," in *Christus*, 95 (1977) 356-362, for the discussion on the addition to n. 219. However his explanation does not appear either sufficient or convincing.

oriental sources that we know today. His written source was the meditation
presented by Ludolph the Carthusian in his *Life of Christ*. It is Ludolph who
suggests to Ignatius the placing of the apparition in the house of Our Lady,
where she is alone [cf. 220 and 209f]: *Sola in secreto domus sedebat* (She sat
alone in a secluded spot of the house). The silence of the gospels is discussed
at length, and the conclusion is summed up in a phrase in which we seem to
hear the author of the Spiritual Exercises: *Et licet hoc ab evangelistis
subticeatur, pie tamen sic creditur* (And though the evangelists pass over this
in silence, this is nonetheless what is piously believed). It would be unthink-
able that the Risen Lord would not appear to his mother when he appeared to
so many others of at least equal rank.

Setting aside the rather doubtful sources of the Carthusian Ludolph, the
colloquy he describes of the Risen Lord with his mother is, however, not
without interest: "So they stand and talk to each other full of joy, while
lovingly delighting in the Lord's paschal victory (Pascha); and the Lord Jesus
tells her how he has freed his people from the powers of hell and what he did
during those three days. See here, then, the great paschal triumph (*Ecce igitur
nunc magnum Paschal*)!" The Carthusian's insistence on the Lord's great
paschal triumph does not allow us to isolate the first apparition from its
"history" [n. 219]—to stop at the details of the apparition, or to dwell
somewhat sentimentally on the mother who sees her absent son once again
after a calamity or disaster. Not without reason does the Spanish autograph
text of the Exercises speak of the apparition of "Christ Our Lord" to "Our
Lady" [218]: the apparition is to be placed on the plane of the *festa paschalia*.

St. Ignatius directs the contemplative prayer of the fourth week towards
the retreatant's asking for "the grace to be glad and rejoice intensely because
of the great Joy and the glory of Christ Our Lord" [221]. The focal point of
the fourth week is the Risen Lord, the Paschal Lamb. The first apparition to
Our Lady becomes in this way a first colloquy with Our Lady that she may
obtain for us the grace which she herself experienced in her first Easter
encounter with the Lord [cf. 63]. For the paschal Joy of union with Christ was
the only meaning of this encounter according to Ludolph the Carthusian's
intuition: *Matri enim Virgini primo omnium apparuit, non ut resurrectionem
suam probaret, sed ut eam devisu suo laetificaret* (He appeared first of all to
his Virgin Mother, not to prove his resurrection, but to give her joy at seeing
him). St Albert the Great wrote in a similar strain: *Christus Matri apparuit*

non ut probaret resurrectionem, sed ut eam visu suo beatificaret (Christ appeared to his Mother, not to prove his resurrection, but to gladden her through seeing him). To express the joy of Our Lady some authors like to use the Song of Songs, the paschal aspect of which is well known. So also to give expression to our joy in union with Our Lady, the prayer *Regina coeli laetare* is taken up by a large number of commentaries on the Spiritual Exercises. At times these commentaries interpret the Marian texts of the infancy gospels in the light of Easter, very much in keeping with modern exegesis. Father Casanovas makes the retreatant pray the *Anima Christi* with Our Lady to the Lord risen "in body and soul" [219].

The Deep and Singular Meaning of the First Apparition

With the silence of the gospels on the apparition to Our Lady and the explicit affirmation of the evangelist Mark that "he appeared first to Mary Magdalen" [16:9], the tendency among spiritual authors, when they come to treat of the apparition to Our Lady, is to "spiritualize" the very words "first" and "apparition." The event is so unique and special that it would be unfair to include it in a general category common to others. St. Albert the Great summarizes this tendency when he says: *Beatissima Virgo non cadit in numerum cum aliis; quia non est una de omnibus, sed una super omnes* (The most Blessed Virgin is not to be classified with others: for she is not one among all others, but one above all others).

The progressive spiritualization of this contemplation inspired by the understanding of faith has grasped the intuition of St. Ignatius, for whom the event of the Lord's resurrection—which is also not described by Scripture—and the event of the apparition to Our Lady make up one single mystery [219]. In his monumental work *Deus semper major*, Father Przywara remarks that the gospel speaks of "the apparition of the angel and of the earthquake (Mt 28:2-4)," but passes over in silence the actual resurrection as such. Since Our Lady is the first to closely follow her Lord in a unique way—a following even to its last consequences—the Easter mystery is accomplished in her silently, yet in divine fashion.

Father Jean Laplace, who entitles the contemplation of the apparition to his Mother, "How the Risen Jesus is Present to His Mother," writes: "It is, in fact, a spiritual understanding that we need to grasp what kind of new world Jesus and Mary have entered." He continues: "They have become one in heart: at the foot of the cross, Mary united herself to the intention of her Son. It is this presence in the Spirit that constitutes their unity. It is this presence that the Resurrection has brought about: Christ is present to those who are united with him in their heart. The body is no longer opaque; it has become the expression and the transparency of the spirit. A new life begins, a new mode of being, this spiritual presence that death cannot interrupt. The world cannot grasp this presence."[15]

This paschal presence—an altogether new form of presence—means that Our Lady consents to the incarnation of the Lord in her even more deeply than at the Annunciation. Present in this new paschal way "to his Blessed Mother in body and soul" [219], the Lord resurrects in her unto eternity. In her he lives again, and she experiences it as "Easter," for, thanks to him, she lives again and already rises to a new life. This spiritual presence cannot be grasped except by the spiritual understanding of faith, as St. Ignatius says. It is not a question any longer, as in the second and third weeks of the Exercises, of living and suffering for Christ, but of receiving the Risen Lord so that he may live in us. This new "announcement" made to Mary will be for St. Ignatius the type and source of all the other apparitions of the fourth week.

Mary, Icon of Paschal Faith

The postconciliar emphasis on the person of Our Lady as "the first believer" does away with the opinion that Our Lady was granted a beatific vision of the divinity of the risen Lord in her first Easter encounter with him. In keeping with the Second Vatican Council some commentators do not hesitate to focus, for Our Lady as well, on the great beatitude mentioned also by St. Ignatius [305]: "Blessed are those who have not seen and have believed." From a theological standpoint, Father Sebastian Tromp suggests that we not forget the commentary of St. Thomas Aquinas on the Gospel of

---

[15] Jean Laplace, *An Experience of Life in the Spirit: Ten Days in the Tradition of the Spiritual Exercises*, Chicago, 1977, p. 172.

John:

It is said, blessed are the eyes that have seen what you have seen.
More blessed, therefore, those who have seen than those who have
not seen. My answer is that there is a twofold blessedness. . . .
Quite another is the blessedness of hope which consists in merit.
Hence, according to this latter type of blessedness, the more blessed
is a person, the more that person can merit. Now the one who has
not seen and believes merits more than the one who sees and
believes.[16]

We must regard Our Lady, then, as the one who believed not only at the
beginning of, or during, her life with Our Lord, but also within the core of
the paschal mystery.

In this sense St. Peter could say even of Our Lady: "Jesus Christ: you
love him, although you have not seen him. You believe in him, although you
do not now see him. And so you rejoice with a great and glorious joy, which
words cannot express, because you are receiving the purpose of your faith, the
salvation of your souls" (1 Pet 1:8-9). The great difference between Mary and
us lies precisely in the grandeur of the Blessed Virgin's faith, for she saw
Jesus humiliated, scoffed at and nailed to the cross. We do not receive our
fulness directly from the fullness of God, but from the death of God in which
through faith Life shines forth. It is faith in the resurrection which permits us
to encounter the risen Lord. Through him, suffering and death, which are an
integral part of our entire life, while remaining a pure mystery, are no longer
an absurd and cruel non-sense. For they have become the manifestation of the
love of God, the paschal journey—journey mysteriously chosen by
God—which issue in the fulness of Life. The funeral creations of the
Byzantine liturgy sing of the faith of Our Lady: "O Saviour, when shall I see
you, exclaimed the Virgin Mother of God, when shall I be able to contemplate
the joy of your return, O brightness without ending, O Light of my soul." "O
my Mother, stop crying; do not weep over me, despite what you see, for I

---

[16] *De Virgine Deipara Maria Corde Mystici Corporis*, Caput sextum, Argumentum
primum, Articulum 1, n.2: "Num Maria viderit Redivivum," Romae, 1972, p. 190 ff.

have freely undergone death to renew mortal men and women after their fall."
"O my Christ, cried the Virgin Mother, what bitterness fills my heart while
I contemplate your humiliation! You who are Life, do not remain buried
beneath the earth!" "Rise, O source of life, said the immaculate Mother,
weeping over her Son who lay in the tomb." It is always in contemplating the
harsh reality of the Lord suffering and dead that Our Lady expresses her faith
in life.

As often in the Spiritual Exercises, so too in the fourth week Our Lady
is for St. Ignatius the icon of the retreatant. With her "understanding of faith,"
Our Lady contemplates the Risen Lord in the light of "his hour." For St. John
as well "to see Jesus" is not accomplished except in an understanding and
penetrating contemplation of the paschal mystery. For this reason those who
have "seen" the Risen Lord and those who believe "without having seen" him
are, spiritually speaking, on an equal footing. The latter will not have lived
and experienced the apparition of the Risen Christ, and yet in faith they will
see him alive. Blessed are those whot the Risen Lord himself gives the
assurance that in faith these latter ones will also be able to see and draw near
to him.

To grasp more fully the meaning of this understanding of faith, what
Father Laplace says in his retreat of thirty days will help us greatly.[17] While
the other apparitions of Our Lord remain "outside" and have a kerygmatic
purpose, the apparition to Our Lady cannot but be "within" and wholly
gratuitous. The risen Lord, who receives his body from Our Lady and rises
from the dead thanks to her, for this is how he willed it, does not remain
exterior to her in his apparition, as in the case of the disciples. It is in her that
he lives again. And Our Lady experiences in a unique manner the "Christ who
lives by faith," as she experiences also in a new way the existence of the
disciple of a risen Lord. This is total presence.

To explain this presence Father Laplace speaks—but human language in
this area is always deficient—of a new presence, not fleshly but spiritual, of
the risen Lord to Our Lady. It would perhaps be closer to the text of the
Exercises to speak of a personal presence in the Spirit, to which Our Lady

---

[17] *Ejercicios de 30 dias*, Presentación de Gabriel Ochoa Gómez, Mexico, D.F., 1969,
pp. 194-197; *Exercicios espirituais de trinta dias*, tradução e adaptaçao de uma Experiêcia de
oraçao por Paul-André Hébert, Sao Paulo, 1981, pp. 188-189.

responds through an experience of faith, that is, through the *credere-videre* (believing-seeing) of the theology of St John. In this presence of perfect transparence all the Marian texts of the Scripture, like so many prophecies, find their filfillment.

St. Ignatius very closely associates Our Lady with the path trodden by Our Lord. We should even remark here that the phrase "his blessed Mother" figures only twice in the Spiritual Exercises: once at the moment when the Lord leaves his Mother ("after Christ Our Lord has bidden farewell to his blessed Mother") [273], and the second time at the moment of a new union in the paschal mystery: "He appears in body and soul to his blessed Mother" [219]. This union does not take place directly with the divinity but, in the very words of St. Ignatius, it takes place "through the true and most sacred effects" of "the most holy resurrection" in which Our Lord now shows himself [233]. These effects are the joy experienced through faith in the Risen Lord, and the consolation which consists precisely in an "increase of faith," "increase of hope," and "increase of love" [316] in Our Lady.

This is the deep meaning of the fourth week; Our Lady is its prototype and icon for all those on whose behalf Our Lord exercises his role of "consoler," thus introducing them into his great Easter experience.

Mary, Icon of the Faith of the Church

In the fifth century, commenting on the *Carmen paschale* in his *Opus paschale*,[18] Caius Celius Sedulius spells out in poetic language the ecclesial dimension of the first apparition of the risen Lord to Our Lady. Mary is the door through which the Lord entered the world. And now, by means of the apparition to Our Lady who represents the Church, the resurrection is announced to the new people of God: "To her [Mary] the Lord showed himself immediately after the triumph of his resurrection, so that, as the kind and loving mother who would spread abroad the witness of such a miracle, she who had been the entrance-door when he was born and came into the world might also be the messenger announcing his coming forth from the

---

[18] *Patrologia Latina*, XIX, 742-743.

nether world."

Father Cusson has stressed this ecclesial character of the first apparition: "For Christ the joy of rising from the dead is not the joy of breathing anew, but that of bearing to the new and liberated humanity his own life, which can now finally be received in its fulness. . . ." And Our Lady alone is capable of receiving this new life immediately and fully for the Church.[19] Our Lady is the ecclesial focal-point where the passage of our sinful humanity to the new humanity of the Risen Christ takes place. In the light of the resurrection of her Son, Our Lady inaugurates the new type of "understanding of faith" that will be the patrimony of the Church that is coming to birth.

Once again the distinction between this first apparition to Our Lady and all the others of the fourth week stands out in bold relief. The aim and meaning of these other "apparitions" is to arouse paschal faith: they give birth to the word that will be the apostolic kerygma. On the other hand, the first apparition of the risen Lord to Our Lady is characterised explicitly by "silence," even the complete silence of the gospels. If in the annunciation the Blessed Virgin speaks, if Our Lady of the Incarnation, as the humble servant, joyfully sings her Magnificat, in the hour of the glory of the resurrection Our Lady effaces herself in the Church (Acts 1:12-14)—the Church which the Lord Jesus entrusts to his apostles. The Risen Lord appears in the faith of Our Lady: she is the fountainhead and icon of the faith of the Church. In her, united as she is in unique fashion to the "paschal mystery" itself, is generated the faith of the Church, which is then hierarchically and sacramentally articulated. The fullness of the Easter grace, as revealed in the first apparition of Our Lord to Mary, Our Lady, takes shape in the Church's message of the great Pasch of the Lord as the only "consolation" of humanity.

---

[19] Gilles Cusson, *Pédagogie de l'experience spirituelle personelle*, Bruges-Paris, 1976, p. 361.

FIVE

THE PASSION ACCORDING TO SAINT IGNATIUS

Introduction

In this essay, I shall discuss some typical Ignatian traits of the Third Week of the Spiritual Exercises. Ignatius has powerfully structured the First Week around the genealogy of sin and that of grace. The Second Week contains the essential elements of what is fundamental to Ignatian spirituality. We run the great risk, on the threshold of the Third Week, of neglecting the specific orientation intended by Ignatius and simply taking as starting point the gospel of the Lord's passion, to give ourselves to the contemplation of the paschal mystery, while ignoring altogether the passion according to St. Ignatius which the Third Week proposes. The danger is all the more real in that, within the spiritual dynamic of the Exercises, the Third Week appears to be just the confirmation of the election, a test of the authenticity of a decision made during the Second Week.

Indeed, a good enough reason seems to indicate that one's prayer during the Third Week be based on the passion according to the evangelists, not on the passion according to St. Ignatius. As a man of his times, Ignatius has his retreatant pray on the gospel texts, but without taking into account the specific theology of the evangelist who produced them: he focuses rather on the events as such, as experienced by the Lord on his way to the cross. To be sure, it is in his paschal event that the Lord saved us, not in or through hermeneutics. Nevertheless, is it not more helpful to leave aside the medieval presentation of Ignatius and pray over the paschal mystery in the kerygmatic perspectives of the gospel of Mark, or in the ecclesial context of Matthew's gospel, or with that personal love of the disciple for the Master that marks the Lucan gospel, or with that theological vision of glory of the gospel according to John?

Yet another reason could make us run the risk of falsifying the prayer of the Third Week. In fact, it easily gives rise to meditating on problems closely connected with the Lord's passion: the sense of suffering, the mystery of the cross, the existence of evil, the scandal or the folly of love of a God who suffers, and the passion of Christ as the first act of liberation. True, such problems exist at the heart of our Christian and human existence in every age; and it would be hard to deny the link of these human concerns with the events of the Third Week. But do they have a place in the spiritual development or dynamics of the Exercises? In any case, such concerns are very far from the goal of the Third Week as defined by Father Gil Gonzalez Davila in his Directory of 1587: "to find the heart of Christ amid the turmoils of the passion, and to rouse us to enter into communion with the crucified Christ, that we may declare: *amor meus crucifixus est*—my love has been crucified."[1]

In sifting through the text of the Third Week, we will try to draw from it some particular traits and so to sketch, to the extent possible, the passion of our Lord according to Ignatius.

Ignatius's "A-temporal" Approach

How shall we proceed in our reading of the text of the Exercises? A text is always the result of a series of choices made by the author from among a certain varied number of possibilities. In order to grasp the meaning and import of a text it is absolutely necessary to know these possibilities—some of them accepted by the author, others rejected—from which were originally made the choices incorporated in the text. The better to grasp the typically Ignatian approach to the contemplation of the paschal mystery, the analysis of the text should grapple with the presence or absence in the text of certain possibilities of presenting the passion. Ignatius had the gospel accounts at hand; from among the possibilities of presentation provided by these accounts, he as author of the Spiritual Exercises made some significant choices. The Third Week is the result of these choices, and so constitutes in very truth "the passion according to St. Ignatius."

And so, to come to the heart of the matter, the reader will at once notice

---

[1] *Monumenta Ignatiana, Directoria Ex. Spir.*, p. 527.

that Ignatius does not preserve in his text any of the indications of time that punctuate the gospel accounts. There is no mention of "when it was evening" (Mt 26:20) in connection with the Last Supper, or of the night of Peter's denial (Mk 14:30), or of the day of the sabbath (Lk 23:54), no word at all about the sixth or the ninth hour (Lk 23:44). There is just one exception, which therefore attracts all our attention: "Jesus remained bound the whole night" [292]. And here, it is rather the duration of the Lord's painful endurance than a simple indication of time. The time as such is not important except in the measure in which it contributes to the passion of Christ. As usual, Ignatius arranges the days and the hours of prayer for the one who is making the Exercises, but the passion itself takes place outside any chronological framework in the eternal present, the today, of God.

The "Way" or Journey of the Third Week

This "a-temporal" aspect, however, does not in any way give to the passion a static character of immobility. No longer does prayer here move, as it did in the Second Week, from the contemplation of one mystery of the life of Christ to another. Ignatius explicitly insists on the retreatant's journeying along the "mysteries" as on a route: "from the Last Supper to the Garden" [290], "from the Garden to the house of Annas" [291], "from the house of Pilate to the Cross" [296]. Starting from the Last Supper [289] right up to the mysteries accomplished "from the cross to the sepulchre" [298], the connecting links indicate a path to be traversed—a path including one or other of the mysteries, at the end including all the mysteries together [209], yet remaining always the passion, the paschal journey of the Lord.

As already remarked by Ignatius in the Second Week [116], this paschal journey does not begin with the Last Supper, but at the moment of the Lord's birth: "from the time of his birth down to the mystery of the passion upon which I am engaged at present" [206]. If then the absence of the indications of time places us within the eternal present of the paschal mystery, the connecting-link indications put us on a journey, on a way of the cross which begins in the birth of him who is the Way. Every stage of this Way is a mystery for the one who desires "to know better the eternal Word Incarnate" [130], right up to the point where these stages succeed one another with such intensity that, as mysteries, they give way to the totality of the passion of "the great sorrow and suffering of Christ our Lord" [206]. This way or path of "labors, fatigue and suffering" is, in the last analysis, the person of Christ our Lord who endured them [206].

The "Kenotic" Change in the Name

This way or journey works a profound transformation in the person of Christ, and Ignatius appears to call attention to this fact even in the very names used for the Lord. The use of the title "Christ our Lord," at times in the abridged forms of "Christ" or "the Lord," largely dominates the whole of the Second Week. Again, on the threshold of the Third Week, it is "Christ our Lord" who celebrates the Last Supper [191]. Indeed, Ignatius explicitly points to the contrast between "the majesty of the Lord" and the "lowliness of Peter" during the mysteries of this Last Supper [289]. Once again, it is "Christ our Lord" [201; cf. "the Lord" in 290, 291, and "Christ" in 201] who lives the mystery of the garden and works the conversion of Peter after his denial [292], but then "the divinity hides itself" [196]. There is in the use of the titles a certain tendency to efface the majesty of Christ before "the most sacred humanity" [196], which is given the name of "Jesus the Galilean" [294] and "Jesus the Nazarene" [296] until that moment when the title of "Christ our Lord" is once again taken up in the mystery of the resurrection [299].

This "kenotic" or self-emptying change in the name—not that it should be taken as absolute, for we are talking, as we have said, of a certain tendency in the use of the name—is confirmed by the same kind of tendency in the Second Week's use of the name of Jesus: there it is reserved, at times in such abbreviated forms as "the child Jesus" or "the child" or "Jesus," for the kenosis or self-emptying involved in the childhood of the Word of God. It is true that on the cross the Lord is without a name, designated simply by the pronoun "he" [297, 298]; but this linguistic fact should not be interpreted as indicating the complete effacement of Christ, for the same thing can be seen also in the other Weeks (cf. "he appeared" in 299).

From the "Creative Activity" of the Second Week
to the "Suffering Passivity" of the Third Week

Of greater importance is the movement in the person of Christ from his creative activity, that the Second Week pulsates with, to His passivity —undergoing pain and suffering—that characterizes the Third Week. The sixteen mysteries of the public life of Christ [273-288], indicated by Ignatius for the prayer of the Second Week, manifest the glory of God. Five mysteries reveal the Son of God; five mysteries highlight in miraculous fashion His divine activity; two mysteries speak of the Lord's power over sin; two are connected with His teaching, and two with the call of the apostles to follow Christ. What shines forth is the icon of the Pantocrator along whose path "sufferings" are scarcely present; the passion is never announced, and it is only in the very last mystery of the Second Week that a certain opposition to Jesus comes to light: "since there was no one in Jerusalem who would receive Him" [288]. But the Third Week, after the mystery of the agony in the garden, marks a sharp change of perspective: a feverish activity prevails all around Jesus along the path leading to the cross, but this "meek Lord" [291], in the text of Ignatius, remains right up to the resurrection either the grammatical subject of a passive verb—"he is led to Annas" [291], or more frequently the grammatical object of an active verb—"Pilate led him forth before everyone" [295]. It is the others who are active in tracing inexorably the way that leads to the cross. The Lord "allows himself to be kissed by Judas" [291] just as the divinity "leaves the most sacred humanity to suffer so cruelly" [196]. There is, however, one exception in the text of the "mysteries": "He carried the cross upon his shoulders," but this activity does not last: "He was no longer able to do so. . . ." [296].

The choice made by Ignatius of the mysteries for the Second Week and his very stylistic presentation of the mysteries for the Third Week point both to the glory of the Pantocrator and the affliction of the Suffering Servant as being the way. The "fifth point" of the first day of the Third Week [196] translates into words the reality that Ignatius has effected by his choice of the mysteries of the life of Christ: the divinity reveals itself in freely hiding itself in the cruelly suffering humanity. The Pantocrator is the Suffering Servant.

Ignatius stresses even more that the divine omnipotence reveals itself in the human powerlessness by the choice he makes of the gospel material. The Christ of the gospels is more active during His passion than the Christ of the Third Week. True, he is dragged to the slaughterhouse (Is 53:7), but he never stops protesting either by word or by His silence against the injustice inflicted on him. In the mysteries of the Third Week Jesus keeps absolutely silent from the house of Caiphas [292] right up to the cross on which he spoke seven words" [297]. The final cry of protest in Mt 27:46—"My God, my God, why have you forsaken me?" is toned down by Ignatius to: "He said that He was forsaken" [297]. All initiative in deed and word belongs to his enemies whom "the divinity . . . could destroy . . . and does not do so" [196]. The perspective of the Ignatian contemplation of the passion is clearly that Jesus "does nothing" [196] and "answers nothing" [294]. It is this Jesus not responding to the questions asked [294], as well as his not reacting to the provocations of his accusers, which Ignatius brings together in the "slap" repeatedly given Him in the face: a "slap" in the house of Annas [291], again in the house of Caiphas [292], and once more in the house of Pilate [295].

In the gospels Christ protests, and thus reveals himself as Son of God and King, but in the Third Week he does not react in any way. And yet, if the almighty power of God hides itself in the powerlessness of Jesus, it only "seemed to hide itself during the passion" [233], for it really reveals itself in the divine gift and pardon of the "meek Lord" [291] on the cross. Jesus is completely at home in his own "house," where His glory bursts forth in pardoning the thief and handing Himself over to His Father [297].

This insistence of the Third Week on the divine powerlessness scarcely differs from that of the Second Week's mysteries of the infancy. Both the human powerlessness taken up in the mysteries of the infancy as well as the human powerlessness freely submitted to in the mysteries of the passion are the "kenosis" or self-emptying of the Lord. Hence the reference to the cross in the mystery of the birth: "making the journey and laboring that the Lord might be born in extreme poverty, and that after many labours, after hunger, thirst, heat, and cold, after insults and outrages, He might die on the cross . . ."[116]. This text already contains the powerlessness in which the All-Powerful journeys from the time of His birth.

Powerlessness: a Passivity of "Positive Desire"

Though insistent here on the mystery of powerlessness, Ignatius by no means considers it purely negative. The three special or typical points of the first day of the Third Week, which contain the entire Ignatian theology of the passion, reflect a decisively positive understanding of this powerlessness. In the fourth point [195], Christ not only suffers in His human nature, but he "desires to suffer." In the fifth point [196], it is the divinity which has all the initiative as it "leaves the most sacred humanity to suffer so cruelly." And in the sixth point [197], Ignatius offers the sole response sketched by the New Testament, in the light of Is 53, to our question: Why suffering, any suffering? He says: "Christ suffers all this" . . . for us, for me, "for my sins." Ignatius presents the gospel account of the passion as a paschal journey of mysteries which all proclaim, in the last analysis, that the path of the *magis* is that of the *minus*—"to be accounted as worthless and a fool for Christ" [167]—for it is in the powerlessness of the "kenosis" that the glory of the All-Powerful is revealed to us. The why of the paschal mystery and the meaning of the cross are like the book of seven seals mentioned in the Apocalypse: only the Lamb that was slain is able to open it for us—"how it is that though he is the Creator, he has stooped to become man, and to pass from eternal life to death here in time, that thus He might die for our sins" [53].

Finally it is not just some past historical event or even a theology that I am here confronted with; rather, I come face to face with the person of Christ on His paschal journey here and now. It is up to me, then, inspired by Christ "hanging on the cross," to "ponder" [53]—that is, to enter ever more deeply, through a heart-to-heart encounter with Him, into the paschal mystery. If this first meditation of the First Week makes the retreatant ask: "What ought I to do for Christ?" [53], the Third Week goes further: "What ought I to do and suffer for Him?" [197]. The encounter with Christ would not be authentic without "sorrow with Christ in sorrow, anguish with Christ in anguish . . ." [203]. It would be spurious and warped if it did not "call to mind the labors, fatigue and suffering which Christ our Lord endured" [206] as the consequences of his desire [195], as something borne "for my sins" [197], as a creative act of the divinity who is love [196], and "how much, as far as he can, the same Lord desires to give Himself to me according to his divine decrees" [234].

Love Alone Explains All

Perhaps it is Origen who puts into words what Ignatius does not want to formulate explicitly, so that we can discover it for ourselves in the encounter and colloquy with Christ on His paschal journey. In his sixth homily on Ezechiel (5,6), Origen writes:

> If He came down to earth, it is out of compassion for the human race [cf. here 107: "Let us work the redemption of the human race"]. Yes, He bore our sufferings even before having experienced the sufferings of the cross, indeed before having taken on Himself our fleshly nature. For, had he not suffered, He would not have come to share with us our human life. First He suffered, then He came down among us [cf. here 102: "since They see that all are going down to hell, They decree in Their eternity that the Second Person should become man to save the human race"]. But what is this passion which He experienced for us? The passion of love [cf. here 338: "the love that . . . comes down from above"].

So if God suffers, it is because of His boundless love from the beginning; it is because He remains faithful to His love for us, even when this love entails the sufferings of His only Son. This reference to the love from above and from the beginning impels us to commit ourselves to it, and so it becomes and remains a confession of faith. Eastern Christianity is very fond of alluding, with Nicholas Cabasilas, to this "mad love of God for man which does not simply destroy evil and death, but assumes them." Yet it does not look upon this confession of faith as the philosophical solution to the problem of suffering.

For this reason Ignatius does not insist on the suffering, but on Christ who suffers [195]. Jesus never stopped combating suffering which He always considered an evil (Mt 26:23-24), and which he experienced in himself with such anguish that in the garden "his garments were saturated with blood" [290]. It is not so much suffering that draws us close to Christ, as Christ our Lord who in His suffering and scandalous death on the cross draws near to our sufferings and afflictions as human beings. If Ignatius then feels obliged to invite us to "begin with great effort to strive to grieve, to be sad, and to weep" [195 and 206], he does not intend some sort of voluntaristic promethean effort regarding the suffering to be experienced. Nor is he aiming at adding to the passion of Christ a new and further weight of sorrow and sadness. Ignatius gives as example the Mother of the Child Jesus who felt compassion for her Son because of the blood He shed in His circumcision [266]. For this compassion to be genuine, great effort is required, as Ignatius says, because the passion of the Lord—that is, to suffer as he suffered—is not connatural to the human person. If, indeed, suffering in its radical absurdity impels the human person to run away from it or to resign oneself to it as inevitable, to take suffering upon oneself as Christ did is, and remains, folly and a scandal.

Faithful to the gospel of the passion, Ignatius never sacralizes suffering or misfortune, but he proposes a compassion that sanctifies all suffering. The difference is based on that love which alone justifies as much Christ's desire to suffer [195], as the paschal event of His divinity leaving the most sacred humanity to suffer so cruelly [196], as also His suffering for my sins [197]. The word "love," which is the sole response to all the challenging questions of the Third Week, appears expressly in this Week only in the mystery of the Last Supper, when the Lord institutes "the most holy sacrifice of the Eucharist as the greatest proof of his love" [289]. But it is love which alone warrants and elicits our compassion [cf.197: "what I ought to do and suffer for him"].

"Compassion" Means Love

The term "compassion" can be risky and ambiguous in a context without "love," signifying then pure sentimentality, a sort of comforting pity in which man consoles even his own self over so much misfortune and misery. Ignatius does not attempt in any way to make this compassion aesthetically tolerable for us by means of some happy turn of phrase—like that of Philarète, metropolitan of Moscow (19th century), who said: "God triumphs over suffering by passing through suffering, or that of the poet Paul Claudel, who wrote: "God did not come to explain suffering, He came to fill it with His presence." The Third Week has a rich vocabulary of words to denote suffering. No aspect or element of suffering is glossed over. But suffering is always secondary in relation to the One who suffers, that is, Christ [203 and 206: "which Christ our Lord endures—or has endured—for people], and always secondary in relation to the folly of love which, according to Ignatius, is revealed in the painful powerlessness of the All-Powerful One. There can, therefore, be no compassion without suffering, but suffering freely taken on by a love that seeks effective resemblance to Christ in wanting to be "poor" and "accounted as . . . fool" for His glory [167], and not some carbon-copy imitation of the passion of Christ.

This compassion calls for an "eternal Third Week," according to the expression of Father Fessard, because in his inmost self—indeed in his very suffering—the human person seeks filfillment. The Last Supper, on which Ignatius insists as a sort of foundation for the Third Week, entails a veritable transsubstantiation of myself in which the old Adam dies to rise to the new Adam in the image and likeness of the majesty of the Lord in existential lowliness at the feet of humankind, in order to make this latter rise to new life as "Paschal Lamb" [289]. The vocabulary of Ignatius, which carries a strong affective charge—sorrow, tears, sufferings, anguish, affliction, sadness—and which insists on "sorrow with Christ in sorrow" [203], is a call to enter into the paschal mystery. This is the paschal mystery which is based on the kenosis or self-emptying of the Word of God, of which Christ's sufferings on the sense level are but painful expressions, so that we may complete by our personal kenosis what is still wanting to the passion of Christ (Col 1:24).

Conclusion

The essence of the gospel, that is of the good news, is the paschal mystery. All that goes before it is only an introduction to and preparation for it. Should we not, perhaps, say the same of the Third Week of the Exercises? Without the First Week, the acknowledgment that the Lord suffers for my sins lacks personal depth. Without the Second Week, the desire to be chosen to suffer with Christ in suffering lacks the concretization of a personal plan and decision. However, it is only in the Third Week, founded on the Eucharist that is Christ's Passover, that the sin which links me personally to the enemies that his "divinity could destroy and does not do so" [196] impels me to a true love-encounter with Christ as he effects his Passover in and with us. Again, it is only in the Third Week that all that has been desired and imagined in the form of concrete life plans and projects becomes paschal reality when His Divine Majesty places us with His crucified Son.

In this way, far from being a kind of sentimental expression of our attachment to Christ, far too from being a simple confirmation of a real but still imaginary desire of following Christ, the Third Week—no differently from the paschal mystery which this Third Week celebrates—constitutes a personalization within me of the Lord crucified and risen, of the Lamb slain and alive, seeing that I have personally acknowledged my being a sinner and personally responded to the call to follow Christ according to the Three Kinds of Humility. In biblical language, heart speaks to heart. Then sadness no longer concentrates on one's sins, then creative joy no longer takes the shape of generous plans and projects—my generous plans and projects. It is Passover, the exodus from one's own narrow self, to be sad and to rejoice with and for the Wholly Other as he is scoffed at, struck, humiliated in that one and only experience of power—his paschal might and power.

And so, the prayer of the Third Week cannot but be disinterested, ready to receive humbly and freely from the God of Jesus Christ my cross —to carry his own cross; ready to receive my Passover as the assault of humble love between God and humankind: to become, for the paschal glory of God, a fool for God. The passion according to St. Ignatius expresses the powerful love of the Lord who saved others in and through his powerlessness, incapable as He was of saving himself (Mk 15: 31). It challenges us to receive, in an act of paschal gratitude, the humility and humiliation of the Lord, for only a heart poor in spirit can make men rich with the richness of the Life of God.

SIX

"CHRIST . . . DESCENDED INTO HELL"

This essay will be dedicated to the contemplation of a mystery which today creates such a problem for us that several contemporary commentaries on the Spiritual Exercises prefer to pass over it in silence. It deals with the descent of Christ into "hell," which St. Ignatius recalls on three occasions. This mystery of the life of Christ is situated right at the center of the contemplation which begins the Week of the Risen Lord [219]. One of its aspects (the mystery of the body separated from the soul) is recalled at the end of the Third Week [208], and the other (the mystery of the soul separated from the body) at the end of the Fourth Week [311].

Problems and Significance

From the dogmatic point of view this mystery of our faith raises so many thorny problems, of which the text of the *Spiritual Exercises* carries traces. It is, also because of such problems, enveloped in so many mythical stories, that it seems at first sight quite difficult to continue to propose it as a first-prelude "history" in view of a contemplation. Father Georges Longhaye (1839-1914), in his famous "Retreat of Eight Days," was able at the time to invite us to limbo to take part in the conversations of the just people of the Old Testament as they wait for Christ, to share their impatience when John the Baptist or Joseph make known to them the latest news, and to see the Lord enter, as King of Glory, gloriously into "sheol." Today, the one who gives the Exercises prefers rather to pass directly from the cross to the empty tomb, from the Crucified One to the Risen Lord, without passing with Christ through "hell." And yet, St. Ignatius, desirous of following his king in suffering so as to follow him also in glory [95], cannot abandon his Lord during the *triduum mortis*, at that exact time when, going ahead of us, he passes from the final suffering of death to the nascent glory of new life. How is one to pass from Good Friday to the first day of the week without uniting oneself to Christ on Holy Saturday? The more so, since the life of the Church, as also our personal life, can be made up of these Holy Saturdays, when neither the acute suffering of the passion nor the overwhelming joy of the Easter feast mark our days and our nights; they are rather that difficult and patient waiting, in the most austere faith, for a Lord *(Kyrios)* who makes himself so long awaited that it seems he might never come. It is the Holy Saturday of a paschal creed which knows that the harvest will be ripe and ready on the morrow, but that, at present the grain of wheat fallen into the earth (Jn 12:24) and buried in it, does not see anything at all of the harvest. It is the *triduum mortis* of the prophet Jonah gone down into the depths, who knows all anguish therein, and yet hopes against all hope that the Living One will make him come up alive. Would not something be wanting to the "knowledge of the true life" [139] of the Lord if we did not allow ourselves to be marked by the sign of Jonah (Mt 12:40), with which he wished to carry to filfillment his existence among us?

Be that as it may, the most recent books of catechesis resume the confession of the descent into "hell," because, as manifestation of a loving *kenosis* carried to its extreme, it alone expresses the radical solidarity of Christ with the law of human death. On the other hand, the growing interest in icons reveals that for the oriental churches the descent into "hell" is the true paschal or Easter image. In this Easter icon the Lord, in one single movement, breaks open the doors of "hell" with his coming and, by means of the dramatic encounter of the New Adam with the first man, frees all the prisoners from "hell." It is, then, the radical solidarity of Christ with our death which is transformed into our solidarity with his resurrection.

The hesitation to contemplate the descent of Christ into "hell" is not unconnected with our existential difficulty of living this double constraint to our spirit, of the cross and the resurrection, of death and eternal life. The confrontation of the nothingness of our existence with its fulness seems to surpass our intellectual powers, and so Christ can only rise from the dead or he has no other aim but to die. A civilization which discards death or chases away the images of death such as old age and illness, loneliness and the night, no longer knows why it should face death; but neither, by that very fact, does it know why to live. It is so difficult to face the tension between death and life that our most beautiful language swings between verbal consolations. It focuses either on the return to the Father, the call back to the Father's house, as if our life had not begun here below, or on eternity as this very day. If resurrection is our "in-surrection," if the kingdom urges us with its present exigencies, then our life has no end in the other life. If, despite our difficulty in expressing ourselves, Easter is not at the same time a radical death and a miraculous resurrection, our convictions can only lead us to illusion or despair. The contemplation of the descent into "hell," where life and death confront each other, rudely awakens the proud who exalt life too much without daring to look absurd death in the face. But it also gives a rude shock to the resigned who only wait for death, for, as St. Augustine says, "life takes away life."

Thus, far from being abstract, purely dogmatic, or mythical, this contemplation of Christ descending into "hell" is situated at the very heart of human existence, where the One who is risen from the dead awaits us.

The Mystery of "Separation"

The first aspect of this mystery will be contemplated on the seventh day of the Third Week with the entire passion as a whole [208]. On this seventh day one should consider as frequently as possible, throughout the day, "that the most sacred body of Christ our Lord remained separated from the soul." It is as though the contemplation of the separated body of Christ became the figure and symbol of the whole passion. When St. Ignatius proposes the mysteries accomplished on the cross [297], he does not recall the death of Christ as such, but draws all our attention to a number of phenomena which echo, as it were, the mystery of "separation": the light is separated from the sun, the rocks are rent, the graves are opened, and the veil of the temple is torn in two. These natural phenomena only reflect the actions of human beings who, in blaspheming, separate themselves from God, and even urge Christ on the cross to separate himself from the madness and scandal that is a shameful death on the cross. In this context, too, are Christ's garments divided and his side pierced with a lance. It is in this separation of everything and everyone which results in the "separated body" to the extreme point that "the divinity hides itself" [196]. Only faith recognizes in it "the most sacred body of Christ our Lord . . ." [208].

St. Ignatius is quite aware of the difficulty involved in expressing this mystery of separation. At the end of the Third Week he makes use of the words *desatar* (loosen, unbind) and *apartar* (separate, divide) [208] to express that the body of Christ, at the moment of his death, was "detached" and "moved away" from the soul. At the beginning of the Fourth Week the use of the verb *separar* (separate) speaks radically of something finished and done: "the body remained separated from the soul" [219]. Is it this radicality of expression that frightened the translator of the Vulgate? He preferred to translate it as "his buried body," and thereby to distort the thought of St. Ignatius. For his part, St. Ignatius takes this separation so seriously that, at the end of the Fourth Week [311], he gives the impression that the Word of God abandoned his body at the moment of death to later "assume it again." Nevertheless, as though he had meditated the *Summa* of St. Thomas Aquinas (III, 52, 2), St. Ignatius takes care to make clear on two occasions that the separation effected is not between the divinity and humanity of the Lord, but within his humanity between soul and body: "the body . . . (though) always united with the divinity" and "his soul, likewise united with the divinity" [219]. Because of this dogmatic distinction, Father Jan Roothaan notes in his commentary on the Spiritual Exercises that the contemplation of this mystery, which is difficult to specify, runs the great risk of remaining *ieiunior*, that is leaving us in our hunger [at 219]. Doubtless, St. Ignatius situates the opening contemplation of the Week of the Risen Lord fully within the dogma of Chalcedon. The hypostatic union, already quite mysterious in itself, does not prevent a separation taking place between the soul and the body of Christ; by this very fact, at least within the Thomistic perspectives of St. Ignatius, the Lord without being "de-divinized" by death is nonetheless "de-humanized" and ceases to be man (*Sum. Th.* III, 50, 4). As a result, this dogmatic view urges St. Ignatius, even while he fully admits the above-mentioned separation, to contemplate the separated soul as "blessed" [219] and the separated body as "most sacred" [208]. These two "divine" adjectives are not applied by chance to the body and the soul of the Lord: they reveal something of the Christian anthropology of St. Ignatius.

Far, indeed, from Ignatius's thought is the idea of terming the soul "blessed" because it has been able to free itself from the body. Commentators at times cite the only phrase in the Spiritual Exercises that would strongly smack of rudimentary platonism—that is, the phrase "my soul as a prisoner in this corruptible body" [47]—to explain in this way the blessedness of the separated soul. But they forget that in the same passage St. Ignatius explicitly insists on the fact that the whole composite human being is as it were exiled here on earth: "I said: my whole composite being, body and soul" [47]. Suffice it to examine all the uses St. Ignatius makes of the terms "body" and "soul" in the text of the Spiritual Exercises to realize that, though fully conscious of the vulnerability of the body because of its virtual connivance with disorder and sin, the book of the Spiritual Exercises contains no word of contempt with respect to the body. On the contrary, its method is based on a great confidence, inspired precisely by an anthropology absorbed in the Word Incarnate, with regard to the composite human being. One single life circulates within our essential duality of body and soul, functioning in the sense of a dialogue signifying a concurrence of forces.

The whole book of the Spiritual Exercises breathes forth an air of confidence in regard to the composite human being. It grows out of the conviction that God will make himself known and recognised when we "put in order" [21] the duality between body and soul in the line of a constitutive and constructive dialogue—not when we reduce ourselves to pure spirit, or when we make rigid this duality in irreconcilable opposition. This is why St. Ignatius is not only not content with remarking on an analogy between the Spiritual Exercises and the physical exercises of the body [1], but spells out a whole spatial strategy and an entire network of time to dispose the soul. He is quite conscious that the human person is involved in space and time through the instrumentality of the body, and that in this the body constitutes the condition for all openness and relationship to the world, to others and even to the wholly-*other* that is God. It is confidence imbibed in the Word Incarnate that underlies a remark such as the following: "When the exercitant has not found what he has been seeking, for example, tears, consolation, etc., it is often useful to make some change in food, in sleep, or in other ways of doing penance. . . . Now since God our Lord knows our nature infinitely better, when we make changes of this kind, he often grants each one the grace to understand what is suitable for him" [89].

"Solitude" not Loneliness

Precisely because St. Ignatius has such confidence in the composite human being, the separation of the soul from the body is not presented as a liberation, but creates a situation of de-humanization, which puts an end to this deep-seated union of soul and body. The human person as such dies, and with preference shown to no one, not even a god. Here we are constrained to take up a comparison suggested by the Spiritual Exercises themselves. Looking at Christ on the cross gives rise to an enthusiasm to "do" something in return for so much love [53]. It is in seeing the Lord die that the Roman centurion at the foot of the cross feels impelled to proclaim a profession of faith. The contemplation of the separated body of Christ leads first of all to a recognition and admission of death which snatches away from us all our utopian exhilaration. God is truly dead, and with him are dead all the hopes that his life in our midst had aroused. As during his stay in our midst Christ was one in solidarity with the living, in the tomb he is one in solidarity with the dead. What is the meaning of this solidarity? The separation of the soul from the body proclaims not only that death is an event which affects the whole human person, but, from the point of view of the separated body, also that among the dead there exists no living communication, only a radical loneliness.

Christ's solidarity with the dead means that he is alone as are the dead, and in total solitude among the dead. The prayer of the Psalms does not hesitate to look straight in the face this truth of the *refa'im* who are such as if they did not exist (Ps 39:14)—"before I go away and am no more." Deprived of all activity and all vitality (Ps 6:6), "no one remembers you in the grave, no one can give you praise in the world of the dead"; living in the land of total oblivion (Ps 88:12) "in the land of forgetfulness." Already on the cross, says St. Ignatius, "he was forsaken" [297]. If Christ had not experienced this state of separation of soul and body, if the resurrection had, so to speak, followed immediately on his last breath on the cross, one could have doubted the reality of his death and the authenticity of a death which would be the final term of his *kenosis*. "God is here, God is present; but he is there only, if one dare say so, to make his absence felt, a need infinitely more necessary than life, and which remains radically out of reach, as though he disappeared and as though He made sport of the thirst he himself had enkindled."

This solitude of Christ in the pangs of death is mirrored in the "solitude" of Our Lady which St. Ignatius proposes for our contemplation. This solitude is not necessarily to be classed along with that of the apostles [208], where disappointment and disenchantment could well prevent "anguish with Christ in anguish" [203]. The sorrow and weariness which, according to St. Ignatius [208], accompany the solitude of Our Lady make us sense that this solitude is a loving relationship to Christ experienced in the inability to have a living encounter with him. In other words, the torture of separation does not lead Our Lady into isolated loneliness, but directs her along the path of soli-tude—solitude, precisely because it entails openness to the other and lives from the desire to be with the other. The love which constitutes the subtle difference between loneliness and solitude is a crucible, in which absence does not create a void but only serves to deepen the presence so desired. Placing before us "the body . . . detached and separated from the soul" of Christ, St. Ignatius leaves us to contemplate it with the solitude of Our Lady in her "great sorrow and weariness" [208].

Expressions of her total desire to be with Christ, this sorrow and weariness make of her solitude a sign of love. It is not the sterile closing in on self of the lonely person, but the painful apprenticeship of a unique desire whose filfillment is possible only in unconquerable hope, in austere faith, and in a love that is stronger than all death. Apropos of this, an author has written: "If ever the day comes on which you will be given true love and affection, on that day there will be no opposition between interior solitude and friendship; on the contrary, it is by this precise infallible sign that you will recognize it." The Lord himself said it in the following words: "The One who has sent me is with me; he has not left me alone, for I do always the things that please him" (Jn 8:29).

All these considerations take nothing away from the fact that the body separated from the soul involves a painful absence which is all the more felt inasmuch as it does not fulfill our desire for the presence of the all-holy God. Something of this solitude of Holy Saturday gets hold of us when we let the silence of the Father rise within our life in the Lord's Spirit, a kingdom which instead of coming seems to be going away, the face of Christ which slowly but surely appears to be obliterated in several countries of our world, a Spirit which no longer seems to fill the universe.

When all around us and within us we see multiplied the signs of an indifference in regard to the Lord and to his Church on the part of a world which organises itself more and more without him and which turns away only to amuse itself, as on the evening of Good Friday as though nothing had happened, the believer runs the serious risk of feeling powerless and alone, whereas in truth these very events ought to unite him the more to the solitude of Christ and to the mystery of his body separated from the soul by death—a death which the Lord "experienced" ("tasted": Heb 2:9) lovingly for all of us.

St. Ignatius invites us explicitly [208] to consider not only the solitude of Our Lady, but also "that of the disciples." This invitation opens out for us the way to penetrate into the mystery of the loneliness of Judas and the mystery of the solitude of Peter, whom the Lord will question about his love [306]. The starting point of this consideration might be found in the key contemplation of the Last Supper when, in the words of St. Ignatius, "(the Lord) washed the feet of the disciples, even those of Judas, beginning with St. Peter . . ." [289]. Without insisting on the fate of Judas, St. Ignatius calls attention only to the murmurings of Judas during the supper at Bethany [286], where the thing (the cost of the perfume) has clearly more importance than the love for a person: "She has wrought a good work towards me." Consequently the kiss of peace becomes the object of bargaining: "The Lord allows himself to be kissed by Judas, and to be seized as a robber" [291]. This will plunge Judas into loneliness even to the point of suicide. Though he went out and wept bitterly, St. Peter, for his part, will experience solitude, because he was "looked upon by the Lord" [292].

Separation, loneliness and solitude: the Spiritual Exercises help us to look the whole reality of death in the face, under the gaze of the Lord, even though this consideration is not at all to the liking of a civilization which, if we are to believe Solzhenitsyn, strives to ignore death while flaunting its slogan: "We live only once; we will never die." And yet, the Spiritual Exercises do not overindulge in the consideration of death, as a certain kind of preaching has at times done. A meditation on death is not suggested in the text of the *Spiritual Exercises* before 1548. For St. Ignatius the human person is not in fact a being vowed to death, even though he well knows himself to be mortal. What alone counts for him is life: the human being is, in his view, destined to live, to progress and to live still more (*magis*). The death of Christ—beyond the death on the cross—is brought in because it questions and challenges all of human life. The third rule is intended to assist one in making a good and correct choice in life [86], not in function of a "good death." The meditation on personal sin arouses a cry of wonder and the discovery that life is pure grace. One reflects on the miracle that [creatures] "have permitted me to live" [60], thus "giving thanks to God that up to this very moment he has granted me life . . ." [61] The Exercises are not meant to lead towards a holy death, but to guide our lives towards "knowledge of the true life" [139]. Within such perspectives of life, St. Ignatius invites us to "consider as frequently as possible . . . that the most sacred body of Christ our Lord remained separated from the soul . . .to consider, likewise, the solitude of our Lady...and also that of the disciples" [208].

Ignatian Accent: Soteriological Significance

Regarding the other aspect (the soul separated from the body) of this mystery, St. Ignatius's theological precision and exactitude contrast with St. Epiphanius's poetic homily for Holy Saturday, which for centuries will inspire the people of God in the Christian Orient (Migne, *PG* 43, 440-464): " . . . a great silence reigns today over the earth, a great silence and a great solitude. A great silence because the King sleeps . . . . God has fallen asleep in the flesh, and has gone to awaken those who for centuries have been asleep . . . ." St. Ignatius's theological precision and exactitude also contrast with the richly detailed meditation on Christ's stay in "hell," which St. Ignatius certainly knew from his reading of Ludolph the Carthusian's *Vita Iesu Christi* (IV, 648-654). The icon of the descent into "hell" is nothing but the visualization of the Easter proclamation: "Christ is risen from the dead; by means of his death he has crushed death and given life to the dead." This icon even today recalls that prolonged meditation of the Church on the mystery of Holy Saturday, which finds its roots in the New Testament and an early imaginative elaboration already in Judaeo-Christian theology. Respecting the powerlessness and privation of all activity proper to the state of death of the Son of God, St. Ignatius does not attribute to Christ any form of action incompatible with this state of his. He is content with mentioning the essential: "From there [hell] he [Christ] set free *(sacando)* the souls of the just . . . [219], "after he had taken them *(sacados)* from there [limbo]" (311). The verb *sacar*, which is to be found elsewhere in the

Spiritual Exercises [295, 306, 312], means simply "to take away" and implies
neither struggle nor confrontation.

The Latin Vulgate version (*ereptisque*) has introduced a certain degree
of violence by translating the original *sacar* of St. Ignatius with the verb
eripere. Thus the contemplation which opens the Fourth Week says nothing
of that which has the power of the icon. In that imagery, a thunderbolt
Christ, resplendent with light and radiating divine energy, leaps down to
trample underfoot the gates of bronze; he then enters triumphantly into the
dark abyss of the prince of that world, to engage him in a fight to the death.
Victoriously, in a movement of glory, he then snatches from "hell" Adam and
our ancestors: a staggering encounter between the two Adams, no longer in
the *kenosis* of the Incarnation but in the glory of life eternal.

Of this great paschal picture, very different from a western iconography
in which Christ seems always to rise from the dead all alone, St. Ignatius has
preserved the soteriological dimension of this mystery which directly touches
our very selves. For Christ not only dies for us; he rises for us and with us.
In this context St. Ignatius clearly distances himself from all those who, like
even St. Robert Bellarmine later, wished to believe in a visit of Christ to the
hell of the damned, or who, like Suarez, thought of a total liberation of all the
dead—the just and the damned. For St. Ignatius "hell" in this mystery is the
place called "limbo" [311], and Christ's meeting takes place with the "saintly
fathers" [311] and "the souls of the just" [219]. This group comprises in the
Spiritual Exercises "the fathers of the Old and New Testaments [275],
classified by St. Ignatius after the group of the apostles and in radical contrast
with "the souls who are in hell" [71], because they did not effectively believe
in the coming of Christ. Thus Christ does not bear the fruit of his resurrection
except to those who await him. Inspiring himself more in the Letter to the
Ephesians (4:7 ff.) than in the enigmatic teaching of the First Letter of Peter
(3:19), which seems to recount a sort of preaching to the inhabitants of "hell"
on the part of Christ, St. Ignatius is content to offer as "history" of the
mystery to be contemplated that which is accomplished in the Lord—the Lord
who, having descended, is the same who ascends to the heights, thus filling
the universe with his Spirit of life and of love, and leading on high the
captives of death. For, as usual, it is in fact a journey which Christ carries
on—as during the passion in the Third Week - from the "holy sepulchre" to
"the place or house of our Lady" [220]. It is a journey also from the

separation of the soul and the body to a radically new life in the Spirit, passing through the pangs of death. This is the theological sense of the expression "made alive in the Spirit," which is found in the first letter of St. Peter (1 Pet 3:18-20) and which St Ignatius sums up in speaking of the "blessed soul" of Christ [219]. And so, in the theological vision of St. Ignatius, the fullness of the divine life which takes possession of Jesus at the moment of his most radical humiliation in death pushes him, so to speak, towards "the saintly fathers" who await him, and towards his body which the resurrecting Spirit penetrates and invades. It is therefore in a movement, a journey, that the text of the Spiritual Exercises situates the resurrection: the sepulchre—"hell"—return to the sepulchre and to the house of our Lady. This journey in space is taken up in time, for St. Ignatius arranges all the events with one simple *despues* ("after") [219 and 311]. From the moment Christ expires on the cross to the moment of his rising and appearing to our Lady, there is a progressive development. He does not mention the biblical indication of time—"the three days"—and so avoids all controversy about the exact instant of the encounter of the Risen Lord with the souls of the just. But the Vulgate translation of 1548 goes beyond the text of St. Ignatius, hinting at a journey which somehow took place in time. In fact, this translation inserts a *demum* into the text: Christ rises "at last" [219].

Total Solidarity in Death—Life

This journey in space and in time includes a theological perspective to which we do not usually give thought. St. Ignatius highlights the fact that Christ is already rising when in "hell" he crushes the absolute evil that is death. If for us the glorification of Christ coincides, so to speak, with the moment of the apparition of the Risen Lord to Our Lady, for St. Ignatius it is the moment of the glorification of his "soul" as "blessed" [219]. This precedes the resurrection that constitutes the decisive paschal event. Starting from this vision "from on high," St. Ignatius does not hesitate to broaden the very concept of apparition. In fact, in writing that Christ "appeared also in soul to the saintly fathers in limbo" [311], the author of the *Spiritual Exercises* violates a rule of semantics. Yet, by that very fact he confers on the apparition of the Risen Lord the width and breadth of a paschal event that surpasses our limits of time and space. Under the title of a "thirteenth apparition," St. Ignatius groups two apparitions together: one to St. Paul which will take place in the future (well after the Ascension), and one to the saintly fathers in limbo, which at this moment of the Fourth Week really belongs to the past. There is also an indefinite number of apparitions to the disciples, which correspond to the present [311]. Just as the Third Week taken as a whole is centered on the separated body of Christ, the Fourth Week from beginning to end is open to the "blessed soul" of Christ who rises and is risen. In other words: the Word of God is made flesh to the point of assuming the whole of human destiny, vowed as this was to death. His divinity hides itself to such an extent that, in the separation of body-soul, his body, while remaining divinely his own, becomes a corpse, and his soul, without being annihilated, passes for us through the pangs of death. This humiliation, which is the final term of the self-emptying of the Incarnation, is seized by the Glory of God, and Christ, according to the expression of St. Peter, is "made alive in the Spirit" (1 Pet. 3:18-20). To put it in the language of the Spiritual Exercises: " . . . the divinity, which seemed to hide itself during the passion, now appears and manifests itself so miraculously in the most holy resurrection in its true and most sacred effects" [223].

"Miraculously" bespeaks the absolute gratuitousness and radical newness of this Life arisen from among the dead. It is the mystery in Christ which St. Ignatius proposes for a prayer of adoration in which "a mortal servant speaks to his Master who is Life and has conquered death" [cf. 54]. But the glory of the living God, which takes full possession of the One who died for us all, is communicated—"its true and most sacred effects" [223]—when the Lord, in his blessed soul, appears (if we are to use the language of St. Ignatius) and manifests himself to the souls of the just. The glory continues when the Lord, in his soul and body, appears and manifests himself to Our Lady and "appeared many times to his disciples and conversed with them" [311], thus going beyond our categories of space and time. It is this dimension that constitutes the Easter feast for us who live on earth, where the Risen Lord exercises "the office of consoler" [224]. It is not the resurrection as such which is at the heart of the Fourth Week from beginning to end; that is altogether impossible to grasp. It is the Risen Lord, in whom we adore the paschal mystery, but who also invites us "to feel joy and happiness at the great joy and happiness of Christ our Lord" [229]. We are called, then, to converse with the Risen Lord "as one friend speaks to another" [54], and in this paschal period as "friends are wont to console each other" [224]. In this way the opening contemplation of the Fourth Week in no way gets bogged down in an intellectual consideration on the confrontation between life and death, but unites us with the disconcerting reality and adorable fulness of the mystery of Christ. This is the Christ who, one with us in our death to its bitter end, makes us one with him in his new life, which is today offered to us as a new earth and a new heaven.

The prayer of the Christian Orient gives this prayerful meaning to Holy Saturday:

> In heaven on a throne,
> here on earth lying in a tomb,
> God our Saviour,
> you unsettled with your death
> the powers of Heaven and of Hell,
> contemplating the unheard-of sight of the Creator stretched out
> in death.
> In order that the whole universe be filled with your glory, you went down
> to the depths of the earth,
> and there I have not been able to hide from you
> my nature fallen in Adam,
> but your burial renews me,
> Lord, friend of humankind.

Conclusion: Life in the Living One

After all this explanation on the opening contemplation of the Fourth Week, must we not admit that, instead of having brought the mystery nearer home to us, this has only served to remove it further away from us? Is it not as though we were witnessing an event regarding the person of Christ which does not concern us except inasmuch as it affects the women and the disciples in the paschal period? This exposé confirms at least what so many other commentators on the Spiritual Exercises have highlighted, namely, that Christ for St. Ignatius is always the eternal Word, the *Kyrios,* the Lord in his glory, never separated from the fulness of his being lived in the plenitude of the Trinity. It is always Christ forever glorious: only the situations change, stressing some particular aspects of his Epiphany. "Though deeply attached to the historical Christ, which makes it possible for Ignatius to reach out to his Lord through the latter's deeds and words and the places he dwelt in while among us, St. Ignatius ceaselessly adores the Majesty of the eternal Lord." His is not merely a refusal to reduce Christ to a human value or to an extraordinary person in his dedication and service to others. Nor is it only a refusal to make of Christ a commonplace companion for life after life, but a call to truly associate oneself with the divine Living One who was crucified and to share his divine passion. St. Ignatius is convinced—at its heart this is the contemplation of the "Kingdom"—that only the Eternal King has the right to ask for the best of ourselves.

Within these perspectives, the mysteries of the descent into "hell" and the glorification of the crucified Lord reveal that life forever—the resurrection—is a purely gratuitous gift. It is precisely this gratuity of the gift of life that contrasts sharply with our growing conviction that we can become increasingly those who hold the reins of life, doing all in our power to disguise death as a shameful failure. Besides, the drama of our civilization is that it engenders death in the very measure in which it wishes to improve or even save life. Why not recognize within ourselves the instinct of death which leads to the rejection of our own life and of the life of others, which leads thus to murder and suicide? To associate oneself with Christ in his descent into "hell" so as to rise up with him entails, then, uprooting from one's heart the complicity with all death and allowing oneself to be seized by the Glory of God which gives life. It means uniting oneself, with a view to being transformed, to the Living One who raises the dead, the Risen One from among the dead.

SEVEN

FOOLS FOR CHRIST'S SAKE

The ruthless war between Iraq and Iran has made us all familiar with the expression "the fools of God." Fanatical and vowed to suicide in their daring deeds, these militant fundamentalists believe they live Islam or a certain kind of Islam unconditionally. They are by no means the first "fools of God" that the Middle East has known. Till today so many Churches there revere and celebrate their own "fools for Christ." In Egypt, the Church of Alexandria honors St. Mark the fool (sixth century). In Syria, the town of Homs venerates Symeon the Fool (sixth century), and the great Church of Constantinople itself sings the praises of its famed fool, St. Andrew Salos (ninth century). With the passage of centuries this contagious folly for Christ's sake moves up north and becomes one of the characteristics of Russian sanctity. Such a foolish way of following Christ would seem to have no more than a tenuous link with Ignatian spirituality, since, in the latter, what appears to be dominant is the balance of the "discreta caritas," the result of a long process of discernment and of well-ordered deliberation. And yet, at the very heart of the Exercises leaps out the cry: "I desire to be accounted as worthless and a fool for Christ" [167].

First Steps in Folly for Christ

At first blush this foolish love for God appears to be no more than a passing phase in the process of St. Ignatius's spiritual maturation. Thus, for example, on his journey from Venice to Genoa, the pilgrim Iñigo's behaviour is all foolishness. He distributes all his money: "all he had was finished" (*Autob*. 50). Then he travels by the road that he knows to be the most dangerous. The Spanish soldiers urge him not to take that road, "but he did not take their advice" *(Autob.* 51). He is then seized and taken for a fool or a spy. Brought before the captain, he uses the familiar form of the second person instead of the more polite and courteous form of respect, indicating thus rather inopportunely an equality of social status *(Autob.* 52). Inevitably the captain takes him for a madman: "This man is not in his senses" *(Autob.* 53). All this manner of behaving like a fool is in the last analysis inspired "by his devotion" *(Autob.* 52) to Christ humiliated and led away.

However, this behaving like a fool on the part of Ignatius, which enters well into the spiritual tradition of "the fools for Christ's sake," is not just a passing folly. *The Pilgrim's Testament,* or *Autobiography* of Ignatius, already shows how it is an inevitable consequence of the Spiritual Exercises. On his return from Flanders Ignatius dedicates himself intensely to spiritual conversations with the students. The word spreads rapidly in Paris that Ignatius, "a seducer of the students," had caused a certain Amador to go mad *(Autob.* 78). In what does this madness, result of the Spiritual Exercises, consist? Amador gives all he has to the poor, even his books; he begs alms and goes to lodge in the hospice of St. James *(Autob.* 77). Some students "go armed" to the hospice and put an end to Amador's foolish stay there among the destitute of Paris *(Autob.* 77).

With this desire of Ignatius to be a fool for Christ so intimately linked to the experience of the Spiritual Exercises, is it any wonder that it never left him? If the *Autobiography* is a sort of spiritual testament of Ignatius, then the experience of what happened in the prison at Salamanca ought to pervade the entire life of the Society. Don Francisco de Mendoza, later to be Cardinal of Burgos, would hear from the prisoner Ignatius himself the answer the latter gave to a lady who had pity on him: "By this you show that you do not wish to be imprisoned for the love of God. . . . there are not so many fetters and chains in Salamanca that I do not want more for the love of God" *(Autob.* 69). The foolishness for Christ's sake contained in these words becomes evident when, taking advantage of a good opportunity, the prisoners all escaped from this prison, but Ignatius and his companion "were found there alone without anyone, with the doors open" *(Autob.* 69). A long letter of Fr. Diego Laínez, written at Bologna on June 16, 1547, to Fr. Juan de Polanco, twice confirms the desire of Ignatius to suffer out of love for Christ: "All the chains and prisons of the world would not be enough to satisfy the desire he had" *(Autob.*

26). More explicitly in terms of foolishness: "he would want to go, as he said, barefoot and his badly affected leg visible, with horns around his neck, but he does none of this just to be able to win souls" (*Autob.* 60). This desire cannot be found wanting in a companion of Jesus; Ignatius, in fact, postulates it in the *General Examen*: " . . . where there would be no offence to his Divine Majesty and no imputation of sin to the neighbor, they would wish to suffer injuries, false accusations and affronts, and to be held and esteemed as fools (but without their giving any occasion for this), because of their desire to resemble and imitate in some manner our Creator and Lord Jesus Christ . . . " (c. IV, n.44). Without professing this desire the candidate cannot join the Society. Ignatius is quite aware of the fact that this desire does by no means come naturally to us. Inspired, perhaps, by his assiduous reading of the *Imitation of Christ* (*de gratia tua . . . desiderii desiderium habeo . . .*),[1] Ignatius requires of the candidate at least the desire of desiring to be a fool for Christ (*Gen. Ex.*, c. IV, n. 45).

Rooted in the Spiritual Exercises

This desire of being a fool for Christ's sake is presented by Ignatius in the Spiritual Exercises in the form of a prayer. The actual wording of this consideration of the Third Kind of Humility reveals Ignatius's difficulty in eliciting a desire which lets itself be gripped by "the Lord [who] desires to give himself to me" [234], or in releasing a love which lets itself be transformed by the love which descends from above [184]. By comparing the Autograph version of Ignatius's *Exercises* with the other versions of the text, let us try to draw out the elements contained in this prayer to be a fool for Christ.

What is striking at the very outset is the marked personalization of this folly for Christ's sake. Whereas the Vulgate version of 1548 weakens this personal note in the Third Kind of Humility by exhorting the exercitant to embrace contempt and the stigma of madness, the Autograph clearly expresses the desire to be a fool like "Christ who was treated so before me" [167: *loco*

---

[1] *Imitation*, Book IV, c. 14, #3.

por Cristo que primero fue tenido por tal]. The accounts of the passion relate how Jesus was made fun of (e.g., Mt 27:31; Mk. 15:20; Lk 22:63 and 23:11). But Mark also tells us how the very relatives of Jesus were convinced that he was out of his mind (Mk 3:21), and John reports that those who heard the words of Jesus believed he was raving mad. (Jn 10:20). Ridicule even to the extreme expression of the cross was the almost inevitable result of the itinerant ministry of Jesus, whose words shattered the image of God dear to most of his contemporaries, whose deeds stood in shocking opposition to the holy law of God, whose Gospel undermined the millenary hopes of a whole people of God. It is this foolish love of what is true life, upsetting all the wisdom and all the assurance which believed its source to be in God himself, that opened "the way" (Acts 9:2) of Jesus—a way so foolish and scandalous that to nobody, neither Jew nor Gentile, does it make sense (1 Cor 1:23). The conclusion that Paul of Tarsus draws from all this is that in order to become truly wise it is necessary to be a fool for Christ's sake (2 Cor 11:1).

Apart from a slight variation in the various versions of the *Exercises*, all of them follow the Autograph in its concern for situating this folly for Christ's sake at the heart of the glory of God. Ignatius does not intend to oppose the folly of the cross to the glory of God as though the one excludes, or sets limits to, the other. In the thinking of St. John (17:1), the hour of this folly of the cross is itself the glory of God. It is from the glory of God that the folly of the cross derives, and it is for the glory of God that it is embraced. Hence glorifying certain expressions of foolishness in or for themselves is out of the question.

St. Ignatius strives to communicate two truths which appear at first sight to be contradictory. On the one hand, since the folly of the cross is the glory of God, it is not possible to be a companion of Jesus without sharing the foolishness of Christ by renouncing what is "wise and prudent in this world" [167]. The Christians of Corinth learned this truth or message of the cross, at once crucified and crucifying, from Paul of Tarsus. On the other hand, convinced as he was that all the concrete expressions of the folly of the cross do not necessarily and in all cases redound to the glory of God, Ignatius makes us beg in a continuing prayer of discernment for the specific effective way of being "a fool for Christ" [167]. By means of this persevering prayer, the companion of Jesus remains open to the unexpected and unforeseen character of the concrete forms of this foolishness for Christ's sake, which the free gift of God's love and the freedom of the passion of Christ inspire. At the beginning and at the end of his letter to the Christians of Philippi, Paul of Tarsus shows how he can face all situations, whether of life or of death, with equal freedom provided only that Christ be glorified. It is in this light that Ignatius's Autograph version of the *Exercises* urges us "to beg Our Lord to deign to choose [us] for this third kind of humility" [168]. The Vulgate version of 1548 completes this prayer by begging God to inspire this choice within us. Borne then by the force of a total availability shot through with prayer, the desire to be a fool for Christ does not automatically and necessarily entail undergoing the sufferings that Christ endured during his passion. Nor does it imply the imitation either of what Ignatius practiced as a pilgrim or of what Benedict Labre experienced as a tramp—no, not even some of those stereotyped forms which express the experience of the famed fools of Eastern Christianity.

Folly for Christ and the Glory of God

Thus Ignatius does not oppose the folly of the cross to the glory of God in the sense that one would truly wish to be a fool for Christ, but then his glory would be at variance with it. There does not exist one Gospel of the glory of God and another of the cross. One and one alone is the triumphant Easter proclamation: "By his death he has conquered death." In the exercise of the Kingdom [95], Ignatius considers the continuing work and mission of Christ as the entering of all humanity into the glory of the Father by its first following Christ on his way of the cross: "in bearing all wrongs and all abuse and all poverty, both actual and spiritual" [98]. To carry out the mission of Christ, which consists in proclaiming the Gospel of the glory of the Father to humankind which understands glory in a totally different way, is to make one's own the Gospel of the cross. This latter does not consist first of all in suffering and death, but primarily in vibrant life that comes through losing one's own self in self-gift and self-surrender so that the glory of the Father may shine forth in the lives of our brothers and sisters. It is the glory of the Father that will give a concrete form and expression to our mission of "carrying his cross."

Well-known is the surprise of some commentators on the Spiritual

Exercises at finding the Third Kind of Humility among the exercises of the Second Week. Would not its more natural place be in the Third Week where Christ is "loaded with insults" [167]? We would do well to recall here that in his *Spiritual Diary* Ignatius acknowledges, on February 27, 1544, that Christ is "completely my God" (*ser todo mi Dios*). It is always the light of the Incarnate Word that shines forth in Christ crucified and risen, hence in all "the mysteries of the life of Christ our Lord" [261]. In this way the folly of Christ is not identified exclusively with the expressions of his suffering. Thus, if one wishes to be a fool for Christ's sake it is not required to reproduce in oneself the acts and deeds of his passion. It is always Christ in his glory that is contemplated from the crib to the cross. "This Son shines with the brightness of God's glory, he is the exact likeness of God's own being" (Heb 1:3).

The response of the human person to the glory of God in Christ is presented in traditional fashion by Ignatius as a sort of hierarchy: the three kinds of humility and, within the third, three grades or steps of poverty, insults, and folly. Rather than build up a glorious ascent, Ignatius feels impelled, in fidelity to the gospel message, to propose a descent even to the point of burial in the *kenosis* of the Lord. In the last analysis, then, Ignatius helps us discover that folly of the glory of God which only divine love is capable of preventing from becoming sheer stupidity. No wonder, therefore, that we find in the Treatise on the Election of Dr. Pedro Ortiz, who in 1538 made the Spiritual Exercises at Monte Cassino under the direction of St. Ignatius, that these three kinds of humility are in fact as many degrees of the love of God.[2] All the elements are thus assembled to bear eloquent witness to what Ignatius leaves us to discover for ourselves, preferring not to proclaim it in the unabashedly strong language of Easter Christianity. That is, namely, "the Creator draws it [the soul] wholly to the love of his Divine Majesty" [330], a love which is *manikos eros*,[3] a mad love of God for man. Metropolitan Philarète of Moscow formulated it beautifully when he said, "The Father is the Love which crucifies, the Son is the Love that is crucified, and the Holy

---

[2] *Monumenta Ignatiana, Ex. Sp.*, p. 635.

[3] Nicolas Cabasilas (Fourteenth Century), *La vie en Jésus-Christ*.

Spirit is the unconquerable force and power of the Cross."[4] Glory, then, is the unconquerable weakness of God in his love. Glory is the life of God who gives himself, who surrenders himself in love. This, therefore, is what, at the invitation of Ignatius, we dare to ask for in prayer: "Give me your love and your grace" [234]. "The love that moves and causes me to choose must descend from above, that is, from the love of God" [184]. Then this love will be transformed by means of the cross; it will be crucified precisely so that God may shine forth in and through it [338]. It will also be rather foolish with the loving folly of God.[5] Requiring a "love which ought to manifest itself in deeds more than in words" (230), Ignatius urges us to ask ourselves how authentic this foolish love for Christ really is. Is it just an enthusiastic way of speaking or must these words be taken literally?

Eastern Christian Tradition

Eastern Christianity does not hesitate to answer in the affirmative: they must be taken literally. This is how the church history text of Evagrius describes the model of a true fool for Christ, St. Symeon of Emesus of the sixth century:

> . . . he strives to pass for a bad Christian and also for an immoral person; monk though he is, he proclaims complete disregard for the precepts of the Church. He does not set foot in a church except to upset the liturgy; he chooses a day like Maundy Thursday to gorge himself publicly at the pastryshop, he eats meat like a godless person. (IV, 34)

This model appears openly to contradict the Ignatian perspective which, in the case of insults and wrongs, specifies the condition "provided only I can suffer these without sin on the part of another, and without offence of the Divine Majesty" [147]. In celebrating St. Symeon the Fool, the Church gives us an

---

[4] *Oraisons, homélies et discours*, Paris , 1894, p. 154.

[5] Cf. Paul Evdokimov, *L'amour fou de Dieu*, Paris, 1973, p. 78.

assurance that the radical nature of his folly for Christ was genuinely evangelical, and that in some pastoral fashion it was aimed at upsetting the then-widespread hypocrisy and formalism. In the 11th century St. Andrew the fool *(salos)*, who takes the folly of St. Symeon as model and prototype, is quite aware of the scandal he causes, and he begs God to pardon those whom he had provoked to ill-treat him. Even while feigning folly, indeed downright madness, Symeon and Andrew are strong personalities, quite aware of being called to an apostolic mission. When St. Symeon exclaims: "I set out in the power of Christ to win over the world," and when the Lord calls St. Andrew to dedicate his life to the salvation of his neighbor "even to the point of becoming a fool for my sake," we seem to hear precisely what Ignatius will later propose in the Spiritual Exercises. It is well to note that even Eastern Christianity takes care to avoid folly for folly's sake. Not every fool is a fool for Christ's sake. Thus instead of characterizing the fool for Christ's sake with the Pauline term for "fool" which is *moros* (1 Cor 4:10), he is just termed *salos,* which stands more or less for "possessed." For the same reason the Russian equivalent for the fool for Christ's sake is not *bouy,* but rather *yourodiv.* St. Augustine, specialist in the tension between "being Christian" and "appearing Christian," in his commentary on the First Letter to the Corinthians, exhorts every Christian to be a fool for Christ. He writes, *Dic te stultum et sapiens eris* (say you are foolish, and you will be wise); only *intus dic* (say it within you), that is, make of it principally a matter of the heart.[6]

At the time of St. Ignatius the fools for Christ, who, while perfectly healthy in spirit, feign madness for the purpose of prophetically proclaiming the truth; e.g., the *yourodivi,* are particularly numerous in Russia. Basil the Blessed, after whom the cathedral in Moscow's Red Square is named, and a contemporary of St. Ignatius, "acts the fool" in order to denounce in Christ's name the inhuman cruelty of Czarist autocracy in the face of which the official local Church remains silent, stuck in its ritual rigidity. Since the folly of the cross is necessarily scandalous, the *yourodivi* cause that type of scandal that in the last analysis humiliates not the fool for Christ's sake but the wise person

---

[6] Migne, *PL,* 38, 436-437. Cf. Irina Gorainoff, *I pazzi in Cristo nella tradizione ortodossa,* Milano 1988, p. 207; V. Rochcau, "Saint Siméon Salos, ermite palestinien et prototype des 'fous-pour-le-Christ'," *Proche Orient Chrétien* 28 (1978) 209-219; V. Rochcau, "Que savons-nous des fous-pour-le-Christ?," *Irenikon* 53 (1980) 341-353: 501-512.

who thinks himself Christian. This particular type of folly for Christ was not
the only one known in St. Ignatius's time. It inspired St. John of God to live
with and for the mentally handicapped and deranged: it gave rise to the
extravagant and original apostolic initiatives of St. Philip Neri.

We need only let ourselves be led by Ignatius's *Autobiography* in order
to discover the spiritual currents which directed him towards this desire to be
accounted as a fool. We must first mention the name of Erasmus of Rotter-
dam: through his publications he accompanied the university student Ignatius
from Alcalá to Paris (*Autob.* 65), but he was frankly allergic to the folly of
the cross. His moralizing doctrine, focused on the difficult human ideal
postulating perfect moral balance, rejected in practice any transgression of that
ideal; it thus did away with the spiritual dynamism that only the folly of the
cross is able to stir up. Erasmus's eulogy of folly—*Moriae Encomium*—is a
masterpiece of irony denouncing all human stupidity; this *laus stultitiae* leaves
no room whatever for the foolish love of God. Any wonder that Ignatius felt
the Spirit of God grow cold within him and his ardent devotion diminish when
glancing through a book of Erasmus?[7] For his reading Ignatius turns rather to
the *Imitation of Christ* in which the influence of the *devotio moderna* makes
itself felt in a way very different from the works of Erasmus.[8] The author of
the *Imitation* does not hesitate to affirm: "You must become a fool for Christ
if you wish to live a religious life."[9] This conviction runs through the entire
history of religious life in its varied forms. In the *Golden Legend* or the *Lives
of Saints* which he read at Loyola, Ignatius came across the "saintly follies"
of the monks of the desert. Twice in the *Autobiography* he mentions the urge
to eat nothing but plain vegetables (nn. 8, 12) probably in imitation of St.
Onuphrios (4th century) who served the Lord "stupidly, in animal fashion" so
as to fulfill the words of the Psalm which prays: "I was stupid and did not
understand; I acted like an animal toward you. Yet I am always with you" (Ps
73/72:22-23).[10] Again, the Franciscan movement of renewal following a path

---

[7] Ribadaneira, *Vita*, FN IV, 172-174.

[8] Cf. da Câmara, *Memorial*, n. 97; cf. *Spiritual Exercises*, 100.

[9] Book I, 17.

[10] Cf. S. Hilpsich, "Die Torheit um Christi willen", *ZAM* 6 (1931) 122.

"considered to be folly"[11] impresses the pilgrim Ignatius: "What if I should do this which St. Francis did . . . ? *(Autob.* 7). It is not just that several Christians in their encounters with Francis exclaimed: "What a fool!" No: the saint of Assisi saw his vocation in this very folly. At the Chapter of Nattes he cried out against some all-too-prudent brethren: "I do not want you to speak to me of another rule, be it that of St. Augustine, of St. Bernard, or of St. Benedict. The Lord has revealed to me that he wants me to be a new fool in the world. He the Lord, has not willed to lead me by any other path but this one."[12]

Originality of Ignatius's Folly for Christ

While clearly integrated into a spiritual tradition to which Ignatius's *Autobiography* bears evident witness, the desire to be a fool for Christ's sake has nonetheless an original trait to it in Ignatian spirituality. This folly always lovingly directed to the glory of God becomes, at least in desire, a quality deemed necessary to be a companion of Jesus *(Gen.Ex.* c. IV, n.44 or *Const.* 101). And yet, compared with Onuphrios and Francis, not to speak of the saintly fools of Russia, Ignatius does not seem at all a fool for Christ. He is the man of discernment. Is not a significant part of his correspondence aimed chiefly at urging his companions against their "saintly follies"?[13] His mysticism is characterised neither by the quiet contemplation of eternal truth nor by the intoxication of the love of God. It is a mysticism of service which does not express itself in rapturous outbursts or ecstasies, but is likened more to "the beam of a balance" at equilibrium (15).[14] Is this then what Ignatius is, with all his desire to be a foolish companion of him who was first taken for a fool?

In our quest for the originality characterizing the folly for Christ according to St. Ignatius, we run into a problem in the interpretation of the

---

[11] *Legenda trium sociorum*, n. 39.

[12] *Legenda perusina*, n. 114.

[13] *Letter to the Scholastics of Coimbra*: May 7, 1547.

[14] Cf. D. Thalhammer, *Grosser Entschluss* 11 (1955-56) 344.

Spiritual Exercises. As long as Ignatius speaks of poverty—the folly of St. Francis—a relevant updating of the Exercises takes place quite naturally even within a socio-economic situation so very different from his own. Even today, not to want to make the most of a technically advanced consumer society seems completely foolish. But Ignatius expresses the desire to be a fool even in the language of honor, very much in line with the thinking of a certain social class in Spain that was jealous of its honor even to the point of folly. At the beginning of his *Autobiography*, Ignatius recounts how much care he took of his own personal appearance—he would even undergo the martyrdom of untold physical suffering just to be able to wear elegant boots[15]—and how "he imagined what he would do in the service of a certain lady" whose rank was higher than that of a countess or a duchess (*Autob.* 4; 6). We hear an echo of this courtly culture in the shame and confusion of the knight who has "grievously offended his lord" [74] and in the ignoble behaviour of the knight who "refuses the invitation of such a king" [94]. Within such a context of honor Ignatius implies that it is not just socio-economic status that makes us "esteem" or "belittle" a human person. Doubtless wealth and poverty contribute largely to founding the scale of values that a human community lives by. But from his own cultural background Ignatius knows well that worth does not depend exclusively on possessions. He himself experienced that a person is perfectly capable of renouncing possessions in order to acquire even greater worth: "And soon the tale grew (at Manresa) into saying more than the truth: that he had given up a large income, etc." (*Autob.* 18). The scale of social worth through honour and contempt changes as fashion does: today's fool may well become tomorrow's or a whole century's wise man. But honor and contempt remain the two closely related poles of that huge deception which all of human society sets up to judge the worth of a human person according to standards and criteria. These hardly correspond to God's truth about man and thus almost compel him to transform what he really is into appearances, to convert his true person into a masked personage.[16]

The meditation of the Two Standards [136 ff.] shows how God through his Son and in their Spirit leads us to "the knowledge of the true life" [139]

---

[15] Ribadenaira, *Vita*, FN IV, 85.

[16] Cf. J. Thomas, *Le secret des Jésuites*, Paris, 1984, p. 175 ff.

by means of a "civilization of love" based on poverty and humility [146]. To these last two Ignatius adds "insults and contempt" because this civilization of love (or of "communion," as our Orthodox brethren term it), far from being connatural to us, comes up against such opposition both within and outside of us that it is seen as a counter-culture. Indeed, it is even deemed anti-cultural and contemptuously held to be sheer madness. When at Alcalá Ignatius tried to live out this civilization of love by means of gratuity, "he began to beg and to live on alms," and people "began to laugh at him and to utter some insults" (*Autob.* 56). To these people it is inevitable that a poor wretch takes to begging, but that someone "in good health" takes to it in the belief that gratuity is a social value—this is sheer madness. And yet, it is only by clothing oneself with the clothing and uniform of Christ who first clothed himself with it that the kingdom of love is built up for the glory of God (cf. *Gen. Ex.* c. IV, n. 44 or *Const.* 101).

This is why the glory of God, far from playing down or soft-pedaling the foolishness for Christ, never ceases rather to stir it up in its most varied forms and ensure its apostolic authenticity. For, in keeping with St. John's perspective, the glory of God does not stand merely for the divine being in the manifestation of its shining splendor. It also represents the radiance of grace and of truth emanating from the person of the Word Incarnate as it continues to shine forth in the work of salvation for the human community—the salvific work in which we are called to collaborate. "It is to the glory of my Father that you should bear much fruit" (Jn 15:8). The greater glory of God, which becomes the passion of Ignatius, consists in being "placed with the Son" (*Autob.* 96) in his mission to bear fruit, that is, to lead men and women to his and our Father. Nothing then can serve the cause of the glory of God that does not form an integral part of the coming of his kingdom of love among us. Hence it is that Ignatius often uses the expression "to produce fruit" in his writings: for every task, every way of life should always be chosen, directed and carried on in function of the fruit which it produces, so that in this fruitfulness the glory of God may be recognized and its cause served.

But then, if it is to bear fruit in the likeness of Christ, the grain of wheat must fall to the ground, to disappear and die so as to rise again. The greater glory of God is achieved in the foolishness of the cross of his Son. In a letter to Duke Ascanius Colonna (15 April 1543), Ignatius desires, for the greater glory of God, the Duke's "complete prosperity," while at the same time coupling with this wish his eager longing to "desire nothing but Christ and him crucified, so that, while crucified in this life, it (the soul) may ascend resurrected to the next." Glory and the cross, the honor of God and folly: it is just not possible to separate the one from the other, or to set them in opposition to each other.

Ignatius's "Discerning Love": Compatible with "Folly for Christ"?

It would therefore not be right to propose the Spiritual Exercises—and the Constitutions—merely within the perspective of effective apostolic fruitfulness (bearing fruit) for the greater glory of God, while bracketing off the foolishness for Christ's sake and preserving it for some exceptional situations. It would also not be right to stress so one-sidedly the indispensable conditions to be truly a fool for Christ. I refer here to the need not to give any occasion for offence to his Divine Majesty or imputation of sin to the neighbor *(Gen.Ex.,* c. IV, n. 44 or *Const.* 101), and the need that equal or greater praise and service be given to the Divine Majesty [168]. Such an overemphasis on reasonableness can result in practically doing away with folly in order to be humanly prudent and reasonable. No doubt the note struck in Ignatius's correspondence is one of moderation; in some of the Society's provinces the companions are conspicuous for their excessive zeal and indiscreet fervor. In his letter of May 7, 1547, to the scholastics of Coimbra Ignatius makes use of a saying of St. Bernard to remind the companions, who were in fact crucifying the new man by excessively crucifying the old man, that "the enemy has no more successful ruse for depriving the heart of real charity than to see to it that it is practiced rashly and not in keeping with spiritual reasonableness."[17] We always run the risk of forgetting that, ever since the glory of God was pleased to reveal itself on Good Friday, this same "spiritual reasonableness" is folly.

Consequently we should not present the Ignatian *discreta caritas* as a sort of perfect balance between love and human prudence, nor equate Ignatius's

---

[17] Migne, *PL*, 184, 327.

"discerning love" with circumspect and carefully calculated tact. The opposite of well-ordered love is not folly but, to use Ignatius's language, "inordinate affection" which, brought about as it is by sin [63], by carnal love [97] and by the vehemence of natural appetite [216], turns away as much from the glory of God as from the folly of the cross. In a word, an affection is inordinate by reason of any motive that is not inspired in that one love which expresses itself as foolish service for the greater glory of God.

The *Autobiography* of Ignatius may perhaps put us off a bit. The folly for Christ appears to belong just to Ignatius's enterprising pilgrim years: it would seem that, once done with the stage of his apprenticeship, he becomes a model of circumspect and cautious competence, notably in the field of government. Very early on, Fr. Juan de Polanco has to shield Ignatius against the accusation of "bending the knee to Baal" in his skillful use, too skillful some think, of human means and resources.[18] Backed up by a whole lot of biblical and patristic references, Polanco states that God wishes to be served as author not only of grace but of nature too: all things, then, ought to be ordered and directed to the glory of God. One particular conviction of Ignatius contained in the *Constitutions* completely does away with any ambiguous interpretation, when he acknowledges that such "prudence" in the use of means is given and inspired by God alone. He writes, "All this can be taught only by the unction of the Holy Spirit and by the prudence which God our Lord communicates to those who trust in his Divine Majesty" *(Const.* 414: IV, 8,8). Foolishness for the sake of the Lord bearing his cross takes God, then, as its starting point even before it is found in our enthusiasm for companionship with Christ. Precisely because this folly is inspired and guided by the Spirit of the Lord, the companion of Jesus makes sure that it does not turn out to be at bottom a perversion of the cross, idolatrous self-will, or self-love, which destroys not just the person himself but the good of another, be he friend or enemy. "Should thy most holy Majesty deign to choose and admit me . . ." [98]: this same proviso is re-echoed in the colloquy of the Three Kinds of Humility [168].

And so, what at first sight appears to be a restriction that would make all foolishness for Christ extremely exceptional, indeed impossible, is in the last

---

[18] Letter to Fr. John Alvarez: July 18, 1549.

analysis a greater availability and openness to all those concrete forms, old and new, that give expression to this desire to be a fool for the Lord. It is a desire to be chosen not on the basis of human conditions, however generous they be, but solely by the choice of God, however unexpected this may be, for the coming of his kingdom among us. In itself it is already folly when persons radically lose their own desires in God's desire for his glory. This is the Ignatian understanding of a lapidary formula that the writers of the Middle Ages took pleasure in repeating, while attributing it to St. Augustine: *Ipse ibi modus est sine modo amare* ("In this, the very measure is loving without measure").

To be authentic, folly for Christ presupposes the knowledge of his true life today among men and women, and hence requires an ongoing discernment precisely in the light of the One who was first regarded as a fool (167). This discernment, as in the case of the saintly fools of Eastern Christianity, can lead to bewildering results, so that we always run the risk of identifying folly for the Lord's sake with these spectacular exploits. St. Basil the Blessed, Ignatius's contemporary, performs all kinds of foolish deeds—he goes about naked in the streets of Moscow, spends the night in a widow's house, smashes an icon of the Blessed Virgin Mary. But those who witness these bizarre and scandalous actions are convinced that, beneath his foolish deeds, lies hidden a "deeply wise" meaning. This is their way of unmasking, especially through a "virtuous" behavior, the influence of Lucifer wherever it disguises itself.[19]

It is not "hubris"[20] and its indiscreeet expressions that frighten Ignatius. If we are to believe Fr. Ribadeneira, Ignatius said in so many words that those who wish to be prudent—too prudent—in what pertains to God rarely perform great and heroic deeds. The reason is, as Ignatius wrote to the Duke of Alba, that "what does not seem to conform to human prudence may very well be according to divine prudence, which is not bound by the laws of human reason.[21] The consequence of this spiritual attitude of Ignatius is that, in comparison with the concrete forms of foolishness for Christ, the glory of God

---

[19] Cf. I. Kologrivof, "Les 'fous pour le Christ' dans l'hagiographie russe," *RAM* 25 (1949), 433.

[20] Cf. M. De Certeau, "Le silence de l'absolu" (*Folles et Fous de Dieu*) *RSR* 67 (1979) 530.

[21] *Monumenta Ignatiana*, Epp. XI, P. 8.

is always greater. It precludes no form a priori; the choice is left to God's glory alone. And because this glory shines forth in the Son of the Father, every discernment of the Spirit of the Lord and every election becomes manifest in the Third Kind of Humility, in which submission to God's glory is precisely a love for Christ to the point of folly. Several commentators have stressed that, by means of the Third Kind of Humility, the entire process of election and of discernment loses the character of cold and logical reasoning to become the folly of irrational love.[22]

Folly for Christ in Concrete Everyday Life

St. Isaac Jogues's letters of August 5 and of August 30, 1643, illustrate well how this Ignatian perspective can be lived in the concrete. His desire to proclaim the crucified and risen Lord among the Iroquois Indians is so ardent that he begs the Lord to wreck the efforts of those who plan to set him free and send him to Europe, "if this was not for his glory" (August 5, 1643). Quite unexpectedly he has a chance of escaping, but Isaac prays the Lord "not to allow me to decide on my own, but to give me light to know his most holy will, for in all and through all I have longed to do his will even to the point of being burned by slow fire." While taking into account his love for the Indians, and "having weighed before God, with all the detachment I was capable of, the reasons that moved me to remain with these uncivilized people or to leave them, I have come to believe that our Lord would be more pleased if I used the opportunity to make my escape" (August 30, 1643). Isaac does not rush to martyrdom as though it were, by itself and automatically, the sole expression of the folly of the cross. It is the salvation of the Indians and his experience in their mission—that, too, foolishness for Christ—that fills his mind and spirit: "All these achievements would die with me, if I did not escape." Though expressing his own preference "to be burned by slow fire," Isaac does not at all exclude the possibility of "escaping" in order to continue, in the face of all odds, the missionary task of proclaiming Christ to the

---

[22] Cf. G. Fessard, *La dialectique des* Exercices spirituels *de saint Ignace de Loyola*, t. I, p. 65; E. Pousset, *La vie dans la foi et la liberté*, pp. 69-70.

Indians.

Thus, Jogues submits to God's glory alone two expressions of the folly for Christ—that is, "to be burned by slow fire" and "to escape" in order to take up again the cross of the mission among the Indians. But he broadens the scope of sharing in the foolish love of God to include every state of human living so as to seek God in all things. The fools for Christ are not only the martyrs or the stylites, but also—and this is Ignatius's originality—those crucified in daily life, in the tasks and sufferings of every day, who unobtrusively radiate the love of Christ through their words, their actions, their silences, their humdrum yes and no. Their very presence and style of commitment brand them as fools in a society that is overwhelmingly hostile, indifferent, or cynical in regard to those who live for a kingdom that is not of this world.[23]

Ignatius reviews in this light of God's greater glory all the activities by which persons try to take their places in human society, the least and most commonplace as well as the most showy and extraordinary. Ignatius excludes nothing from this Third Kind of Humility, in which the foolish love of God is embodied, in imitation of the One who was first regarded as a fool. For it is in each and every one of these activities that Lucifer, the "rebel chief," tempts and lays his snares [139; 141]. It is also in each and every one of these activities that "the true Commander" [139] inspires the ability to collaborate in the building of the city of God by means of the paschal cross which is the abiding law of true life. To share in this work of God through Christ in their Spirit of love [236] is in itself already folly. It is "choosing to accept at the heart of the most ordinary kind of life all the humiliations, injustices, ill-disguised refusals, and unpopularity, on condition that no other inconveniece may follow and only my own self-esteem be at stake. . . ." It is ". . . the summit of the Exercises."[24] Thus living by his faith in Jesus, one finds oneself in a situation which enables him to go beyond all mere self-interest and, in imitation of Christ, to prefer what is foolish and senseless for the sake of the life of one's brothers and sisters. "The wisdom of God

---

[23] Cf. K. Rahner, "Die ignatianische Mystik der Weltfreudigkeit," *Schriften zur Theologie*, III, p. 346; cf. O. Clément, "Après Hiroshima et Auschwitz: La croix du Christ dans l'histoire des hommes," *Le Supplément*, 152 (1985) 72 ff.

[24] F. Varillon, *Beauté du monde et souffrances des hommes*, Paris 1980, p. 200.

flowing into man, produces in him, as it does in Christ, the folly of love and universal salvation."[25] The feel for the universal that constantly marks the spiritual experience of Ignatius makes the folly for Christ applicable to the daily humdrum life of the silent majority of the people of God. But at the same time it also expresses itself in ways not infrequent in our days. One thinks of the need born of love to denounce a social injustice through a hunger strike, to go against what seems to be well-established custom in order to give the best to the poor, or to perform prophetic gestures like the saintly fools of Eastern Christianity in order to unmask the anti-evangelical compromises of the people of God. It is to identify with the marginalized as so many saints have done; to accept, even without self-defence, a transfer as the result of a false accusation or a total misunderstanding; to welcome ridicule, even being "branded," because one does what one believes must be done in the name of the Lord; to take on tortures and imprisonment. Some will interpret all these as aberrations and almost a sacrilegious understanding of the word of St. Paul: "We are fools for the sake of Christ." Others will see in them the power of the Spirit who is building up, against the opposition of so many, the civilization of love in Christ for the glory of the Father.

In all this one loses oneself in foolishness; only God's greater glory comes out triumphant. This kind of folly would be a forbidden path if Christ had not been the first to be regarded as a fool for love. Small wonder, then, that St. Ignatius and his companions were rightly wary of their apostolic activities if these did not bring about opposition, astonishment, even persecution. "Master Francis complains that there is no persecution [in Portugal], but he gets comfort in the thought that he will have them in India, for to live long without them is not to do faithful battle for God."[26] Small wonder, too, that particularly in religious life such painful tensions and conflicts cannot be wanting. Not because these are sought for or in themselves, not at all. Rather, as the Second Vatican Council suggests, how does one bear witness "that the world cannot be transfigured and offered to God without the spirit of the Beatitudes" (*Lumen Gentium*, 31) without coming

---

[25] J. Laplace, *L'Esprit et l'Eglise*, Paris 1987, p. 182.

[26] Cf. *Saint François Xavier, Correspondance, 1535-1552: Lettres et Documents, Collection Christus*, n. 64, p. 56.

into conflict with the cultures and civilizations of our day, which parade as the wisdom of our times?

If, under this wise pretext, religious life ceases to denounce the world of our time as deformed and disfigured, and that foolishly, in the name of him who was first regarded as a fool; if it ceases to strive existentially and communally to transfigure this world with vigor and fervor by means of the paschal mystery, then, without a shadow of doubt, religious life fails in its vocation and its mission to be foolish and senseless for the sake of Christ. If this were to happen, religious life would also be depriving the people of God of that visibility of a love for God and for the neighbor to which so many Christians bear witness, as veritable fools for Christ, in the hiddenness of their daily lives.

Thus, in a great variety of vocations and of missions, so many fools for Christ—men and women—share in the manifestation of God's foolish love, of which Eastern Christian tradition has said that "perhaps only this incomprehensible self-emptying of a divine person on the cross can convince man of God's foolish love for him."

PART TWO

"TO GAIN SOME UNDERSTANDING":

ANALYSIS

EIGHT

A LINGUISTIC INTERPRETATION OF
THE *SPIRITUAL EXERCISES* OF ST. IGNATIUS

The text entitled *Spiritual Exercises* has been circulated in an incalculable number of editions and is still being translated into more and more languages. Right up to our own day this small work continues to stimulate commentaries and study guides intended to enrich it with all the new perspectives that Vatican II received from the Spirit. These perspectives include both dogmatic and biblical aspects as well as the practice of spirituality and pastoral liturgy. Still more impressive is the huge throng of men and women who, with the help of this little book, have experienced a personal encounter with their Lord. It has led them to further authenticate their lives and realize their true personalities, by discerning their vocations to a mission of ecclesial service to the coming Kingdom of God.

In this introduction to the spiritual text authored by Iñigo Lopez de Loyola, we shall examine all the "actors" associated with utilizing and practicing the text of the *Exercises*. These actors are four in number: first, there is the one who has produced the text, second, the one who employs the text in order to pass it on personally to another. Third is the one who, although having no direct access to the text, still appropriates personally that which has been proposed to him. The final actor is the Lord who has been petitioned to complete the challenge which the text facilitates: that is, to know how to recognize the choice that my Creator and Savior desires me to make in response to his love.

There is one hypothesis—a familiar and seductive one—that would present these four actors as "authors." Thus there would be a literary author, a semantic author, an allegorical author, and the author-by-analogy who transforms the literal text into a mystical one.[1] But to accept this working hypothesis unreservedly runs the risk of obscuring the specificity of each of the actors in their relations to the text. This can lead one to oversimplify the very nuanced and complex reality involved in the respective communications of these four actors who produce the event of the Spiritual Exercises.

The Author of the Text as "Actor"

The first actor is the author of the text. Undeniably responsible for the literary product, Ignatius both gives himself to and removes himself from the text; he makes himself both useful and superfluous. It is significant that the letter of pontifical approbation of the *Spiritual Exercises*, dated July 31, 1548, clearly mentions Ignatius as author, even though in September of that year the work was published anonymously. Although Ignatius made much of that bull of approbation—an exceptional form at the time—he seems not to have intervened either in the composition of the text to be submitted to the Holy See, or in the editing of translations. Curiously, two very different Latin translations were proposed and approved. One of these had as its point of departure a rough draft entitled *Todos exercicios breviter en latin*: it renders an original Spanish *verbum verbo* into a "word-for-word," which resulted in a stiff and awkward Latin. The other translation, finished in March by the French Jesuit André de Freux, who rejected the word-for-word method while assuring fidelity to his technique, launches into a *sensum sensui*. He sought above all to compose a smart and elegant Latin, especially by a refined choice of words and by a systematic refusal to repeat verbal or nominal forms. Ignatius as author did nothing to certify the fidelity of these translations. However, five years later, Ignatius would regret the corrections made according to a Spanish text, "seeing that the Latin text had been approved by the pope" (*MI*, 321).

Ignatius has left no manuscript of the *Spiritual Exercises* that might be from his own hand; the text commonly called "autograph" is only a copy, probably from the pen of a Portuguese Jesuit. However, thanks to some thirty

---

[1] Cf. R. Barthes, in *Sade, Fourier, Loyola*, Seuil, Paris, 1971, 45-80.

additions in the form of precisions and corrections from the hand of Ignatius himself, the autograph more or less merits its title. But even if the autograph is a favorite working research instrument for any kind of study of the *Spiritual Exercises*, no one has been able to establish any connection between that copy and the Latin translations. It must be acknowledged that Ignatius's indifference regarding his own authorship of the text is largely responsible for the fact that the editorial history remains in the realm of hypothesis, in practically all its stages.[2]

Moving from the history to the text itself, a quick reading of this small manual reveals that Ignatius is not communicating a history of his own mystical life. If Ignatius had not begun, barely three years before his death, to impart some confidences about his mystical adventure to a companion, it would be difficult if not impossible to reconstruct it out of the text of the *Exercises*. A more thorough analysis of the text illustrates a removal of the personal character originally impressed upon it. The first person pronoun "I" never refers explicitly to its author's personal experience of God. Sometimes the "I" is of a didactic nature, used to clarify some affirmation that leaves itself open to misunderstanding. Take, for example, the text "seeing this whole human composite as being in exile . . . I say, the whole composite of body and soul" (SE 47, 6). Sometimes the "I" urges a more personalized identification, abolishing the distance which the third-person pronoun permits in relation to the text. This interplay of pronouns can be observed several times over.

In the meditation on sins, Ignatius returns to the objective order of things by inviting the retreatant to consider what humans are when compared with the angels and all the saints, and to reflect on what all creation is in comparison with God. This objective stance alternates with the strong personalization shown in his penchant for "I": "What am I, in comparison with all other human beings, and then I alone, what can I be?" [58]. This logic of humiliation does not remain aloof in pure consideration, but rather arouses the experience of the mystery of iniquity deep within the self. I should also mention in this context the expression that is repeated at several points: "to ask for what I desire" [55, 4, passim]. The author does not demand that retreatants, in prayer, should align themselves with his desire, but that they

---

[2] Cf. ARSJ, Rome, 1987, 303.

ask according to their own personal desires. This invitation to accept one's own responsibility before the Lord is one of the characteristics of the *Spiritual Exercises*. It rules out every identification between the personal experience of Ignatius and that which the text intends for someone else.

On this precise point at least, Ignatius helps us with one of his rare confidences. "He tells me [says the confidant of his narrative] that he had not made the *Exercises* all at one time, but that certain things that he observed in his soul and found useful to himself and potentially useful to others, he put down in writing" (*Autob*. 99). Thus, as a service to those who sought his help, he chose certain of his observations on how to make progress along the way of the Lord.

The result of this policy of usefulness will thus be a text both functional and manifold, as well as disconcerting. That is, the principle of utility, if rigorously applied, produces a book that no one ever reads. But this text is neither a narrative to be followed from beginning to end nor an exposition of spiritual theology which progressively sets forth a theory or a doctrine. The preface to the 1548 edition, approved by the Sovereign Pontiff, says it in lapidary fashion right at the outset: *non tantum lecturi sed facturi*—not a mystical experience destined to be read about, but one to be put into practice. Ignatius's concern to aid us on our personal way to God thus commands the choice of a certain number of notes belonging to different literary genres: there are some schemas of meditations and biblical fragments for contemplation, as well as some widely varied methodological notes to be used in order to discern God's project for us. There are some annotations and rules, some brief tractates for understanding the discernment of spirits and for examining one's conscience. But one also finds rules for distributing alms, for knowing how to treat scruples, and especially for taking the right direction in the Church militant.

The utility of this diverse collection is not immediately transparent, but it is clear that all this material, the fruit of a mystical experience, is being put at the free disposal of anyone who may have to accompany persons in search of the will of God in their lives. This utilitarian character makes itself felt down to the very letter of the text. So many mystical texts make use of poetry, but the text of the *Exercises* does not merit even a mention as literature. It aims throughout at linguistic economy and sobriety of expression, such as the systematic use of the Spanish gerundive; this makes for economy of expression, but at the same time for more complex translation and interpretation.

As a service to one who is searching for God, Ignatius has composed a book for the director, the one who gives the *Exercises*. The originality of Ignatius's initiative lies in the idea of addressing himself in written textual form to a person who intends to give the *Spiritual Exercises* by word of mouth to one who wishes to make them. By thus creating a distance between the author of the text and that which will happen in the exchange between master and disciple-exercitant, Ignatius wanted to prevent every form of servile imitation or mere copying of his mystical experience. The director is to proceed in the clear conviction, as I have mentioned, that the Creator "should act immediately with the creature and the creature with its Creator and Lord" [15]. Ignatius himself had undergone this experience: "God behaved with him in the same way that a schoolmaster behaves with a child; that is, he taught him" (*Autob.* 27).

As a testimony to the divine origin of his personal experience, Ignatius does not hesitate to make a daring statement: "These things that he saw gave him strength at that time and gave him once for all a powerful confirmation of his faith. In fact, he often reflected thereafter that, if Scripture had not taught him the matters of faith, he could have decided to die for them purely because of what he had seen" (*Autob.* 29). It is important to point out here the delicate question of dogmatic and spiritual theology in relation to the knowledge of what stands first in Christian faith. Considering Ignatius's ecclesial reference to Scripture and tradition and to the spiritual person who existentially lives the faith, it is enough to underline how, thanks to his experience, he holds every mystical adventure to be incomparably personal (*Autob.* 364). Out of respect for each person's quest for God, Ignatius seeks only to lay down some markers on the way towards union with God.

The sole original way in this little work is certainly that of the spiritual exercise. One of Ignatius's early collaborators clearly observed even at that time that in the text of the *Exercises* there was practically nothing—*nihil fere*—that had not already been found in the spiritual inheritance of the people of God, from the monastic tradition to the *devotio moderna*.[3] In actuality, even the noun phrase *"Spiritual Exercises"* is not of Ignatian origin. It may be that,

---

[3] Cf. Nadal, vol. V, Rome, 1962, 90.

during his stay at the abbey of Montserrat in Catalonia, Ignatius had come to know the *Compendio breve de exercicios espirituales* drafted by Fray Garcia de Cisneros and intended since 1522 for the use of pilgrims to the monastery. But the long history of "exercises" does not deprive Ignatius of his own originality, since he was the first to organize the expression "spiritual exercise" into a way of pedagogy. Nor does it weaken the challenge of this expression. So accustomed are we to the phrase that we tend to forget that it describes a union of two realities at first believed to be mutually exclusive.

If we follow a semantic analysis of the word *ejercicio* as understood at the time of Ignatius's Spanish writings, this shows us that the term fully retains its semantic value for the practice and techniques of humanistic methodology. The young Ignatius himself records his great delight in the exercise of arms (*Autob.* 1). Later, in the *Constitutions*, he recommends the exercise of letters (*Const.* 369) and other scholarly exercises (*Const.* 375) that he had practiced himself at the University of Paris. In the text with which we are concerned, Ignatius in no way spiritualizes the word "exercises," but defines it explicitly from the side of corporeal activity, evoking an increasing intensity: "to walk, to travel, to run" [1]. In spite of the radical incompatibility between any organized human technique, even spiritual, and the purely gratuitous gift of an encounter with the Lord in the Spirit, the author of our text not only relies on the material and corporeal foundation of exercise, but rather builds it into a system—a paradoxically spiritual system.

When one peruses the text, it becomes apparent that the word *exercises* does not stand alone, but produces an entire semantic field. All human faculties and the entire environment of concrete daily events are mobilized and judged apt to be transformed into "exercises." The use of the light of day and the way in which we take our meals, the reading of certain books and the meticulous distribution of one's time—all these are called up to give fullness and effectiveness to the word "exercises." Certain methods are proposed to focus the imagination, to explore the memory, to requisition the understanding, and especially to guide the will to be able to love and to abide in love. At the risk of being considered obsessed with detail, Ignatius gives a fuller sense to exercises in their corporeal and material reality.

However, if we are dealing with "spiritual exercises," does not the entire systematization rely on a simple preparation which remains, in the final analysis, merely external to the encounter with the Lord? Would not all this movement be a kind of scaffolding, no doubt useful for ascetical self-mastery, but finally outside the mystical meeting in which only the Lord is master? Fittingly, however, on the level of vocabulary, everything happens as if the exercise has already been grasped by the Spirit. The use of a verb like *mudar* (to change or modify) sets up a relationship between "exercise" and encounter with the Lord. In reality, when it happens that the exercitant does not happen to find what he or she desires—the response of the Lord—it is often helpful to introduce some changes in diet, sleeping patterns, and other ways of doing penance. The deep reason for these changes in the exercises is that a person might be taught by the Lord what exercises will be of greater help to unite one with him. Because, Ignatius insists, "As God our Lord knows infinitely more deeply what we are, he often gives to each one, by means of such changes, to perceive that which best suits him" [89]. The election in the Exercises is not given over to the effectiveness proper to the means employed; rather, the choice is made by the one who knows us better than we believe we know ourselves.

Consequently, Ignatius will not say that it is unimportant for someone to perform an exercise seated or standing, prostrate on the ground or on one's knees, or with face turned to heaven [76]. But what he does say is that I must sense what bodily posture the Lord has chosen for me as a means to find what I desire. In this way, the Exercises are not a means of infallible competence to give us that which can be only a gift of God. But, paradoxically, the Exercises deploy a methodical activity which conducts us, in the grace of God, to a receptive and submissive passivity seized by that divine grace. To put it another way: the human faculties in exercising themselves do not create prayer through a kind of artifice which would like to actively force God to respond to us. Rather, they discover that God was already present in them, in their hearts and in their activity. The point is to maintain exercises of any sort in a movement of availability, choosing only that which the Lord has chosen for us, including particular concrete exercises.

This development brings us back to the syntactic "spiritual exercises," where the adjective "spiritual" clearly indicates that the whole exercise from beginning to end is an active, open invitation to God. Using "spiritual" in this way, Ignatius can speak of a spiritual life [350], a spiritual person [326], and even of "spiritual things" [9, 189, 325], to the degree that these realities open us to an encounter with the Divine Majesty.

If, in the noun phrase "spiritual exercises," the term "exercises" has produced a semantic field in all details and particulars, it is the same case with the second element of the phrase, the adjective "spiritual." Since the exercise is entirely comprehended through the spiritual, the two semantic fields are not separated in the text, even though they are clearly distinguished. The semantic field "spiritual" assumes that of "exercise" in reality, but dynamically opens it to the universal, and especially to the "universal Lord" [97, 1]. This dynamic power should be understood within a certain preference for comparative adverbs: the whole corpus of Ignatian spirituality seems to be summed up in the "greater," the *mas/magis*.

In actuality, the Exercises address those who would "more fully offer their hearts and distinguish themselves in the full service of their eternal King and universal Lord" [97, 1]. From this comes an offering of greater value and greater worth. [97, 2]. All these intensive comparatives give to the text a certain quality of unfulfilled need; they reinforce the recognition that the glory of God will never be great enough, and that God, always the greatest, will never be sufficiently "praised, reverenced and served" [23 , 1]. They also give weight to the conviction that the human person will never sufficiently exist in the image and likeness of the "Eternal Word Incarnate" [109, 1]. By means of these adverbial constructions, the text is emphatically open to a synergy with this God who never rests, but labors and works in all created things on the face of the earth [236].

All the same, this use of the comparative should not lead us to forget the superlative, to the degree that the text attributes it to the human person. By means of this syntactic construction, the text is open to a radicality that appeals to a largeness of heart and to a great generosity towards the Creator and Lord, offering him all one's will and liberty [5]. This fragment which makes such ample use of *todo*, the "all," depicts that which the superlative envisions as "the greatest spiritual poverty" [146, 2], the poverty of Christ born into our midst [116, 1]. Also, in sober linguistic style, Ignatius produces the semantic field of the spiritual as the active and unbounded openness to the universal dimensions of the work of God, "who acts as one who labors" [236], and who wills to need our choices in life and our labors.

So much for the text of the author, Ignatius. It does not yield much of a personal nature: the narrative which he will later give of his life and the few pages of his *Spiritual Journal* reveal a mystical experience of which the

Spiritual Exercises bear undeniable traits without actually relating them. On the contrary, Ignatius simply offers that which can be useful to us, by placing in the text an original process in which ascesis and mysticism, represented by the two semantic fields—exercise and spiritual—dispose one to search for and to find [1] the life and state in which the Divine Majesty wills to employ us [135, 4], in the *pure* service of the eternal Father [135, 3].

"The One Who Gives the Exercises"

The intended reader of this book is the one who gives the Exercises to a third person. In the preface of the edition approved by the Sovereign Pontiff in 1548, this purpose is clearly enunciated. The little work is not to be read but rather practiced—*non tantum lecturi sed facturi*—and this *facturi* is then made more precise by *potius aliis tradituri*, which means to assist others to make the Exercises. Having brought out some aspects of the author of the text, the moment has come to understand further the function of this giver to whom the Ignatian text is directed.

Given Ignatius's taste for linguistic economy, it is rather astonishing that he designates this person without exception as "the one who gives the Exercises." Nonetheless, in place of constantly using the subordinate phrase, the vocabulary available to Ignatius allows another possibility. Semantically available to him were the word "preacher" (*Const.* 281) as well as "master." (*Const.* 363, 2) But Ignatius retains the expression, "the one who gives the Exercises." The same point applies to the retreatant: the word *ejercitante* was not excluded—the directories place faith in it (*Dir.* 4 and *passim*)—but the text always refers to the one who receives or makes the Exercises.

We attempt first to examine the connection between the text and the one who gives the Exercises. To begin with, we must note the fact that we are discussing a person who has already undergone the experience of the Exercises. Now, accordingly, the text explicitly calls upon this person to adapt—*aplicar* [18, 1]—the experience to the one who will undergo it. That is, this potential director should consider the other's capacities for making the Exercises in light of his or her age, culture, and personal gifts. The transmission of the Exercises is grounded in a strong personal relationship between the one who gives and the one who receives them. Still more important is the fact that, for Ignatius, this communication between the two parties makes sense only insofar as it begins with a reciprocal [231] communication between God and the person who seeks God. The consequence of this intention is that the one who gives the Exercises must take a place in the background in such a way that the Creator can communicate himself to the one who makes the Exercises, with a view to entering the way upon which he or she will be better able to serve the Lord in the future [Cf. 15, 4].

To arrive at this goal, the text of Ignatius renders the one who gives the Exercises an "actor" without making him an "author" of them. For on the one hand the text maintains the one who gives the Exercises within the pedagogical structure experienced by Ignatius: that is, it thereby prevents a privatization focused only on the oral encounter with the exercitant, in which the subjectivity of the giver might dominate the process. The latter will thus commit himself to the exercitant to lead him along the Ignatian way. Consequently, the giver is never the author of a new text, even if he must so act that the text might lead the exercitant where God wills him to go. This supposes a great flexibility and an unlimited diversity which Ignatius himself has clearly foreseen. This responsibility demands so much generosity and such creative ingenuity that it is understandable how Ignatius could look upon that person only as one who gives himself in the process of giving the Exercises.

The other verbs which set the boundaries of the one who gives the Exercises can be distinguished according to the two semantic fields that ground the whole work of Ignatius. Regarding the one part, the Exercises, to assure that the exercitant remains on the way laid out by Ignatius, the giver of the Exercises should frequently question him in detail about how he is making them [6, 2]. On the other hand, in dealing with the semantic field of the spiritual, he should neither incline nor dispose the exercitant toward one side or another [15, 5]. Outside of the time of the Exercises, he can and should have his preferences, but within this search for the will of God he should show himself fully available and docile to the good pleasure of God and of the one who is making the Exercises. Both of them should suspend the tendencies of their own wills, in order to let God take the initiative and weigh in perfect balance those things that mark out the direction that leads to the praise and glory of God [15, 5 and 179, 3]. The one who gives the Exercises is like the friend of the bridegroom, who, imposing neither himself nor a fixed system, actively accompanies that which the Bridegroom will accomplish in the spiritual experience of the one who receives the Exercises. In following this direction, he should not preach a retreat, since the task at hand presupposes a one-to-one contact. Nor should he act like a teacher transmitting knowledge or a doctrine, since it is not a great deal of knowledge that fills and satisfies a person in search of God, but the feeling and taste of God's presence [cf.2, 5]. But neither should he be a mere witness, who, with the neutrality of a competent psychiatrist, is content merely to follow that which is being accomplished in the exercitant, but rather the kind of person preferred by Ignatius. That is, he is to be constantly active to assure that in full freedom the Lord can communicate himself directly [15, 6] with his creature. The one who gives is thus one who gives himself as an intermediary guiding the retreatant along the path, while remaining unobtrusively in the shadows.

All the verbs which describe this original and unique responsibility point in this direction. It is an engagement strongly marked by a disengagement, with the result that the exercitant will always find the one who gives the Exercises elsewhere, in places where he does not expect him. Thus, the exercitant in desolation will find a consoler [7], and the one in full spiritual euphoria will inevitably find a restrained questioner along the way [cf. 14]. Because the text of Ignatius is conceived as a manual intended for both the one who gives and the one who receives the Exercises, its whole message is explicitly about the spirit of confidence that should mark the dialogue between the two [17]. However, Ignatius lays down a condition, elementary yet significant: one must always save the discourse of the other [22]. Looking to the one who gives the Exercises as well as to the one who receives them, Ignatius is well aware that their entire relationship will take place by means of words. He thus seeks to warn that every piece of discourse can give occasion to misunderstanding or suspicion and thus can cut off the indispensible dialogue. Since this is a spiritual dialogue, it calls for a compassionate understanding and a ready benevolence: even at the level of exchange of words, the partners of the dialogue mutually give themselves in their very language.

"The One Who Receives the Exercises"

In this investigation of the one who gives the Exercises, the one who receives them has never been absent. The text calls this person "the one who receives the Exercises," without forgetting "the [self-exercising] "exercitant" [6, 9, 13]. The verb "to receive," *recebir*, has a double in the verb *tomar*, and the translations do not distinguish them, even if these two verbs are in no way synonymous. If *tomar* (to take) marks the decision to take hold of the Exercises, *recibir* (to receive) marks still more strongly the reception reserved for that which is given. These two verbs go side by side in the prayer of offering which shapes the final point of the Exercises, which petitions *tomad, Señor, y recibid toda mi libertad* (take, Lord, and receive all my liberty) [234]. This prayer says quite clearly that it is not enough that, in a heartfelt impulse, I say to God, "take"; it must always be the case, because he is always Lord, that he wills to "receive."[4] A third verb accompanies these two others, since the exercitant "makes" (*hazer*) the Exercises.

The verbs which characterize the one who receives the Exercises seem to be intended to strengthen him. The reflexive verbs, which indicate that an action falls back upon the subject of the proposition, can be found abundantly in the text. All the activity to which the text invites us is that of exercizing, [130, 5], imagining [143], representing [151], and perfecting oneself [173, 2] in order to subject one's spiritual condition to consideration [59, 1°].

Another series of constructions is significant for describing the activity of the exercitant: to behold myself [53, 2] and to reflect on myself [114, 1]. This concentration on the self takes the forms of an intense personalization of the history of salvation. Thus one reads, in the mystery of the nativity, "all this for me" [116, 3]; in the mystery of the cross, "for my sins" [53,1]; in the mystery of the passion, that Christ has endured it "for me" [203]; the mystery of a Lord who "desires to give himself to me" [234, 2]. The text thus recounts such an intense personal relationship that I constrain myself to grow sad and cause myself distress because of the great sorrow of Christ our Lord [206, 3]. In this context, it is interesting to note that the Latin translation of Frusius, approved by the Holy See in 1548, emphasizes a personalization that could be less clear in other editions. In place of calling oneself to rejoice intensely in a contemplation of the risen Lord, the Latin translations,

---

[4] G. Fessard, *La dialectique des "Exercices spirituels" de saint Ignace de Loyola*, t.1, Aubier (Théologie, 35), Paris, 1956, 162.

especially that of Frusius, insist on the fact that the point is to share the immense joy of Christ and of his Mother [221], thus closing the distance between myself and the One who becomes more intimate to me than I can be to myself.

This incorporation into Christ, desired by the Exercises, already prevents exercitants from closing themselves off or adopting an individualistic spirituality. Thus it forestalls the criticism of individualism, which even more completely loses its foundation when the analysis of the text takes note of the two semantic fields. If the first field, that of exercise, exposes itself to criticism by formulating its purpose as "to overcome oneself and to order one's life" [21], the spiritual field opens this individual practice to the universal fact of salvation history. In this light, individual sin is situated within a death-dealing history in which I participate and to which I join myself through my own connivance with it. If Christ calls me as an individual to join his task of evangelization, this is intended for the life of the world. The fact that sharing in such an evangelical enterprise occurs unavoidably, according to Ignatius, through one's yes to the person of Jesus, does not limit the appeal to an individual involvement, but on the contrary integrates it into the ecclesial communion of the apostles and disciples. Without doubt it is from me myself that the Lord awaits a personal offering of my heart in the election, and that each man and woman should discover where the Lord has chosen them to be. But that personal incorporation in the design of God verifies an enrollment in the history of salvation which God is lovingly writing and wants to write along with us.

These perspectives are those of the text of the *Exercises*, right from the Principle and Foundation to the Contemplation to Attain Love, passing through the meditation on sins and the contemplation of the Kingdom. To incorporate oneself through love in this history the exercitant will be moved by the good spirit as well as tempted by the evil one. In this discernment of spirits, the exercitant will be the actor only by being in the spirit. Ignatius does not use the expression "spirit of man." Sometimes this absence is explainable as a consequence of bad experiences that Ignatius had lived through because of the trouble caused by the *illuminados*. Linguistically at least, it is more probable that Ignatius has the whole person and not simply the person's spirit facing good and evil spirits. The whole person and not simply the spirit is the locus and context of the spiritual combat. In fact, Ignatius speaks semantically in a different way, by referring to the thought which is my own, born entirely out of my freedom and my own will [32, 2]. The semantic field that explains the exercise proves the faith of Ignatius in an incarnate spirituality that lays hold of the whole person. It situates one's physical, psychic, social and historical condition in the presence of the One who "wholly and completely is my God" (*Diary*, Feb. 27, 1544), the Word incarnate, Son of God and Son of Man. It is in this Spirit that it is proposed to the exercitant to be an actor, and in pedagogical dialogue with the One who is Creator and Lord.

God as the Ultimate "Actor"

This trusting conversation between the one who gives himself or herself in the ministry of the Exercises and the one who receives and makes them has no other meaning than to initiate a dialogue. It enables the encounter which comes about appropriately in speaking with God "as a friend speaks to a friend, or a servant to his master" [54, 1]. Here we meet the final actor in the adventure of the Exercises, namely God, who, despite appearances, is the One who initially addresses his word, first to Ignatius and then to other actors. In testimony to this there is the important biblical material contained in the book of the *Exercises*. According to the characteristics of the two semantic fields under discussion, Ignatius, on the one hand, abridges the biblical text in order to transform it into an exercise. On the other hand, however, he allows it to expand and to manifest its spiritual sense in much greater depth. He reminds the one who gives the Exercises of "the Gospel itself" [261], but he does this by summing up the "points"—usually three [261]. These condensations should then be accompanied by a brief or summary explanation [2, 1]. At this distance from the letter of the biblical text, all knowledge and all exegetical curiosity are set aside so as to mobilize the human faculties in view of acquiring the interior knowledge—not of the biblical word—but of the Lord, the Word of God [104].

All of this goes on as if Ignatius is supposing that the literal is well known and is thus aiming at a personal assimilation made present by the One of whom the entire biblical text speaks. *Facta Verbi verba sunt*: to contemplate the meaning of each of the words [cf. 249] is as much as to contemplate the mysteries of the life of Christ [261 ff.], for in the fuller sense, which is spiritual, the mystery of Christ, the Word of God, speaks to us. Even if it is strongly attached to the Jesus of history, who permits Ignatius to approach him, to hear and converse with him, he is always, in all his acts and gestures, the eternal Word [130] who is present and turns to us in the very actuality of our existence. The *Exercises* do not aim at a historical restoration to assist our memory and imagination to grasp that to which the biblical text witnesses. Their purpose is rather that we perceive in the present moment that which the Lord wants each of us, deeply within our hearts, to live out in his Church. Thus, he desires to speak to us in an entirely personal way through the same mystery which he lived for us in another moment in time.

As he lets the discourse of God come to life in the freedom of a colloquy, enabling us to receive the word that enables us to respond to such a generous king [94], so much the more does this Lord, as eternal King [95], seek to enter into a loving communion [231], as a friend with a friend. The very text of the *Exercises* reminds us that this colloquy, being based on an interpretation and a spiritual actualization in the fuller sense of the Word of God, is not limited to biblical language. Some indispensable fragments for the process of the Exercises are drawn up without a direct reference to Scripture. Such is the case with the Principle and Foundation, even though it is conceived in the light of the covenant. So too with the recapitulative Contemplation for Attaining Love, developed from Johannine perspectives [23 and 230]. It is possible to speak personally to God and to our Lord in a spontaneous and free manner.

It is here that the text of the *Exercises* leaves the one who makes them alone to be united with the Lord [cf. 20, 9]. In that conversation that Ignatius calls colloquy, it may be that the word of God is born of movements in which one finds oneself so close to "the infinite sweetness and fragrance of the divinity" [124]. The one who makes the Exercises learns through discernment how to translate this language of God into human words and choices. Guiding the traveller toward that communion with God, marking out the way toward that encounter, the text of the *Exercises* does not reflect the language of mystical poetry or prose in the the words of the colloquy with one's Friend and Lord. Rather, the "dark night" Ignatius will simply call desolation: night is for him merely a moment on the clock. Neither is there a "living flame," and fire is simply the fire of hell. It is significant that at one of the rare places where the reader does find a mystical power in the text, the reading becomes uncertain. That text is about the communion of the Creator who communicates himself to the exercitant, according to one reading, "by embracing him in his love," and according to another reading, simply "by embracing him" [15, 4].

In every way, this presentation of the four actors of the drama assumed by the Exercises proves clearly how everything is called upon to dispose the one who receives them to enter into the way where he or she will be better able to serve his Divine Majesty [cf. 15, 4]. In this spirit, it is good and proper to celebrate the 1548 pontifical approbation of the little work of Ignatius, the master of the Spiritual Exercises.

NINE

LANGUAGE AND ANTHROPOLOGY

The *Spiritual Diary* of St. Ignatius

It would certainly be difficult to deny the evolution and progress of the human sciences in which, obviously, a truly anthropological dimension ought to assert itself. But beyond the fact that every human science has adopted its own often partial or even biased anthropology lies a further problem: obsession with attaining scientific precision as well as the fascination of formalism. These have often ended in the development of a methodological discourse in which man's humanity, far from constituting the center of reference, is condemned little by little to disappear. This evolution can be clearly observed in the human sciences with the most human of objects, i.e., general linguistics, the science of language and of languages.

In choosing to study a great spiritual text—St. Ignatius's *Spiritual Diary*—we shall ask ourselves how far the application of a linguistic discipline allows us to have access to the humanity of the founder of the Society of Jesus, as it reveals itself through meticulous, precise, and original language in the account of a spiritual experience.

In the first place we must examine the linguistic project itself, as it has been developed historically in relation to certain great authors. Next we shall submit the text of the *Spiritual Diary* to a study which specifically considers its language. Finally we shall ask ourselves whether we are not in the presence of a going-beyond-language when faced with the phenomenon Saint Ignatius calls the *loquela*.

Language and Speech

For linguistics to become a true science, did not de Saussure's project consider it indispensable to abstract from man, to remove from the scene, as it were, the person who speaks? And this effort directly to exclude any anthropological taint from general linguistics led an expert in the field to write that the area of linguistics is a knowledge conditioned by that which knowledge does not want to know anything about—the area of the human. Consequently, at this point the most efficient repression meets the most penetrating lucidity. And this methodological shelving of the person who speaks has made it possible—according to the famous formula of de Saussure's program—to "study language in itself and for itself."

But in all fairness to the founder of modern linguistics we should not forget one important point: when de Saussure made a distinction between "language" and "speech," he did not intend to stop at a linguistics of language. Rather, he concentrated his efforts entirely on the structures and mechanisms of the linguistics of language, on its tools and basic elements. This gave him only a glimpse—in a curious study of "anagrams"—of the range of the linguistics of speech, in which the speaking subject would no longer be able to avoid detection.

What had been at first only a distinction between language and speech in the development of de Saussure's plan was thus progressively transformed into an out-and-out separation, indeed, an extreme opposition, between these two elements. General linguistics underwent the same ineluctable evolution which other human sciences had suffered: the establishment of a science at the cost of a fiction. In fact linguistics—the science of language and of languages—considers its object as if human beings did not use languages to speak and say things to one another.

We know that while linguistics was developing in Europe, a school was being formed in America based on the research of ethnologists who had come to linguistics out of necessity, through their wish to describe the Amerindian languages. The procedure they had to resort to was purely formal as well: distributionalist or taxonomic; it segments the linguistic chain and the classification of the resulting elements, again leaving no place for the person who speaks. The meaning that persons give to their speech is thus reduced to the effect of a regulated articulation of elements and of determined categories.

Chomsky's revolution was a reaction to this empiric formalism of the American school: laying aside a science which confined itself to the domain of pure forms and a mere statement of these forms, it developed a new general theory of linguistic structure. One could have hoped to welcome in it a return to the anthropological dimension, and consequently a return to a recognition of our humanity. But what it accomplished was to extract from the reality of language a linguistic theory which accounts for the functioning of the majority of known and emissible grammatical phrases. Thus, generative and transformational grammar does not examine a limited "corpus," but relies on an operative hypothesis which reflects man's linguistic creativity. Curiously, it calls on a milieu well known to spiritual theology, i.e., the milieu of Port-Royal; that is, the generative theory—in an initial moment, at least—conceives of the person who speaks as a kind of profound structure developed and defined in terms of a universal logic. Thus, as an expert in linguistic systems has noted, in spite of the apparent rejection of earlier theories, Chomsky's paradox simply picks up de Saussure's paradox all over again, while paying a new price.

But humanity infinitely surpasses itself: this statement, too, comes from the Port-Royal milieu and, more specifically, from Pascal. Since then, in spite of the categorical judgment by which the linguistics of language and the linguistics of speech are "two roads which cannot be followed at the same time," present-day linguists are increasingly forced to recognize—at least in the praxis of their science—that speech and language cannot constitute two completely autonomous domains. And yet, in the theory directed towards establishing a scientifically (i.e., rigorously) homogeneous linguistic coherence, the interaction of the language system with the speaking subject (the locutor, the person who speaks) appears to be still largely disregarded or downrightly rejected.

Starting from the praxis of this science and under the rubric of the quite imprecise term "pragmatic," several studies aimed at a kind of linguistics of speech have since been developed to recover the acts of discourse. But the swing of the pendulum so well known in the history of the sciences, along with an excessive reaction towards an exclusive linguistics of language, causes this linguistics of speech in its turn to forget a vital truth: speech is inconceivable outside the systems of the language it uses. Moreover, the texts, whatever they may be (even spiritual texts), present themselves as a codified result and cannot be separated from the source from which they spring, i.e., the linguistic code. Clearly the creative and operative activity of the dialogical person is situated in the polarity between language and speech: thus he renders the linguistic code manifest in his discourse.

We have just spoken of the separation between language and speech, and have clearly seen that to separate in the person that which should only be distinguished leads to eclipsing the anthropological dimension. But many linguistic studies, e.g., those on the Latin of Christian texts, to mention only one category, show that this pitfall can be avoided.

Language in the Spiritual Diary

Nonetheless, when a linguist opens a dictionary of spirituality and reads the article on the "language of spiritual persons," his professional conditioning creates a problem for him. It is difficult for him not to classify the contributions he finds there within a linguistics of speech which takes little account of the data of the linguistic code behind the resulting spiritual texts. Do we not immediately ascribe this language to a witness who has experienced God? We tend to have direct recourse to the allegorical nature of the spiritual texts, thus inevitably creating metaphors and hardly escaping metonymies. We have such an interest in the poetic function which lies within the framework of the language of spiritual authors, even if we may not necessarily consider their writings poems or literary texts. In this do we not too quickly give up defining spiritual language on the basis of linguistic forms, and too hastily identify the specific features of a spiritual word with the one who was its author, simply because he is a spiritual master?

The few observations I shall take the liberty of making concern the spiritual text I have intentionally chosen—the *Spiritual Diary* of Ignatius Loyola. Without claiming to resolve the problem presented here, perhaps my remarks may give rise to a discussion and eventually provoke studies or research which will go beyond the competence attained by this article. In this way Ignatius's *Spiritual Diary* would at least provide the necessary pretext for drawing attention to some of the problems which the anthropology of spiritual masters may have in common with general linguistics.

We can present Ignatius's *Spiritual Diary* briefly. It is made up of two autograph notebooks: one 27 pages long, the other 24; the first contains notes from February 2 to March 12, 1544, while the second consists of a new series of notes which follow on those of the first notebook and end on February 27, 1545. In the course of drawing up the *Constitutions of the Society of Jesus*, Ignatius was engaged at this period in resolving a problem concerning the regime of poverty of the new religious order; his search for enlightenment on this point fills the whole of the first notebook.

As the days go by, this search is accompanied by a mystical experience which bears witness in Ignatius to the constant availability of his will to the Holy Trinity through the mediation of Our Lady, for the most part centered around the eucharistic celebration. The number of editions, translations, and commentaries which have been made of this text is proof enough of the interest it has created among spiritual theologians. However the text has nothing allegorical about it on the level of speech; it does not borrow the language of spiritual marriage. Furthermore its poetical function is limited to a passing alliteration—*parte o puerta* (*Diary* 31)—or to stereotypes of the "heavenly music" genre (*Diary* 224). Would not language, in the sense of code, be of greater interest for grasping its meaning?

Some linguists in particular have already shown an interest in the linguistic facts contained in this spiritual text. The system of phonemes and morphemes, the syntactic and semantic structures which underlie it, are linked to the system of the evolving Castilian language; but the many oscillations and variations reflect the singularity of an author whose mother tongue is also Euschara (Basque) and whose apostolic work was expressed in the Italianizing language of Rome. The fact that this same author had access to spiritual theology through the Latin language is betrayed by his borrowings from this language. Thus, for example, one reads *loquela* (*Diary* 221) or a Pauline "Dominus scit" (*Diary* 65), or again the use of certain scholastic distinctions such as *mediate vel immediate* (*Diary* 102) in an attempt to specify the nature of a vision of the Trinity. There is the enigmatic expression *ad utramque partem* (*Diary* 91), not to mention a certain number of liturgical quotations. This strongly idiolectal nature of Ignatius's *Diary* is reinforced by the accumulation of nominal phrases, present participles, and infinitives (as a whole constituting more than seventy percent of the verbal material), whose syntactic linkage is often ensured by the conjunctions of scholastic jargon.

Ignatius, as we can see, did not ignore the compost of language. He did not wish to assure the mastery of language by subverting its laws in order to translate his mystical adventure and to express the inexpressible linguistically. The reader of the *Diary*, if he disregards alliterations such as "Our Lady, who is the part or portal of such a great grace" (*Diary* 31), will find no clear recourse to the poetic function, even though some consider it indispensable for evoking mystical experiences.

All the linguistic elements in Ignatius's *Spiritual Diary* can be easily identified and located as normative elements or variables of a given linguistic system. This being the case, if so many sentences of this *Diary* do not openly deliver to us the information they convey, it is because we lack the reference points or the necessary connotations to be able to co-produce their meaning. Ignatius was aware of this difficulty in reading; but we should remember that he was writing this intimate journal about himself and for himself. This is also why the manuscript of the *Diary* contains a certain number of non-linguistic signs in the margin of the text—graphemes in the form of double strokes, crosses, underlining—for which Ignatius does not provide us with an interpretative key.

This reason alone, which is intimately linked with the comprehension of the text itself, is sufficient to prevent certain passages of the *Spiritual Diary* from providing us with all the information we would expect from them. Thus, after receiving consolation and joy, Ignatius wrote on February 21, 1544: "So great an achievement did it seem to have untied this knot or accomplished something similar (*cosa simile*) that I could not stop repeating to myself, with reference to myself, 'Who are you?'" (*Diary* 63). In this sentence the absence of the thing referred to (is it the Trinitarian problem or his doubts concerning the confirmation of his decision on the subject of poverty?) and the obliteration of a precise connotation (this "something similar") makes our reading decidedly uncertain. But it is not that Ignatius deliberately wanted to make his language enigmatic. On the contrary, the many deletions in the manuscript prove his constant effort to express his ineffable mystical experience as clearly as possible for himself.

For far from believing that linguistic mechanisms must be shattered and the communicable deserted in order to really express a mystical experience—following the principle that "all true language is incomprehensible"—Ignatius felt the need to translate the "visitations" (*Diary* 127) of the Holy Trinity by means of resources of language. This led him to a struggle on various levels and, in the first place, to a difficulty, i.e., the fact that he felt the impossibility of putting his mystical experience into writing. Thus on Friday, February 14, 1544, he wrote: "At the consecration, she [Our Lady] showed that her own flesh was in that of her Son, with so many intuitions that they could not be written" (*Diary* 31).

A week earlier, however, Ignatius had experienced such satisfaction from the way he had described a vision—marked with a double stroke—that he avowed: "When I read over what I had written and saw that it was accurate, fresh devotion came, not without tears in my eyes" (*Diary* 9). But a few days later the light was so blinding and the benefit received so great "as to be inexplicable" (*Diary* 21).

At times Ignatius admitted to a kind of despair in regard to writing: "Feeling the Son very ready to intercede, and the saints, I cannot put in writing how I saw them, as I cannot explain anything else of what happened" (*Diary* 27). The reason for this impossibility is certainly not language itself, but the understanding of the mystery of the Most Holy Trinity, which enlightens the spirit in such a way that its expression is quite beyond the possibilities of a whole life of study (no. 52). Thus Ignatius can find "neither memory nor the understanding to explain or expose them [the intuitions]" (*Diary* 185). But he refused to the very end to have recourse to the subversion of language in order to communicate the unfathomable nature of the visitations of the Holy Trinity.

This respect and confidence where language was concerned are confirmed by another spiritual phenomenon mentioned in Ignatius's *Diary*. The visitations of the Holy Trinity caused him "often to lose the power of speech" (*Diary* 72), but they did not destroy it. Every time Ignatius uses the expression "to lose the power of speech," he evokes the manner in which he "converses" with a divine person, the Holy Spirit for example, through the liturgical "word" of the Eucharist (no. 14). During the eucharistic celebration he willingly "held back from speaking whenever this was possible" (*Diary* 7). More often, however, he "could not keep the power of speech for long before losing it again—with many spiritual intuitions" (*Diary* 27). On February 17, which must have been Sexagesima Sunday, Ignatius noted that he often lost the power of speech, "especially during the whole long epistle of St. Paul which begins *libenter suffertis insipientes* (*Diary* 40). Ignatius never dealt systematically with this phenomenon, but what he tells us about it seems to lead to an alternative: either the Holy Trinity's visitation is accomplished in speech, or else it leads to a loss of the power of speech.

On February 14 Ignatius mentions these two modes of visitation without adding any comments: "Often I could not keep the power of speech for long before losing it again—with many spiritual intuitions; finding easy access to the Father when I spoke his name, as the Mass names him . . ." (*Diary* 27). On the following day he feels "an inner sweetness" . . . when I named the Eternal Father" (*Diary* 28). And precisely because of the visitation accomplished in speech—"every time I mentioned God as *Dominus*" (*Diary* 164)—Saint Ignatius exclaimed on February 22: "I am not worthy to invoke the name of the most Holy Trinity" (*Diary* 64).

From the time when the Father placed Ignatius "with the Son" (*Diary* 67) at La Storta, it was normal for the name of Jesus to have a special place in the account of "visits" by the Holy Trinity. This name so "impresses itself on me" (*Diary* 68), he wrote, that on February 23 he was "impelled to speak and felt intensely moved from within" (*Diary* 69). On the following day "the name of Jesus was shown me" (*Diary* 71), with "exclaiming spiritually" (*Diary* 72). What was not said about the name of the Father is then said about that of the Son who "communicates himself" to Ignatius through speech (*Diary* 73, 76). And the words Ignatius pronounces in the liturgy transform themselves into Jesus' words. Ignatius's *Confiteor Deo* takes on, in the gospel for the day (*Diary* 76), the plenitude of Jesus's *Confiteor tibi*. Consequently, when Ignatius pronounces his prayer to the Father, it is Jesus who not only presents it but accompanies it (*Diary* 77). In this way, and also in words which do not belong to the liturgy, Ignatius receives visitations from the Holy Trinity (*Diary* 178).

The more Ignatius reunites with the Holy Trinity as being everything, the less the visitation appears to "come down to the letter" of the liturgical text: "Yet this visitation seemed to be interior, midway between their seat on high and the letter" (*Diary* 127). Instead of descending into speech, the visitation sometimes makes it difficult even to pronounce the first words of the Mass (*Diary* 101). But, during Mass, the visit often signifies "loss of the power of speech" (*Diary* 166).

The Presence of the Loquela

And here we must face the problem posed by the use of the term *loquela*, a term which appears unexpectedly in the *Spiritual Diary* on Sunday, May 11. *Loquela* is clearly part of the liturgical celebration of the Eucharist (*Diary* 221). But the term appears on several consecutive days until May 28 when it disappears, while the loss of the power of speech continues to be present in Ignatius's spiritual notes (*Diary* 308, 367, 414, 416). Evidently *loquela* as a term is taken for granted, since it is not translated, as it would be to indicate the strangeness of the phenomenon. According to Father Louis Beirnaert's interpretation,

[i]t is really the locution of the Mass which becomes the *loquela*, when the meanings efface themselves to give place to the voice and to the other modulations of the signifiers in the depth of the silence of the Other. Ignatius is possessed by this dimension of the signifiers, which turns them towards the void of the Other, contrary to the dimension which is orientated towards meaning.

Ignatius uses a technical term here, which is new in the *Diary*, and which appears only over a definite period of days. It is surrounded by a musical type of semantic field: harmony (*Diary* 222), heavenly music (*Diary* 224), sonority or the mere sound (*Diary* 234). While the visitations of the Holy Trinity in speech are disturbed by people who are talking around him (*Diary* 107, 144), the *loquela* is hampered by "someone whistling" (*Diary* 227). What is most important however, linguistically speaking, is the fact that Ignatius tries to insert this *loquela* into speech through a double articulation: "I was taking excessive pleasure in the tone of the *loquela,* that is, in the mere sound, without paying sufficient attention to the meaning of the words and of the *loquela*" (*Diary* 234). The "spiritual visitation" to which this effort explicitly refers cannot "teach" or "instruct" Ignatius on the part of God without "a word" being received in it. To separate the meaning attached to the sound and cling to the mere sound can only be a temptation of the evil spirit (*Diary* 234). This is not the first time that Ignatius receives "a new sensation, a fresh devotion" (*Diary* 127) "divinely granted" (*Diary* 221). The *loquela* too appears to be situated between God's "seat on high and the letter" (*Diary* 127) of the eucharistic liturgy (*Diary* 221). At all events, the two experiences (on March 7 and in the month of May) have in common the fact that Ignatius, like an *infans* ("someone who does not know how to speak")—*ego sum puer* (*Diary* 127). Thus does he receive a word that can gratuitously enter into the liturgical word (*Diary* 127).

If we limit our analysis to linguistic phenomena, the *loquela* and the spiritual visitation which descends into the "letter" (of the text of the Mass) are the only "spiritual exclamations"—*riplicas espirituales* (*Diary* 72) mentioned in Ignatius's *Spiritual Diary*. On the one hand, the employment of the personal pronouns in the *Diary* leaves no doubt about the dialogical procedure Ignatius uses to express himself. Unlike the autobiographical account written in the third person, in which Ignatius calls himself the pilgrim, the *Diary* is clearly couched in the first person, supported by nominal constructions, "I felt within me no desire to rise" —*sentia en me no querer levantar* (*Diary* 38). On the other hand, the passages in which the second person is explicitly made present to complete the dialogue are rare. Once Ignatius answers the tempter: "Get to your place" (*Diary* 151), and once he asks himself, "Who are you" (*Diary* 63)? Twice he questions the Lord: "Where do you wish to take me, Lord?" (*Diary* 113), and "Lord, where am I going?" (*Diary* 114). And again he prays the Lord twice: "Confirm me" (*Diary* 53); "Give me loving humility" (*Diary* 178). But a "you" addressed by God to Ignatius never appears. The "visitation" of the Holy Trinity is therefore not of a linguistic order, unless we accept, through an abuse of language, that "everything is language." On the other hand, the 165 times that Ignatius receives the gift of tears over a period of 40 days (from February 2, 1544, to March 12, 1544) are the Spirit's answer, the visitation of the Holy Trinity. It is as if Ignatius were straining to exploit all the possibilities of language to begin the utterance of his sentence, and as if God only offered his answer through completing this sentence in a non-linguistic manner, filling the language of *koinonia* with being: "Only to those who worship the Word are given words and speech" (Gregory Nazianzen, Or. 41, 1).

I have deliberately omitted the properly semantic dimension of Ignatius's *Spiritual Diary* in this reflection on language as such. In fact, this dimension rarely escapes the erudition and competence of experts in spiritual theology when they co-produce the sense of the texts they are studying. Exhaustive research on the semantic material of this *Spiritual Diary* would certainly lead to important discoveries. And these will soon be able to profit, through intertextual comparison, from the systematic computerized listing which is being made of all the lexical material in Ignatius's letters; we are hoping to make this material available on the occasion of the Ignatian Year (1990-1991).

Conclusion

I would like to conclude this study by referring my readers to a passage in the book of Genesis in which both spiritual theology and linguistics have recognized for centuries the place of their origin. It is the solemn moment when the Lord God leads the animals to man "to see what he would call them" (Gen 2:19). A quick comparison with the parallel passage in the Koran reveals, in the book of the origins, the autonomy granted to man in the use of his speech through languages. In the Koran, however (Koran II, 29), man is content to call the animals by the name God teaches him to use. This Koranic verse, which is in no way satanic, is the basis of the divine origin of the Arabic language up to the present day.

But if we grant anthropology all the value of a recognized autonomy, it is left to the spiritual master to testify to the fact that this autonomy itself has been received in its entirety: for our humanity transcends the knowledge and awareness which we can cull from it, and by ourselves we can no more produce our end than we can our origin.

A realization of this kind, of which St. Ignatius has been our privileged witness, is far from impeding the establishment of the exact sciences and the human sciences according to the scientific laws proper to them. But such a realization simply invites these autonomous sciences to recognize their dependence on the person, thus opening the way for a true anthropology, and so to recognise their dependence on the Lord of all. If our humanity thus remains the open horizon of all scientific research, science will escape from its suicidal and narcissistic tendencies.

TEN

IMAGES AND IMAGINATION
IN THE *SPIRITUAL EXERCISES*

I would like to attempt a modest contribution in an area in which we are not, and perhaps cannot be, very faithful to Ignatius. I refer to the whole area of images and imagination in the *Spiritual Exercises*; and by imagination I understand the ability of the human mind to produce, preserve, reproduce, combine and create images, even in the absence of perceived objects. We find in the *Spiritual Exercises* plenty of imaginative and figurative material suggested for prayer: from the Temporal King to the Two Standards, from the ignoble knight to the poor little unworthy slave. Indeed, Ignatius gives such importance to the imagination that Roland Barthes could speak of a radical imperialism of images in the Spiritual Exercises.

Ambivalence of the Imagination

This area of the *Spiritual Exercises* has suffered and still suffers because of the contempt or suspicion with which the level of the imaginary tends to be regarded, if one does not restore to it an ontological function, if one considers it to belong to the unreal and purely fanciful world. Naturally we should distinguish between fidelity to the imaginative sketches (e.g., Christ as "eternal Lord") and the images themselves (e.g., the "parable of the temporal king"). Thus, for example, in the case of the temporal king, suppressing the images provided by the Ignatian text would be quite different from substituting for them other images closer to our culture or even with biblical images. The following is Fr. Francis Varillon's response to a query concerning the application of the senses:

I offer no more than very discreet suggestions and, at times, simply
leave this out altogether: this is not the essential thing. What matters
is the choice of those images that are most apt to help one enter into
the knowledge of the true God. There is no thought without an
image, as all university graduates know. There is need, then, to
guide the imagination, because some true ideas can give rise to false
images; besides, since what is first received by the human spirit are
the images, they can well obstruct the ideas. The use of images
needs to be at once prudent and controlled. And the retreatant must
soon enough accept the experience of "emptiness," seeing that he is
before the mystery of God and that he must discover for himself that
there are no images that are adequate to the revelation of the
mystery.[1]

We must remark, all the same, that in the case we have mentioned of the
temporal king, we are dealing with applying the spirit not so much to the
mystery of God as to that of the Kingdom, for which the Gospel offers many
images (cf. Mt 13).

On the one hand there is no thought without images, but, on the other,
the core of the spiritual journey or of life in the Spirit is the transformation of
the intellect and of the will in a union with the invisible God, in which case
the imagination could well lead us astray. The importance which Ignatius gives
in the *Exercises* to the field of the imagination indicates at least that he intends
disposing the whole person to enter into the mystery of God. This entry will
not be real unless the imagination is also integrated into the spiritual
movement that such an entry supposes.

Some think that this importance given to the imagination in the *Spiritual
Exercises* should be attributed purely and simply to the particular psychology
of Ignatius, and that therefore the imagination ought to be set aside or
by-passed in the case of persons who do not have his imaginative capacity or
do not share his "baroque" fascination with certain images of his day. It is
true that his biographical data show us Ignatius as a man gifted with a more

---

[1] François Varillon, *Beauté du monde et souffrance des hommes*, Paris, 1980, p.
194.

than ordinary imaginative sensitivity, whose spiritual development is marked throughout by a flood of images. The *Book of the Hours* which he uses at the time of his conversion, the *Life of Christ* on which he meditates and the "Golden Legend" which inspires him—these three illustrated books will be, thanks to the purification of Ignatius's imagination, at the root of the great images of the *Spiritual Exercises*. But even without illustrations the text of the life of Christ and of the saints is enough to make Ignatius "think for two and three and four hours without realizing it. . . . he pondered over many things that he found good" (*Autob.* 6, 7). The figure of "our holy father Onophrius" haunts the imagination of Ignatius.

But, in the course of his spiritual adventure, Ignatius experiences the ambivalence of the imagination. On the one hand, in the story of his conversion, the imagination acts as a "deceptive influence" which not only conceals the reality from him, but ceaselessly tempts him, even while on the brink of contemplating suicide, seducing him to the point both of holding him captive to certain images and of closing him up forever in thoughts of death (*Autob.* 24). But, on the other hand, the imagination is also "the place of the projection of the unconscious" (as is exemplified in the already cited *Autobiography* and in the symbolically poor Trinitarian images of the *Spiritual Diary*); indeed, the imagination drives Ignatius to search for different figures and sets him in the presence of the purest figure—the icon that is Christ—which leads to the One who is beyond all figures and images. Ignatius recognizes, in the "Rules for the Discernment of Spirits" [314] that the enemy makes use of the world of the imagination to "fill with sensual delights and gratifications" so as better to keep a person imprisoned in the deadly revery of sin. But he has in fact discovered the positively creative power of the imagination which can make Christ present to a person and that person contemporaneous to the mystery: "Imagine Christ our Lord present before you upon the Cross . . ." [53]. Thus, paradoxically, the imagination can open a person to the very core of reality. Undoubtedly Ignatius here is communicating his own personal experience which is strongly characterized by his desire to "see" the Lord, at times even to the point of a love-filled obsession, as when he yearned to see "on what side the right foot [of the Lord] was, or on what side the left" at the moment of his ascension (*Autob.* 47-48). Yet Ignatius is also giving witness to his unshakable trust in a human faculty which, while conscious of its ambivalence, he does not disregard or do away with, but rather "evangelizes" so that it can play its part in leading us to an intimate knowledge of the Lord [104].

Ignatius's Sober Use of the Imagination

Situating the personal experience of Ignatius in the context of his times is not without interest. In the classical description of Johann Huizinga in his work "The Decline of the Middle Ages," the sixteenth century is presented as the century par excellence of the "worship of the image." Seeing the world around them crumble, people appear to cling to religious representations without worrying too much about their content. And so a way is opened to the purely imaginary, to the superstitious. The "Rules for Thinking with the Church" contain allusions to these deviations. With all that, however, very much in the spirit of Ignatius, such deviations call not for an iconoclastic attitude but for the proper use of images: "We ought to praise . . . images and veneration of them according to the subject they represent" [360]. In the *Spiritual Exercises* Ignatius clearly distances himself from that abuse of imagery that was so characteristic of his ambience. Exercises such as those on hell and on the birth of the Lord, which have express recourse to "seeing in imagination" [66 and 112], are extremely sketchy and jejune in the explicit role they assign to the imagination.

The recent work of Frei Betto, *Fidel y la religion* (Havana, 1985, p. 150) makes it clear that President Fidel Castro remembers the Spiritual Exercises merely as "a punishment in which what mattered was to stir our imagination to the extreme . . . as regards hell, the heat of the fire of hell, the sufferings in hell, the anxiety and despair of hell . . . a sort of mental terrorizing . . . in a word, stirring up the imagination." But this excessive appeal to the imagination which bothers President Fidel Castro, and which consists in exploiting all the horror which our phantasy can arouse, should not justify the other extreme of disincarnating to the utmost the spiritual experience of hell that Ignatius proposes—particularly if we realise that the application of the imagination is always for Ignatius inserted into a concrete spiritual movement. The different approaches to God and to his mystery should not be mutually exclusive; in fact, they rather complete one another in the unity of human consciousness. Indeed, the sobriety of Ignatius in regard to the creative power of the imagination is so much the more remarkable in that Ignatius himself—the story of his life and his *Spiritual Diary* bear evident witness to this—lived his own personal experience of the life in the Spirit at an intense level with the aid of many images. Well known, for instance, is his devotion to any image whatsoever of Our Lady, but preferably to that of the Mother of Sorrows. And yet, when it comes to the Spiritual Exercises, where there is no dearth of opportunity for it, Ignatius never imposes his own preferred images. The same is true of his images of the Trinity and of Christ. He wishes to allow the Creator to deal directly with his creature, without any intermediary, and the creature directly with its Creator and Lord [15]. Ignatius is ever ready to withdraw into the background. This also happens when Ignatius brings "the person who is contemplating" [2] face to face with the biblical images. The few variations from the biblical text—like the ass of the Nativity contemplation [111], or the apparition to Our Lady [299] and to Joseph of Arimathea [310], or even the call of the temporal king [91]—are an invitation not to shut oneself up in the reading of biblical texts alone, but to give the greatest freedom possible to the imagination "to experience and relish the truth interiorly" [2].

The insistence of Ignatius on the part which the imagination should play in the Spiritual Exercises does not mean, therefore, that Ignatius wishes to impose or rigidly determine the ways in which it is to be used. Some commentators of the *Exercises* have surely good reasons to mistrust certain visual representations of hell, to free themselves from the "outdated symbolism" of the Two Standards and to reject the "dead letter" of the parable of the king. But this is not the same as rejecting the very imaginative sketches of which we have spoken earlier; much less does it mean doing away with every form of "seeing" and every recourse to the imagination, or reducing every gospel contemplation to a mere intellectual interpretation of the mystery, or substituting for the first prelude of "seeing the place" [91] an explanation that entails a precise investigation of the scriptural texts with the help of biblical criticism. What is the "solid foundation of facts" [2] that Ignatius demands as starting point for a faith-inspired listening to the Word of God? In his letter to the Churches of Europe Fr. Clodovis Boff writes (*Il Regno*, 15 February 1985, p. 55):

There exists the danger of shielding oneself against the Gospel by means of a culture of exegetical, historical and sociological erudition, without ever letting oneself be wounded by "the sword of the Word." The problem will always be: how much have we understood of the Gospel and how much of it have we assimilated? The Gospel is Good News only when it is read with the eyes of the poor and with the heart of children, or, in other words, when we believe it simply. Doubtless, the Gospel does not dispense with critical understanding; but it is an illusion to think that the latter can guarantee our essential grasp of the Gospel. We need, therefore, to go beyond, and further than, mere criticism. Only thus will the Gospel be read with a rediscovered innocence, a second innocence.

As Ignatius would say in concrete language: "I will make myself a poor little unworthy slave and, as though present, look upon them, contemplate them, and serve them in their needs with all possible homage and reverence" [114]. Nothing prevents us, in this becoming contemporaneous to the mystery contemplated, from giving to this "poor and unworthy slave" all the spiritual depth that the Gospel accords to "the child of the Kingdom"—image of a faith that has surrendered all security.

Contrariwise to those who would like to free themselves of the imagination, other commentators favor the role of images in the *Spiritual Exercises*, having recourse to photo-language, slides, and films in order to rouse the imagination. Thus, for example, the use of photograph albums of the countryside or of the family is suggested as a way of visualizing the "meaning" of life and its discovery in the consideration of the "Principle and Foundation" [23]. Again, as an aid to the contemplation of the King in all its fullness, the use of a whole collection of reproductions of works of art on Christ is proposed, to say nothing of the present-day use of icons. At times the commentators consider this recourse to figurative material absolutely necessary, because the attack mounted on modern man by the bombardment of images runs a great risk: it either atrophies the human ability to produce images or causes total confusion between the external images provided by television, publicity and the audiovisual media on the one hand and the internal images of the imagination on the other. In order that we may also make use of the imagination in our discovery of God, we must at times have recourse to certain strong and vigorous images and spend a certain amount of time in "fixing one's gaze" on these images so as to activate the imagination as the place of the projection of the unconscious. In this way, in the contemplation of the Gospel, we will assure the transition from the body which the Incarnate Word chose for Himself to the intimate knowledge of the Incarnate Lord. There is need then to step out of the flood of images which invade a person day after day, but not indeed to eliminate the imagination. This imagination plays its part even in that exacting task of making a good choice, in which "as far as depends on us, our intention must be simple, considering only the end for which we are created, that is, for the praise of God our Lord and for the salvation of our soul" [169]. Or, as is set forth in the second way of making a choice in the third time, "[t]he love that moves and causes me to choose must descend from above, that is, from the love of God, so that before one chooses he should perceive that the greater or less attachment to the object of his choice is solely because of his Creator and Lord" [184]. And so Ignatius suggests that "I should represent to myself a man whom I have never seen or known" [185] to help him with advice regarding his life, or "to consider . . . if I were at the moment of death" [186], or "to picture and consider myself as standing in the presence of my judge on the last day" [187]. Careful to take in all the dimensions of man, Ignatius makes use of the imagination in the journey towards him who is beyond all images.

Role of the Imagination:
Ignatius and John of the Cross

Is Ignatius's daring trust in the imagination justified, given its bad reputation in East and West? Is it Ignatius's intent to "save" the role of the imagination in prayer so as to help in the struggle against "distractions," and then to reject the imagination once it has served this purpose? Ignatius trusts the imagination and, in this sense, he is regarded differently from his contemporary John of the Cross. The latter incessantly repeats that, if one is to know God really, one needs to go radically beyond "distinct knowledgeable data, forms and images" and remain before God *en vacio de todo aquello*, in the void or emptiness of that entire world. Nevertheless, even John of the Cross accepts that man must pass through these images, but that he must "so pass through them as not to encounter obstacles to his attaining the living reality—*de ir a lo vivo*" (*Ascent of Mount Carmel*) III, 15, 1-2; cf. also *Spiritual Canticle* A, prologue, 1). According to John of the Cross the image is a transit port or a door, a place of passage. It would be a mistake to stop halfway, or to expect to hold on to God on the level of the imagination. Prayer moves towards the wiping out of images: "meditation . . . is a discursive act with the help of images . . . for example, we imagine Christ crucified or bound to the pillar . . . or God seated in splendid majesty on a throne, or his glory as most beautiful light, etc. To attain to divine union the soul has to strip itself of none of these images and remain in darkness . . ." (*Ascent of Mount Carmel*, II, 12,3).

It would be less than just to oppose an "iconoclast" John of the Cross to an "iconophile" Ignatius. Both mystics acknowledge that the praying person must traverse the path of images and that the one who contemplates cannot short-circuit the imagination. For both spiritual authors the image stands at the crossroads of the perceptible world and the world of thought. While the image no longer belongs directly to the sense-perceived world, it is not as yet precisely thought and does not belong to the world of thought. The terminology of the *Spiritual Exercises* seems to reflect this openness of the imagination, this mediation between body and soul. The imagination has its roots in the bodily sphere even though it does, and should, open to the realm of the spiritual. Hence, when referring to the imaginative seeing—*vista imaginativa*—and the seeing in imagination—*vista de la imaginación*—[cf. 47], Ignatius does not strictly distinguish between the visible and the invisible, and allows a person "to taste the bitterness of tears, sadness and remorse of conscience" [69]. The images of so many hellish situations—signs, all of them, of the absence among us of a society and culture of love—will suffice to make us grasp the reality of the fire of hell. The function of images and of imagination in this vision of hell is not, indeed, to inflict terror.

In his *Structures anthropologiques de l'imaginaire* (Grenoble, 1960, p. 124), Gilbert Durand shows how every image mitigates the harshness of one's lot: "To portray an evil, or represent a risk, or symbolize an anxiety is already to master them by the dominion expressed in my *cogito* or act of reflection." Here we discover once again the mark of mediation that characterizes the image, with the result that negative images always connote their contraries. How is one to portray a prison without setting up a contrast between its darkness and some light, be it ever so distant? How represent hell without thereby connoting heaven? Only the imagination can express the simultaneity of those contraries that spiritual experience has necessarily to set over against each other: light and darkness, heaven and hell, sin and grace. It is necessary, then, to control the imagination—the additions in the *Spiritual Exercises* [74 and 81] insist on this—and not to allow it to deteriorate into hallucinations and illusions, but by no means to do away with it, for the imagination makes it possible for me to see myself as a "knight . . . filled with shame and confusion" and a "prisoner bound with fetters" [74]—"to consider who I am . . ." [58]—and, above all, to see the Lord: "While one is eating, let him imagine he sees Christ our Lord eating with His apostles . . ." [214].

Though Ignatius and John of the Cross are at one on the constructive function of the imagination in prayer, they still have different emphases. The two authors see themselves as gifted with different vocations. Prayer, it is true, moves towards the disappearance of images once the icon of the invisible is lit up. But—and this is to simplify matters greatly—in the case of Ignatius, taking up and transforming the images without destroying them, while in that of John of the Cross, freeing self from every attachment to concrete images and places of devotion, as it were jumping over the wall of the imagination to leap towards the Bridegroom. Hence the advice of John of the Cross: "Let the soul know for sure that the more it is attached possessively to the image . . . so much the less will it see its devotion and prayer rise up to God" (*Ascent of Mount Carmel*, III, 35, 6); while, for Ignatius, the application of the senses contributes, in his spirituality of incarnation, to the transformation and transfiguration of the imagination into the sentiments of Jesus Christ.

Application of the Senses:
Mediatory Function of the Imagination

Since Ignatius takes the mediatory function of the imagination quite seriously, without ever isolating either one of its two poles, and concretely integrates the ambivalent character of the imagination, viz., the real made present in an unreal way, he conceives of the application of the senses as one total experience of body and soul, by means of which the praying person progresses towards the Lord and lets himself be seized by him. This Ignatian anthropology was not taken seriously from the beginning of the history of the Society, and so certain problems were raised which imply a completely different conception of the imagination. We should study the mediating function of the imagination in the application of the senses without ever isolating either one of its two poles. To wish to know whether the application of the senses is easier or more difficult, for beginners in the spiritual life or for the proficient, whether it is inferior or superior to meditation, whether it is intended as a help to take things more calmly at the close of a day or to gather up the entire fruit of a day filled with prayer, is in the last analysis to probe the very nature of the application of the senses. The official *Directory* published by Father Aquaviva situates itself very definitely on a plane above the imagination: "When the soul is already satiated with the knowledge of higher things and finds itself full of fervor and piety, it gladly *comes down again* into those things perceptible to the *senses* and finds in them its nourishment, so that even what is lowest or *least* may help it on towards love and consolation" (*MI, Dir.*, p. 681). Father François Courel puts things more positively in his translation of the *Spiritual Exercises*: "In this way St. Ignatius proposes the application of the senses at the end of a day's striving in prayer as a help to gather up all its fruit. Such a form of prayer marks a definite *progress* over the discursive and even affective forms of meditation" (*Exercices Spirituels*, Paris 1960, p. 76). The latest French translation of the *Spiritual Exercises* (*Exercices Spirituels*, Paris 1985, p. 220) situates the application of the senses within the context of the understanding of 2 Cor 3:18: "None of us, then, reflect the glory of the Lord . . . and that same glory, coming from the Lord who is the Spirit, transforms us into his very likeness, in an ever greater degree of glory." There is no comparison between the object perceived by our senses and the object imagined. What is represented by the imagination is, as such, extremely simple in the case of every person. In this connection it would be quite a mistake to think of the application of the senses as an exercise possible only for those gifted with a powerful imagination. Many persons, it is true—particularly a large number of adolescents—are accustomed to cultivating their ability to phantasize in extreme fashion. But it is an error to identify the imagination with mere fantasizing activity. Indeed, there is no question here of filling up an interior void with the products of one's fantasy, even if this is seen to be devout.

Some Aspects of the Imagination

This is surely the point at which it would be helpful to focus on certain aspects of the imagination as such, the more easily to grasp the intuition of Ignatius: characteristic of the imagination is the ability to *render present even that which is absent*. The image makes present what is absent. How are we to restore to the life of Christ, which historically belongs forever to the past, all its human reality as experienced in His flesh and in his heart without the aid of the imagination, which alone can help us discover past history as actually present here and now in the contemporary reality of our life? The figure of Jesus of Nazareth, such as is presented by the gospels and the Exercises, cannot be bypassed. Without this reference to Jesus—and not merely to Christ—the mystery of God is, for us, beyond our reach. Ignatius's invitation "to see the way from Nazareth to Bethlehem, its length, its breadth, whether level, or through valleys and over hills" [112] is not aimed at exercising the probing curiosity of the imagination or at encouraging a search for descriptive details, as would be the case of painting in representational art. Rather, it is meant mainly to guarantee the sense of presence of the Gospel as an actual event taking place here and now.

The imagination will always have an aspect of "phantasizing" to it, but it is also and above all *the capacity to produce symbols*—that is, forms that conjoin the visible and invisible, able to make present the encounter between God and man. Ignatius suggests making use of the surrounding atmosphere—"closing the shutters and doors" [79]; "to make use of pleasant or disagreeable weather" [130]—to awaken the senses, then proposing "gospel scenes" to the imagination so that in it may spring up the symbols that prayerful faith can hold on to. The symbolizing function of the imagination makes the one who contemplates capable of *being transformed into the Gospel*—capable, that is, of experiencing in the "gospel scene" the "mystery" of Christ, and of "putting on Christ" while taking an active part in the present reality of the Lord.

Contemplation of the Mysteries of Christ: Recent Objections and Ignatian Orientation

Even recently this form of contemplation of the Gospel has been criticized as not really suited to the pragmatism and empiricism of our day. Contemporary man wants facts and, as is often said, we have no image of Christ that gives us an idea of his true traits and features, nothing that guarantees that He actually pronounced the words attributed to Him in the gospel or even those attributed to him by our imagination—"to hear what they are saying, or what they might say"—[123]. Then again, the burgeoning of several forms of oriental meditation has evidently called into question the very contemplation of the Gospel: such an approach would call for a liberation from all content that is the object of the senses or of the imagination, finally even all that is conceptual, in order to conform to the simplicity of God—in the case, at any rate, of a Christian type of oriental meditation. A form of prayer, such as the one described earlier on as contemplation of the Gospel, would be acceptable merely to beginners who initially consider Christ as an object of meditation before experiencing him at the heart of the contemplation itself. On the other hand, the fact that the *Spiritual Exercises* conclude with a "Contemplation to Attain Love," which is related not so much to Christ as to God present in all creation and at work deeply within us, is considered an indication that even for Ignatius Christian mysticism has to go beyond the stage of the contemplation of the mysteries of Christ, in which the imagination necessarily plays its part. Nor is there wanting, together with these current opinions, a certain reaction against a conception of prayer in which only the Christ of faith is taken into account, to the complete neglect of the Jesus of history.

Without wanting to define these various positions inflexibly, and keeping in mind that the problem is far more vast and complex than the whole question related to the imagination, we need nonetheless to call attention to the fact that the reality of God and of man in Catholic prayer will always remain the mystery of Christ in the indissociable union between God and man that is true of the Lord Jesus. As Ignatius refuses, in the contemplation of the Incarnation [101], to separate what is historically incarnate from what is in every age Trinitarian, the same Ignatius assumes fully what is historically the object of the senses. Human beings, in fact, ought never to completely break away from it, but rather should shed only those images which are the product of inordinate attachments. In this way he is able to get to that surrender of self which is the attitude of spiritual indifference [23], and which makes it possible for God's plan of "saving the human race" [102], deeply written into the core of our being, to be accomplished in and by us in the likeness of Christ. Ignatian contemplation, which finds its place within patristic and medieval tradition, is a being plunged into the mysteries of the new and eternal alliance which transforms us from mere spectators into present-day partakers of the life of Christ. Without water and blood, the Spirit alone is of no avail (1 Jn 5: 6). Contrary to a human being's experience, which runs the risk of closing it up narcissistically upon itself, the contemplation of the Gospel makes man get out of himself to encounter Christ. Ignatius focuses only slightly on the "I," just enough to discover in it the sinner; it is rather the life of Christ that is the ever-fresh existential dimension of his trinitarian prayer, which unfailingly takes off from the concrete historical event to leap towards the eternal now of God.

This contemplation of the humanity of Christ is admirably suited to beginners in the life of the Spirit, but it equally sustains the great mystics who have already been initiated into intimacy with the Word. The activity of the spiritual senses is linked to the spiritualization of inner consciousness, and admits of various degrees ranging from that of the beginner to that of the spiritually perfect person, who rises effortlessly from the plane of the senses to the spiritual and mystical plane. The contemplation of the gospel scenes certainly has in itself elements appealing to the imagination that facilitate the work of contemplation. But the purification of this imagination remains always difficult if one is to arrive at truly seeing how the Word is entirely present in his "mysteries" and how in every detail the whole mystery of his love is revealed. Finally, even though the imagination is in itself on a lower plane, it ought to be gripped all the way from top to bottom or from within to without. For it is the imagination which perceives what God had to do to become visible and to make himself audible; it is the imagination which experiences on the sense level even what of God is beyond the senses. The application of the senses cannot be understood except in the context of the whole human person. Hence "the application of senses can assume many modalities, of quite different depth, ranging from a contemplation of a more simplified and affective nature to a more or less profound intuitive apprehension . . . whose quality is gauged according to the measure of God's gift."[2]

Instead of relegating prayer in isolation to this or that level, Ignatius probes all the energies of persons to transform them into availability to the coming of the Lord in us. Nothing is excluded from it; everything is integrated in the measure in which his Divine Majesty grants us to make use of it. Ignatius wants to make sure that the person enters into the mystery of the Incarnation with all his heart; and in this heart, taken in the biblical sense, the imaginative powers have a role to play which, however, will depend on the here-and-now situation of each person.

This freedom of Ignatius in regard to the forms of prayer, and the care he takes to mobilize all the potentialities of the person so that they can be seized by the Spirit of the Lord, explain as well the ambivalence of "the three ways of praying" [233-260]. The Eighteenth Annotation [18] considers them suited to "those who have little natural ability or are illiterate," while Annotation Four [4] appends them to the Fourth Week with the Resurrection and the Ascension. They are, in fact, placed at the very end of the *Exercises*, following the Contemplation to Attain Love [230 ff; 238 ff.]. Nowhere is the fleshly reality and down-to-earth aspect of the human person so clearly underscored as here: the very material and content matter of the commandments, the harsh reality of the capital sins, the meaning of words,

---

[2] Cf. H. Coathelem, *Ignatian Insights*, Taiwan, 1961, p. 157.

the rhythm of breathing and all the bodily senses. This rich text of the three ways of praying inserts the whole human reality into a movement of prayer developing from the exterior to the interior; but all this human reality can be the manifestation of the new person captivated by the love of Christ and transformed by his paschal mystery. Then it is that one's respiration breathes in the Spirit, words give expression to the Word, and the observance of the commandments as well as the desires of the senses manifest the love of the Father. The application of the senses as well as the three ways of praying allow of two interpretations, from above and from below, because they express the totality of the human person as saved by God-with-us.

From Mirror Image to Icon Image

The application of the senses thus reaches its filfillment not just in the production of our images by our imagination, but in the transfiguration of our powers of loving by the love of Christ. On the plane of the imagination such a transfiguration means the "epiphany" or manifestation of the icon of God that is the figure of Christ. Of set purpose, then, must we speak of the icon. For images, inasmuch as they are products of our imagination, can easily be mirror images in which we keep on looking at ourselves. After all, one cannot rule out in principle that we could well project ourselves into a gospel scene. It is a very different matter when the products of our imagination are icon images by means of which we aim at seeing the light "in your light." Ignatius offers an illustration of this in the call of the temporal king [92-94]. The image of the king somehow embarrasses us, and we dearly wish to move beyond it. And yet, this image is placed between two invitations: on the one hand, one is "to see in imagination the synagogues, villages and towns where Christ our Lord preached" [91]. On the other hand, one should in reality "see Christ our Lord, the Eternal King . . ." [95]. Indeed, the invitation "to place before my mind a human king" [92] is intended precisely to elicit this movement from a mirror image of the Gospel—"a sentimental walk, with a flower in the buttonhole, through the gardens of the Gospel or of Scripture as a whole" (Jean Laplace)—to an actualization by means of the icon image of the experience of the living God revealed in Jesus. The desire to be with the other, as well as the desire of the other to be with me through suffering which opens out onto glory, is a desire called forth by the image of the human king, and it must be evangelized. To this human capacity of desire is given, in the deeds and actions of Jesus, the possibility of seeing the icon, the true figure of a freedom without fetters, because here the desire of man and the desire of God coincide perfectly.[3] The application of the senses mobilizes the whole of the human person to see in the Gospels the Epiphany of the Icon of God.

The term icon image is very much to the point. It is well known that the icon, in contrast to the portrait painting, attempts to elicit a maximum of presence with a minimum of strokes. It is worthwhile calling attention to Ignatius's constant sobriety when it comes to tracing certain features of the gospel. "After that he appeared to James" [309]: this single stroke, for example, is aimed at lighting up the icon of the risen Lord and his encounter with us. But the most notable characteristic of the icon, as compared with the portrait or the mirror, is that of "looking" or "gazing." And so Ignatius looks at God dwelling in creatures, and at humanity created in the likeness and image of the Divine Majesty [235], but the human face does by no means become for him the only image of spiritual life. Far from tending towards the figurative image, the icon is accompanied by the presence of the Invisible and gazes upon us, all the while transforming us.[4] The application of the senses, therefore, entails disposing the imagination to welcome and receive the look of Christ so as to be transformed into him. By no means does it signify being filled with images: it is rather the look of Christ gazing upon our desire and our history, as the icon that is the visage received through grace.[5]

---

[3] Cf. Joseph Thomas, *Le secret des Jésuites*, 1984, p. 153.

[4] Cf. Charles A. Bernard, *Theologie symbolique*, Paris, 1978, pp. 133 ff.

[5] Cf. Olivier Clement, *Le visage interieur*, Paris, 1978, p. 58.

Conclusion

After all that has been said so far, there will be no more need to insist that the *Spiritual Exercises* is not an awkward, outdated deposit of images. Rather, this text affords us a path through our mirror images and portrait images towards the seizure of the whole of our being—body, soul, imagination and understanding—by the Icon of the Invisible that is Christ Jesus. A path through our images: the contemplation of the Nativity confirms this when, instead of stopping at a beautiful picture of the crib, it makes us see with the gaze of the imagination the way from Nazareth to Bethlehem, symbol of this journey even unto the cross [112 and 116]. A path through our images: The contemplations of the Third Week are in fact and precisely a journey on which one never halts—"from the garden to the house . . ." [208], "from Herod to Pilate" [208]: they aim to shatter our own images and transform them into an actual resemblance of the bruised and broken figure of Christ.

That such a task is also apostolic is affirmed by the Thirty-Second General Congregation in its Decree 4, n. 26 a):

> Certain false images of God which prop up and give an aura of legitimacy to unjust social structures are no longer acceptable. Neither can we admit those more ambiguous images of God which appear to release us from our inalienable responsibilities. . . . For our own sake, as for the sake of our contemporaries, we must find a new language, a new set of symbols, that will enable us to leave our fallen idols behind us and rediscover the true God.

ELEVEN

THE WORD: A WAY TO GOD
ACCORDING TO MASTER IGNATIUS

Introduction

The more one becomes familiar with the *Spiritual Exercises*, the more one is struck by Master Ignatius's faith in speech as a means for meeting God. At the crowning moment of prayer Ignatius does not propose silence or mental reflection but a colloquy, "as one friend speaks to another, or as a servant speaks to a master" [54]. A colloquy is in fact a conversation, an informal communication through words. At one point Ignatius proposes that we pray "contemplating the meaning of each word of a prayer" [249]. This implies taking a term, a word, and savoring its sense; relishing a term like "father," for example, for as long as devotion lasts, because Ignatius believes that this way of dealing with the word "father" will lead us to a true meeting with him, our Father. Again, the author of the *Spiritual Exercises* places great confidence in speech as an instrument, a way, which helps us to meet God. At the end of the *Spiritual Exercises*, while observing that love must be applied more to deeds than to words [234], the Contemplation to Obtain Love ends in a vocal prayer, in a composite formula of words, as an offering of one's whole heart: "Take, Lord, and receive . . ." [234] Is Ignatius's trust in words as a means to meet God justified?

At all events this trust is not obvious. Some mystical schools in Asia are convinced that speech is merely an obstacle, hence the need to eliminate it, because "He who knows, does not speak; he who speaks, does not know."[1] "The Tao which has nothing to do with words."[2] "A Zen master, tormented by one of his disciples, withdrew into absolute silence. "But, Master, kindly answer me." "I have answered you," the Master said. In this mysticism

---

[1] Joseph Masson, *Mystiques d'Asie. Approches et réflexions*, Desclée de Brouwer, 1992, p. 199.

[2] *Ibid.*, p. 203.

everything concurs to shatter human language, because it can only distort and prevent true encounter. Human speech is not to be trusted.

We find this distrust, or at least these reservations, in the schools of Christian spirituality too. Though he was a master of speech who handled the instrument of language admirably, Augustine had to confess that "language says what it can; it is up to the heart to understand the rest."[3] Augustine gives St. John as an example: among the evangelists he appears the most refined and precise in the use of human language when speaking of the mystery of the Incarnate Word. However, "I venture to say, my brothers, that John himself has not said what is, but he too said what he could, because he was only a man and spoke of God, a man who was undoubtedly inspired by God but nevertheless a man."[4] This confession of human inability to "say" the mystery of God and the advice to honor what is ineffable in silence, lead to Augustine's prayer: "When we will have reached you, these words which we multiply without reaching you will cease. . . ."[5] Many saints who, like St. Augustine, were artists in the skill of speaking and describing, never ceased expressing their fear of being caught up in the game of fine words and failing thus to meet God, covering up the experience of God with fine words without really discovering him. Ought not Ignatius, convinced as he was of an "ever greater God," understand more than other people that to really meet God one has to go beyond terms and words? However, Ignatius considered vocal prayer an integral part of the Spiritual Exercises [2] and systematically suggested that the contemplation should end with the recital of an Our Father [117].

To sum up our linguistic situation today, words are slowly but surely losing their symbolic dimension, whereas in fact they ought to reveal a meaning by hiding it, or protect a meaning while revealing it. In view of this refusal of the symbolical dimension of language, hasn't the way to God through words been interrupted? Hasn't the capacity to pray been suppressed or, at least, hasn't prayer been reduced to a silence in which no word disturbs the awareness of self or of the presence of the Other?

---

[3] *Sources Chrétiennes*, 75, 231.

[4] *Homélies sur l'Évangile de saint Jean*, (*Bibliothèque augustinienne*, 71, DDB, 1969, 129.

[5] *La Trinité*, II, p. 567; 15.28.51; cf. André Manaranche, *Des noms pour Dieu*, 1980, p. 88.

Ignatius on Himself

After recalling certain attitudes concerning speech past and present, we would now like to consider further the role of speech in Ignatius's religious experience and its influence on the Spiritual Exercises. We are concerned in particular with the people making them today, whose linguistic culture is very different from that of Ignatius. Ignatius did not like to speak about himself. Many years and the insistence of many people were needed before Master Ignatius decided to tell his life story. In 1553, on the morning of Friday, August 4th, the eve of the Virgin of the Snows, Ignatius began to "dictate while he walked" to Fr. Luis Gonçalves de Câmara, who memorized his words and then wrote them down in his room according to the custom of the time.

We should note two aspects of Ignatius's way of giving an interview. First of all "he spoke in a manner which indicated that God had clearly shown him that he had to do it. He had to reveal everything which had occurred in his soul until that day." For Ignatius speech was important. Though he was not concerned about saying things well, he always measured—in the presence of God—what he said. Hence this other aspect Father Louis recorded: "I have made an effort not to add any word I did not hear from the Father. Where I fear I may have committed an error is when, in order not to stray from the Father's words, I was unable to communicate the strength of certain words."[6] In spite of the limitations imposed by the technique of the interview, Ignatius did not tell any stories, anecdotes, or curious facts concerning his life: through the wise choice of his words and the breath—"the strength"—which inspired them, he communicated his experience of familiarity with God, a God who irrupted into his life and, changing his best plans, was at the origin of all the events referred to. For a long time this story remained unknown within the Society of Jesus. Recognizing the inspiration of this interview, many people today have or repeat their own experience of God, drawing inspiration from the strength of Ignatius's words. These words undoubtedly highlight Ignatius's person, but only in order to show how he was led by God. He did not try to

---

[6] *Prólogo de la Autobiografía, BAC,* 1991, p. 98.

"speak of" himself, and even less to propose himself as a model,[7] but his words convey and suggest a way—a specific way—towards God, which each one of us can use for personal conversations with God. This observation implies that we read Ignatius's autobiography not as a body of information but as a collection of stories each of which throws light on this collaboration between God and Ignatius in the most ordinary things of a life. It was such an extraordinary collaboration that Ignatius wrote down all that happened every day, at least while he was drawing up the *Constitutions*.

Only a fragment of this quite imposing sheaf of documents has reached us, in the form of two notebooks in Ignatius's own hand which we call *The Spiritual Diary*. Though they contain the whole discussion concerning the poverty the Society of Jesus must live, they also reveal the life Master Ignatius lived with the Trinity through consolations and desolations, tears and illuminations, and also words. The most important testimony for our study is that of Friday, March 7, 1544. Ignatius celebrated the Mass of the Holy Trinity, starting with the words *Beata sit sancta Trinitas"* (*Diary*, 127: (bis) March 7). He immediately felt a great devotion, or rather a "new devotion."

The Holy Trinity "visited" him. Ignatius willingly chose this word, with its biblical richness—"God visits his people"—to express the inexpressible experience. He went even further. He felt as if suspended between the Holy Trinity up above and the words of the Missal down below. "Not by elevating my attention to the Divine Persons, as far as they are distinct, nor for distinguishing them, nor lowering it to the wording [in the Missal]. But the interior consolation seemed to me to be between its place on high, and the words of the Missal" (*Diary* 127: March 7), between the space on high and the formula, i.e. the first words of the Mass of the Trinity. Ignatius felt "midway" (*Diary* 128: 25, March 7) because "I did not think that it gave me leave to gaze higher"—no one can see God—and on the other hand "the spiritual lights . . . did not descend to the formula." (*Diary* 127: 25, March 7) That is, he did not remain trapped in the text on the level of words. This "midway" experience brought "very great and increased devotion" (*Diary* 128: 25, March 7).

If we too want to draw inspiration from this experience we must place

---

[7] J.C. Dhôtel, *Ignace de Loyola. Ecrits*, 1991, p. 1018.

it in the context of Ignatius's *Diary*. Ignatius had to confess several times that he had lost the power of speech. "Just before Mass, during it and after it, there was a great abundance of tears, devotion, and heavy sobbing. I could not attempt to speak without losing the power to do so. I had many spiritual lights." (*Diary* 27: 13, February 14) Overcome with emotion at hearing this or that word, Ignatius could not continue reading. Occasionally he made a note of these texts.

At times he did not even begin celebrating the Mass: "I found great difficulty in saying the words "In nomine Patris . . ." (*Diary,* 101: 31. March 3) And why? Because on another occasion when he started the eucharistic prayer with "Te igitur," the word "Te," (you, Father) provoked a luminous vision of God (*Diary* 121: 34, March 6). If, as children of our scientific century, we ask ourselves what happened when Master Ignatius pronounced words, we have to say that for him, in terms of linguistic theory, the "signifier" was immediately the "signified." That is, the very name became the reality. The father does not necessarily have to be called father; Jesus called him "abba." The word is not the thing, but it is still true today that human beings can identify the word with the thing. Our ancestors, living in the forests, did not dare to call a bear by its name for fear of summoning it by the mere fact of pronouncing its name. So they called it "brown." In many cultures, and for many centuries, God's name existed in order not to be used. This was a linguistic taboo: the divine name is God, and so, among the people of God, the name that is the person must not be pronounced and one reads "Lord" instead. This linguistic taboo still exists today. Moderns could not scandalize another person or blaspheme without the interdiction which is placed on a certain number of words.

This capacity human beings have of identifying the name with what the word is saying is quite characteristic of St. Ignatius's time. And so it should not surprise us that his intelligence would remain more easily than ours suspended between the persons up there and the formula down here when pronouncing *beata Trinitas*. He wrote in his Diary: "I thought that every time I named God, Lord, etc., I was penetrated through and through with a wonderful and reverential respect and humility which seem to defy description" (*Diary* 164: 1.a.1., March 17). Ignatius stressed in this confession that for him speech was like the point of departure of a mystical experience which then did not allow itself to be told in words.

We read in Ignatius's Spiritual Diary that these words were not necessarily liturgical texts or prayer formulas. On Sunday, March 30, he prayed, "Give me loving humility . . ." and never stopped repeating these words. Then, as he himself says, he "received fresh consolations in these words." (*Diary* 178: 14.a.1d, March 30) The same thing occurred when Master Ignatius asked for confirmation of his decision concerning poverty in the Society: "Holy Trinity, confirm me. . . . I said this with great earnestness and with much devotion and tears, very often repeated and very interiorly felt . . ." (*Diary*, 48: 17, February 18). This was a real conversation with the Holy Trinity, just as his conversation with the evil one, Satan, was real: "Answering at once, without any disturbance, as if to a beaten enemy, 'Down, where you belong!'" (*Diary* 151: 30 (bis), March 12) Then, as he spoke with himself: "I could not stop repeating to myself, with reference to myself: 'Who are you?'". . . (*Diary* 63: 20, February 21).

On the other hand his attention to words was so intense that the slightest noise disturbed him; he observed that grace had diminished during the greater part of the Mass "because of the sound of the talking from the room" (*Diary* 107: 32, March 4), or "because of the noise" (*Diary* 93: 30, March 2), or because he was "at times bothered by water being thrown on the fire" (*Diary* 129: 25 (bis), March 7) because it was too hot in the chapel. These details are not only picturesque. They show how this mystical experience requires a certain condition of life and fits into the normal capacity of human beings to soliloquize or speak with other people through words, which, though they come from below—i.e., are totally arbitrary—can nevertheless be identified with their sense in order to say the Unutterable.

Thus words serve for the union with God which Ignatius modestly called "feeling intensely united,"or also "I thought my mediators had interceded for me" (*Diary* 3: 3, February 4). On the one hand he could trust this experience to the written word, "Reading this later, and thinking it was good to have written it out, a fresh devotion came upon me" (*Diary* 9: 7, February 8), and yet "in such a way as cannot be written about, any more than other things can be explained" (*Diary* 27: 13, February 14th). If speech makes rising towards the Holy Trinity possible, a *loquela*, a word "from above" which seemed to him to be more divinely bestowed, appeared at a given moment in the *Spiritual Diary* (*Diary* 221: 46.a.1, May 11). Ignatius was prudent: who could assure him that this wordless voice did not come from the "evil spirit"? He mistrusted the "tone of the *loquela*" and attentively trusted "the meaning of the words and the *loquela*" (*Diary* 234: 57.a.1., May 22). In fact, Ignatius felt that all these linguistic or super-linguistic phenomena came from God only when he thought that he was "being taught how to proceed, with the hope of always finding further instruction as time went on" (*Diary* 234: 57a.1, May 22).

Ignatius Helps Us to Say "God"

This incursion into Ignatius's intimate *Diary* offers us more profitable access to the Master's advice in the *Spiritual Exercises* on how to say "God." In the first place it elucidates a passage which commentators usually neglect or ignore. A whole paragraph is devoted to speech in the general examination of conscience "to purify the soul and to aid us to improve our confessions" [32]. Even though Ignatius does not invent anything in this small penitential, after reading the *Spiritual Diary* we are not surprised to encounter an Ignatius who takes words seriously, especially the word of God, and who insists on this sacred word being used according to truth, out of necessity and with reverence [38]. He is interested less in "useless oaths" than in oaths which truly call on God, the supreme witness to truth.

After all this, we should not be surprised at Ignatius's distinction between swearing on the Creator—calling on God's testimony—and swearing on creatures—calling on a reality of the world insofar as it is the work of God: "by God," "by heaven." Ignatius then observes that perfect people can swear more easily on creatures than imperfect people. For by invoking creatures, Ignatius reasons, we risk not expressing clearly enough the fact that human beings can legitimately swear only on God. Consequently perfect people who are in the habit of discerning the Creator's presence in every creature can swear on creatures without failing in truth and reverence, unlike imperfect people who do not contemplate this presence of the Creator in a creature. Since—like the people of his time and culture—Ignatius had greater facility in identifying the word with the thing it signifies, not only does God's name evoke his presence but the word for a creature evokes the presence of the Creator.

This passage of the *Spiritual Exercises*, which we risk neglecting because it seems very strange to our way of thinking, announces the contemplation of God in all things. For Ignatius, perfect people, by constant contemplation and illumination of their intelligence, consider, meditate and contemplate the fact that God is in every creature according to its specific essence, presence and power. He does not except the creature speech from this belief. We see God in all things: even in the true, necessary, and reverential word [38 and 39] which reveals God.

It is therefore not surprising that Ignatius wrote in his *Diary*: "Every time I named God, Lord, etc., I was penetrated through and through with a wonderful and reverential respect and humility, which seem to defy description" (*Diary* 162: 1.a.1, March 17). And so, far from being extraneous to the book of the *Spiritual Exercises*, this short passage on words included in the general examination of conscience [38-41] is an integral part of it. It announces on the one hand the contemplation "ad amorem" [230-237] and on the other the second method of prayer [249-257].

The Second Method of Prayer

This method of prayer is a linguistic operation. It starts from a word, no matter what word as long as it is the word of a prayer. The prayer then allows itself to be guided by the words. When contemplating the nativity the eye of the imagination reconstructs the picture of the evangelical scene. In this second method of prayer the whole mechanism of speech is made to bear fruit: the meaning of each word of the prayer, the comparison with other words, the connotations of relish and consolation [252]. If we follow Ignatius's text a whole itinerary opens up: a word in a prayer, the contemplation of its contents which open to other realities in keeping with the word, the capacity to relish and savor, i.e., to derive pleasure from this harmony of words which reveal the mystery of the Word Incarnate. To explain this method of prayer in terms of modern linguistics, we need to start from the fact that a word is rarely monosemic, i.e., having only one meaning. Undoubtedly this is a possibility and the sciences all do their best to reduce the capacity for several meanings of a word to one only in order to avoid any ambiguity or misunderstanding.

Ignatius himself does this when he defines his words: "By the term 'Spiritual Exercises' is meant . . ." [1]. Without this definition "exercises" can mean equally "taking a walk, journeying on foot, and running" and "meditation, contemplation, vocal and mental prayer," and without this specification of "finding the will of God in the disposition of our life," the expression "spiritual exercises" could indicate contemplative monastic prayer.

Terms have to be polysemic, i.e., they must have several meanings, for the simple reason that the reality which surrounds us is indefinite and that the words at our disposal in a given language cannot function in an unlimited number. Here we must point out that the problem does not lie only in the words themselves. A single word may be too much or too little. A single word, on its own, is always ambiguous. But the following sentence presents no ambiguities since Ignatius does not leave the word "king" as an isolated term: "The call of an earthly king will help us to contemplate the life of the eternal king" [91]. In order to assume its entire sense and function fully a term must fit into a semantic field which gives it its sense through the play of correspondences and oppositions.

Consequently a word draws other words into its wake, to the point of constituting a small world of its own. The Spiritual Exercises give us a fine example of this. Ignatius notes the importance of listening to the call of the good king and observes that "if anyone would refuse the invitation of such a king, how justly he would deserve to be condemned by the whole world, and looked upon as an ignoble knight" [94]. The Spanish expression *perverso caballero* evokes all the loyalty and valor of noble chivalry. Ignatius's translators made the expression change its social field. The 1548 translation gives "a vile soldier": the expression no longer evokes the world of chivalry but the picture of an army which relies not on valor and loyalty but on duty. The translation commonly called "first translation" couples soldier with "subject": "and [shall be] looked upon as an unworthy subject and soldier" [94]. The term "subject" takes us away from a purely military setting but it stresses the fact that this soldier had nothing to do other than be subordinate and carry out orders. We are still further away here from the stimulating image of a knight who passionately serves his king. This example clearly indicates that the words "knight," "soldier," "subject" belong to different semantic fields and can therefore evoke different worlds, drawing in their wake words with completely different meanings.

To return to Ignatius, it is clear in the first place that the author of the *Spiritual Exercises* limits his semantic field: he takes words, to be prayed one after the other, but within a sacred text and the limits of a prayer like the Our Father, the Hail Mary, the Creed, or even Soul of Christ and Hail Holy Queen [253]. An hour is assigned for reflecting "upon this word as long as he finds various meanings, comparisons, relish, and consolation in the consideration of it" [252]. The linguistic mechanism which sustains this method of prayer is explicitly indicated in the words "meanings" and "comparisons"; the difference is marked by "relish" and "consolation." For example, we like a literary text; a poem which fascinates us gives us the pleasure of reading. When reading, the reader is never completely passive towards the text; it is also true that the reader co-produces the text, i.e., the sense of this reading is the result of a co-production of the words read and of the reader's understanding.

At times we are caught up by a text, at times we have trouble understanding it. Sometimes the text interests us and sometimes we rapidly skim over it to discover its message. A book can fascinate us and even obsess us, and a volume can bore us completely. At all events the result of this exercise we call reading is always the fruit of a collaboration between the reader and the act of reading, of a co-production of meaning: between what the text evokes and what it receives from the reader. Most texts are in the third person, but some make use of the first or second person—I, you—to involve the reader in an explicit dialogue. All the texts Ignatius advised for this second method of prayer propose a conversation of an "I" with a "you": "I believe"; "Soul of Christ, save me"; and, in the plural, "Our Father"; "Hail Holy Queen . . . our hope"; "Hail Mary . . . pray for us."

Though these texts are pieces of an "I - thou" dialogue, they are prefabricated: the person who prays them allows himself to be guided, instructed, remodeled, almost unknowingly, by the language of the Church, by the texts common to the people of God. There is a certain decentralization and a gratuitous concentration on a sequence of words which another person's devotion has formulated under the inspiration of the Spirit. "It is not I who compose the text: these are words which the Spirit has inspired, and by which I allow myself to be moved in prayerful listening." Ignatius imposes a whole attitude—kneeling, sitting, eyes closed or fixed on a given point, for an hour—which leads to a reading of the text which will not be a linguistic analysis, the search or desire to know, but the welcoming of a word of God which, while it tells us of one aspect of the experience of God with man, guides us towards other words in order to finally reach Him who is the Word of God. It is very important that we bear in mind that this word is no longer a dictionary term but an instrument of the communication which God lovingly seeks with man and which man has found in order to converse with his Lord. In Saint Ignatius's time this method of prayer was taught and was very widespread, and curiously enough most of the publications give the Our Father as an example. Thus Fray Ambrosio Montesino suggests the beginning of the Lord's Prayer as an example of this way of meeting God, taking as a whole the expression: Our Father who are in heaven,[8] insisting on the sense of "in heaven" which, as an expression, can evoke the assembly of saints. God who dwells among the saints and the just, but is also in the completely unknown dwelling of his Majesty: "truly God is hidden" (Is 45:15). God is also our future, because our country is in heaven.

Ignatius insists on "without permitting them [the eyes] to roam" [252] and on not being "anxious to go on" [254] if we have found "relish and consolation" in a word—because the virtual polysemics of each word can easily provoke dispersion. More, it would not be a good idea to follow linguistic procedures to cull all the meanings of a word: we should not, for example, want to stop at the word "I believe" starting from all the prepositions (or none at all) which can accompany it. Even if this linguistic consideration makes us discover that our faith is not only adherence to a truth but, above all, adherence to the person of Christ, the matter is more complex than that. Such a method of prayer implies a growing prayerful—and biblical—culture. Thus, when the word "hour" is mentioned in prayer, one does not stop at the sixty minutes indicated by the term but culls the entire breadth of the hour, after the Johannine understanding of an event in the passion of the Lord.

Not satisfied with only the meanings of a word, Ignatiu0s also invites us to find comparisons for it [252]. Since this whole method of prayer is strictly

---

[8] *Vita Christi*, 1.37.

connected with the *lectio divina*—the prayerful reading of the Scripture—these comparisons often, though not exclusively, will have their origin in Holy Scripture. The "Our Father" can be compared with the prodigal son's father, with Isaac's father, with Absalom's father, without excluding the father we have known in our own personal experience. These meanings and comparisons introduce us to the considerations which should nourish our conversation and dialogue with the Lord, even if this colloquy will consist more in listening to what God has to say to us: "Apply yourself, I beseech you, to meditating each day on the words of your Creator. Learn to know God's heart in God's words."[9]

A more recent author echoes the same exhortation, qualifying this whole method of prayer as an inner confrontation between the Word and the heart.[10] This method of prayer has a linguistic aspect, but its essence consists in bringing the mechanism of language into dialogue with God because, as Dionysius the Carthusian said in the wake of many others, "each book [of Scripture] is like a letter from the Holy Spirit destined for us and, when we study it, it is God who is speaking to us."[11] Through prayer we speak to God; through reading it is God who speaks to us.

From the beginning of this conference we have seen Ignatius's great confidence in speech, insofar as it is capable of being inhabited by the presence of God. The author of the *Exercises* has no doubts concerning the presence of "relish and consolation" [252 and 254] in this method of prayer. The 1548 translation appears to mistrust these words of Ignatius and translates them as "spiritual enjoyment and other movements of devotion" [252] and "inner consolation" [254]. We know the pleasure of a text as an experience. We read or reread a book, a periodical or a passage from a letter or newspaper with pleasure. Some publications have fired and inflamed people. John Gerson—to whom Ignatius attributed his favorite daily reading, *The Imitation of Christ*—already believed that man will not be judged on his knowledge but on his heart, and consequently must neither study nor read anything . . . which is not directly or indirectly disposed to inflame the

---

9 Gregory the Great, *PL*, 77, 706.

10 A. Louf, *Seigneur, apprends-nous à prier*, 1972, p. 73.

11 *Opera omnia*, 1909, 38, 368a.

affects.[12] The expression "non tam scientiam quam saporem" (not to know but to relish) was often used in the Middle Ages. Jerome stressed the dimension of welcome in this contemplation of the sense of words, writing in one of his letters: *non ad laborem sed ad delectationem* (not for work but for delight).[13]

Ignatius fits into this tradition, but it would be easy to be mistaken about his thinking. The word "relish" immediately connects us with the semantic field of delicious food and the word "consolation" evokes the perceptible comfort of suffered pain. In both cases something must be felt. It is to avoid this stumbling block that Ignatius's translator specifies that the relish is of a spiritual order and that the consolation is inner and a movement of devotion. This precaution was unnecessary because Ignatius had already defined "consolation" as an inner movement which inflames us with love of our Creator in such a way that we can no longer love any creature on the face of the earth for its own sake, but only in the Creator of them all [316].

Here we are dealing with a form of vitality which does not necessarily involve any sentiment, a vigor of the entire heart which does not necessarily entail a perceptible savor. By discovering God's heart in God's words our outlook on the world, on ourselves and on our life will be marked by an increase in faith and hope [316]. Physical suffering or painful moral trial is of little importance; the presence or absence of pleasure in the text and of joy in reading are of little importance. What matters is a growing familiarity with God's words, which brings us a security—according to John's expression—which nothing can take from us. So it is normal that this "consolation" in the Ignatian sense should create a preferential bond with one or another word. A word which does not say anything to one person can be the condensation of another person's entire personal experience with God. There is nothing surprising in this! When God bends down towards humans speech is his favorite means. And so it is fitting that when we try to meet God we seek him in the words of his Word. The second method of prayer, as Ignatius presents it after experiencing it himself according to the testimony of the *Spiritual Diary*, leads to this savoring of God of which Father J.-J. Surin says:

---

[12] *De libris legendis a monacho*, 1706, 2.707.

[13] *D. Hieronymi Epist.* 130, 15.

"When the soul will have instructed itself through reading . . ., if it sees that it has reached the savor of God, it will be enough if it reads little and savors greatly. . . ."[14]

Wordless Confirmation

We have clearly demonstrated Ignatius's great trust in speech as a means for meeting God. This is rather unilateral, however, for in a colloquy or conversation both people must speak. But when in the *Spiritual Exercises* Ignatius multiplies encouragements and injunctions to speak to God, doesn't this speech remain unanswered? If we examine the colloquies we see that Ignatius fills these conversations with God: asking him for favors, blaming himself for misdeeds, making known his affairs to him and seeking advice in them [54], presenting petitions [199], obtaining grace or knowledge, giving thanks to him for granting life, resolving to amend for the future, extolling the mercy of God our Lord [61]. Ignatius mentions only indirectly what he expects from the companion of this conversation, from God: a grace, forgiveness, advice [54], to be chosen [157], a deep knowledge [63].

Ignatius did not expect an answer in words. He once said that "I must have a colloquy thinking over what I ought to say to the Three Divine Persons" [109], but nowhere did the author of the *Spiritual Exercises* anticipate what we can expect of God, friend and Lord [54], as word of life. Does this mean that the colloquy ends in silence? Many spiritual authors have experienced and studied this. The word "silence" is almost absent from the *Spiritual Exercises*; it appears once in opposition to the noise the good and bad angels make or do not make [335]. However, God does react, and Ignatius, although abandoning every form of term or word as a reaction from God, notes that God will confirm our decision and choices. Thus he writes, "After such a choice or decision, the one who has made it must turn with great diligence to prayer in the presence of God our Lord, and offer him his choice that the Divine Majesty may deign to accept and confirm it if it is for His greater service and praise [183].

---

[14] Jean-Joseph Surin, S.J., *Guide spirituel pour la perfection*, Desclée de Brouwer, 1963, *Coll. Christus*, no. 12, IV, 3, p. 176.

We know that Ignatius willingly identified himself with the life of the apostles. Therefore it is not surprising that he considered the Pentecostal coming of the Spirit the confirmation of their mission to go and preach in poverty (*Diary* 15: 10, February 11). He waited for a sign from God as a reaction in confirmation of his words. But this confirmation was not committed to terms and words. In the *Spiritual Diary* Ignatius registers the phenomenon of *loquela*, of words which come from on high, according to Ignatius's own testimony, detached in some way from their meaning and very close to heavenly music (*Diary* 224: 47.1.d, May 12; 234: 57.a.1, May 22), a vocalization which produces no meaning but with a pleasing tone (*Diary* 234, *Ibid.*), because given more divinely (*Diary* 221: 46.a1., May 11).

What it is important to establish here is how on the one hand God's confirmation approaches speech and how on the other it moves completely away from it. This beautiful music is merely a rather extraordinary form of God's reaction to our words. It more usually consists in motions and movements in which words can play a role: "Throughout the Mass, I had various feelings in confirmation of what I had said [concerning poverty which must be radically observed]"; "I felt fresh movements of devotion and spiritual joy"; "As I held the Blessed Sacrament in my hands, the word came to me with an intense interior movement never to leave Him for all heaven and earth. . . ." (*Diary* 69: 22, February 23). The gift of tears, which Ignatius distinguishes from the more ordinary phenomenon of moistened eyes, belongs to the extraordinary quality of God's reaction to our speech (*Diary* 141: 28 (bis), March 10). If we want to express the whole of this experience in a few simple terms: being confirmed by God signifies that Ignatius sees and feels that he must maintain his decision and continue in his resolution, comforted by an increase of faith, hope and charity [316].

This is a real reaction on God's part, a real confirmation - even if it does not pass through terms and words. Even though not all Christians undergo Ignatius's extraordinary experience in the course of their lives, each person opens himself or herself to realities of a spiritual order during the colloquy, feeling their effects in the form of consolation and desolation. Ignatius teaches us through his own vast experience how to discern God's answers in all these motions. Thus prayer and colloquy will never be the explanation of self to self but an interpersonal conversation in which two freedoms become allies: one

freedom which expresses itself in words, one freedom which arouses a communion of hearts.

Ignatius does not seek fine language or words as decoration and
ornament. The unliterary value of the text of the *Spiritual Exercises* is proof
that he considers language simply as an instrument and a means. His trust in
this language is the trust of a craftsman in his materials: hence its total use
through prayers and colloquies, through meditations and considerations in
order to complete a language addressed to God as the receiver of a message.
The colloquy would not be a dialogue but a monologue if God were not to
receive the message or if God were not to offer in exchange a language to
decipher. There is something dramatic about this because God, the receiver,
cannot use the instrument of language, even though he can signal to us
through means which belong outside specifically verbal language. Consequently, during a colloquy, we must speak in ignorance of the end of the
sentence we have begun, or of the way in which God will give his nonverbal
answer.

This dramatic nature is all the more evident insofar as Ignatius tries less
to converse with God during the colloquy than to obtain an answer from him
in order to know his will. He wants to know whether God is or is not in
agreement with his choice. To use the terminology of an author like Roland
Barthes, Ignatius seeks less a theophany (a manifestation of God's presence)
than a semiophany (a sign God gives him to follow or not follow his choice).
Hence a conversation, a colloquy based on *caritas discreta*, on charity—from
one friend to another—on clear-sighted charity, which knows how to discern
and distinguish the Master's sign to his servant [54]. Ignatius himself gives as
an image of this conversation the extremely sensitive "balance at equilibrium"
that our language must be for God to be able to bend and incline it where he
wishes, marking it with his own desire [179].

The Spiritual Exercises are sometimes presented as the apprenticeship for
the question to be put to God, and the *Spiritual Diary* as the book in which
one can discover the divine code, the forms which God's pressure on the
balance can take. However this divine code is already present in the *Spiritual
Exercises* in all that is said on consolation and desolation. If anything, we
should say that the *Spiritual Diary* illustrates this code with Ignatius's personal
case, with the true code of the gift of tears. But the book of the *Exercises* contains all that is necessary for the statement that the colloquy is a true dialogue,

even if man's part reveals itself as verbal and God's part reveals itself as non-verbal. God and man signal to each other, the latter through human language, the former through acting on man's heart by means of movements and motions. If Ignatius places such trust in speech in this colloquy it is not because he believes that multiplying words is the surest way of obtaining an answer from God—this would be against what Jesus himself says (Mt 6:7)—nor because he relies on the magic power of enchantment of words to move the heart—this would be abandoning oneself without discernment to the evil spirit—but in order to incite the person to "speak of himself with the clarity and precision which words normally impose, to express one's desires and anxieties, so that God can use them and mark them with his desire. Only a well-formulated question can receive a well-constructed and relevant answer. Since all Ignatian mysticism is oriented towards the service of the greater glory of God, the question is less "Who is God?" than "What does God want of a human life?" Hence this preference and this trust in the means of language.

God's Silence

And God's silence? This silence in which God is truly God? Where all words and all language turn in on themselves without reaching the Ineffable and Unutterable? Roland Barthes[15] seems to say that Ignatius transforms the deficiency of the sign into a sign and that thus the divine void, God's silence, is no longer a threat. "Listening becomes its own answer." "Returned to its significance the divine void no longer can threaten, alter, decentralize the fullness which belongs to every closed language." The question is asked so prettily that the pleasure of asking the question is already its answer. A retreat or a prayer develop in such a pleasant environment that this joy becomes in itself the fruit of the retreat, God's answer. It is rather like what Jesus himself observed concerning the behavior of men who pray in order to be seen: the honor they receive is already the reward, the answer to their prayer (Mt 6:5).

---

[15] Roland Barthes, *Introduction des Exercices Spirituels* (1972, pp. 5-53).

Undoubtedly the deficiency of the sign is a sign: when God no longer speaks, the people of God are desolate and ask themselves what this means. But Roland Barthes is wrong to believe that this is the only sign. God lets us know his will if we live with him. God signals to us, speaks to us, if we know how to listen to him. Out of respect for our freedom, God is not in the habit of crushing us or violently imposing himself on us. On his part there is a call and on our part there is the trust of faith. Every interpersonal conversation is based on faith and trust in the other, and God wishes this to be so between himself and us too; hence we find this respect for our freedom and this refusal of mathematical or automatic evidence in God's signal.

But there is a lack of absolute clarity and technical precision in the human signal too. If Roland Barthes believes that the language man uses to address God is closed in on itself he does not take into account the symbolical nature of every religious language. When Ignatius invites us to contemplate hell, all the words he uses must evoke horror without being able to denote it. The word "howls" [67] indicates and designates a precise reality—he who howls does not sing—but in using this word in connection with hell we must attribute something unmentionable to it. The same is true of the word "sulphur" [68]: a solid lemon yellow, tasteless and odorless metalloid, whose atomic number is 46; when contemplating hell "sulphur" loses its chemical characteristics and takes on a terrifying dimension.

Just as in poetry, even though we use everyday words when speaking of our conversations with God we must give them greater breadth than they normally have in order to make them say what they do not say and not say what they do say. In the "Two Standards" Ignatius shows us the chief of all God's enemies "seated on a great throne of fire and smoke . . ." [140]: this is a satanic truth which the symbolic words "great throne, fire, smoke" evoke on condition that we deprive them of their obvious meaning.

Thus religious language is not closed in on itself even on a linguistic level; on the contrary, it is open to stammering the ineffable experience. In this sense human speech contains a confessed silence when speaking of God or speaking with God. When we say "God speaks," we know that we are not telling the whole of this reality. This is why the language we use to speak to God is never closed in on itself: it is a kind of synthesis which opens speech to God's verbal silence. In this sense Ignatian words are a synthesis of conversation and silence: due respect is given to this friend who lets me talk but who, nevertheless, is the Master and Lord in the presence of whom everything imposes on me the silence of adoration.

TWELVE

THE LETTERS OF ST. IGNATIUS:
THEIR CONCLUSION

I close, praying that the most holy Trinity by its infinite and supreme goodness may bestow upon all of us plentiful grace to know [= to have the sense of] its most holy will and perfectly to fulfill it.

(Letter of St. Ignatius to Teresa Rejadell: 18 June, 1536)[1]

Introduction

Starting a letter, ending a letter—these operations are sometimes simple and sometimes complex. The more the recipient of the letter is familiar with its author, the greater the freedom of choice. If, on the contrary, the letter has to be sent to a person with whom we are not on familiar terms, to deal with official business, the beginning and end of the letter must give the recipient his or her due importance, and the choice of expressions is limited to stereotyped formulas, circumstantial greetings, and formal titles of social usage. Even today the formulation of the beginning and end of letters is so fixed, that is has a meaning only if the author of the letter changes something in the usual phrases. Their presence is taken for granted and no longer signifies anything; their absence can cause surprise and may even be quite significant.

Ignatius's Correspondence

In his time Ignatius probably had a little more freedom than we have, but

---

[1] This quote is an example of the epistolary style of Ignatius, and of his practice of ending a letter with a prayer.

these remarks hold good for him too. To know Ignatian spirituality it is not enough to explore the *Exercises* and the *Constitutions*, to meditate on the *Autobiography* and the *Spiritual Diary*. There is also the mass of his 6815 letters: all that is left of a correspondence which undoubtedly was even more voluminous. The first letter we have was written in 1524—three years after his conversion—and, after a period for which we have only one letter a year, the correspondence increases up to three letters a day. Almost 7000 letters written over a period of 32 years have been preserved (Ignatius died on July 31, 1556). It is not easy to make the best use of this material for a greater knowledge of Ignatian spirituality. To begin with, Ignatius had some secretaries, and it is almost impossible to distinguish clearly what Ignatius wrote in his own hand or what he considered confidential or strictly private. Ignatius continued to "determine" or fix the essential core of his letters, even though he willingly delegated the broad lines of their development to his secretaries. An exception must perhaps be made for at least part of the correspondence with certain ladies whom Ignatius guided spiritually. The work of exploring the letters is further complicated by the fact that we know that we often have an extract of a letter, with the essential part of its contents, but without the beginning and end which here interest us. Finally, we must bear in mind that from March, 1547, Ignatius had the assistance of an exceptionally efficient secretary in the person of Juan Alfonso de Polanco, who gave his correspondence a more administrative turn of phrase and a more systematic treatment.

Conclusion of the Letters: Three Categories

Bearing these facts in mind, why should we be interested in the last lines of Ignatius's letters? Leafing through the twelve volumes which contain them, we observe that the endings of the letters belong to three categories. The first category is dominated by the verb "to recommend." "May your Lordship recommend me insistently in Our Lord to the kind remembrance of the lady Doña Isabella, the gentlemen her brothers, and the whole household" (Aug. 11, 1548). This category continues its stereotyped existence in the well-know form of "on this, I recommend myself to the sacrifices and prayers of your Reverence. . . ."

A second category contains good wishes and greetings with which the author concludes his letters. This kind of ending corresponds to the good wishes and greetings which generally mark the beginning of the letter. Thus, writing to Margaret of Austria, Ignatius opens with the wish: "May the sovereign grace and eternal love of Christ our Lord greet you and be with you," to end as follows: "I will bring this letter to a close, asking and humbly beseeching of the goodness of God our Lord to guard and rule your excellency in all your actions by his divine and eternal goodness" (Aug. 13, 1543). While favoring personalized wishes, this category also makes use of short and conventional forms such as: "May the Lord be with you all" or *Vale in Domino* (Be well in the Lord).

A third category interests us, too, because it appears to have been composed by Ignatius and to sum up his spirituality. From the point of view of form it is simply a variant of the second category (i.e., wishes) but it stands out among the other possible forms for its frequency and its structure. Already the first of Ignatius's letters known to us ended with a prayer. "May it please our Lady to intercede for us . . . and obtain this grace for us. . . ." (Dec. 12, 1524: corrected date). Four years later the poor pilgrim Iñigo wrote again to his Catalan benefactress Inés Pascual—now as Iñigo, poor in goodness—and ended his letter as follows: May the Lord of the world . . . ever remain by this goodness in our souls, so that his will may be always fulfilled in us" (Mar. 3, 1528). We then have to wait four years for a letter from Ignatius to his brother Martin García de Oñaz to find the basic structure of that conclusion to the letters which, under various forms, remained unchanged until a letter of July 22, 1556: "[Pray the Lord] "to give us the grace to know [= to have a sense of] his most holy will and the strength perfectly to fulfill it" (end of June 1532).

This structure with its many variants stands out for its frequency. Of the almost 7000 letters (6815), almost 1000 (992) end with these wishes of Ignatius. This frequency diminishes considerably in the time of St. Ignatius's successor, insofar as we have been able to check it. But the answers to the letters of congratulation which Father James Laínez received on his election as superior general use St. Ignatius's ending and, differently from the letters received by Ignatius, some people, writing to Rome, use Ignatius's final greeting.[2] St. Francis Borgia rarely uses the Ignatian final formula.[3]

Third Category: Basic Structure

As Ignatius conceived it, the basic structure of this conclusion of the letters is extremely limpid. It is a prayer which asks for the grace of knowing and accomplishing God's will. Fundamentally it is a development of the prayer the Lord taught us: "May your will be done!" A great many variants are grafted onto this basic structure. Ignatius was more at ease writing in Spanish (573 times out of 992); the translation of his final prayer into Italian (369 times) or Latin (50 times) immediately brought about variants. The translation of *sentir* presented real problems; rendering this verb as simply "to know" weakened the rich force of the Spanish verb. Ignatius's style was sober; his secretaries liked to have balanced phrases. They could not tolerate an adverb alongside the verb "to fulfill" —to perfectly fulfill God's will—without also accompanying the verb *sentir* with an adverb—to *always* have the sense of God's will. At times Ignatius intervened in the work of these secretaries. In a letter to Don Juan de Vega (12.04.1550) the secretary had asked the Lord for *su copiosa gracia*. This quantitative abundance did not please Ignatius, and he had the letter end with his favourite expression: *su gracia cumplida*, his perfect grace. A whole series of variants was brought about by the adaptation of this concluding phrase to the particular circumstances mentioned in the letter. Thus, writing to Francis Borgia about the plan already set afoot of proposing him [Francis] for the cardinalate, Ignatius, who opposed it firmly with a conviction born of the discernment of God's will, was satisfied to end the letter with a prayer: "Let us leave the whole matter in the hands of God our Lord, so that His holy will may be done in all our affairs." (June 5, 1552). This is thus a sentence which contains the essence of the usual basic structure, but which is adapted to the matter of conscience dealt with in the letter.

---

[2] Letters 791, 792, 862, 872 in *Mon. Laynez III*, pp. 208, 210, 351, 372.

[3] *Mon. F. Borg V*, letter 844, p. 327; letter 904, p. 474; letter 999, p. 671.

Its Core Element

The core element of the basic structure is precisely "his most holy will." This nucleus is what is least exposed to variants, and the entire movement of the basic structure is geared towards it. To have the sense of, to fulfill, to obtain grace: all in function of God's will. In the first place the fact that this short treatise on God's will belongs to a correspondence of which more than ninety per cent (5639 letters out of 6815) were devoted to ordinary affairs, not to mention letters on financial matters and contracts (142), is of primary importance. The clause then, which is entirely in the spirit of the *Spiritual Exercises*, is not satisfied in the accomplishment of God's will simply to having a global sense of being God's creature, or of being made by God, or of being under God's universal law. More, Ignatius places the content of the letter within the context of a divine plan which manifests itself in precise and specific decisions, in strictly personal choices, in entirely material details. Thus one letter, in which much is said about the revenues in ducats of the first colleges, concludes, by order of St. Ignatius, with a prayer to God and Father of our Lord Jesus Christ, that he may open our hearts to his most holy will and give us the strength to fulfill it (June 4, 1545). In fact, the generosity of so many nobles and so many cities is a sign of God's will, to which we must be open and devote the best of our strength.

Even while transforming the fulfillment of God's most holy will into daily decisions, the conclusion to the letters, which ask for God's grace for everyone, refuses, by means of this very prayer, to harden and rigidify the decisions taken. We have a beautiful example of this in Ignatius's letter to the mother of a Neapolitan novice, Ottaviano Cesari. Cesari's mother would like to see her son again and Ignatius states frankly that to satisfy her request would be "to go against the will of God Our Lord." "We must therefore comply with his holy will." "May God's supreme goodness grant all the grace always to know his most holy will and carry it out perfectly" (Jan. 28, 1554). This is followed by some interventions—as the letters prove—and, after listening to popes, cardinals and princes, Ignatius changes his decision. Finally, two months before Ignatius's death, Ottaviano leaves the Society, which he had chosen "more out of youthful infatuation than under the impulse of God's spirit." In praying to the Lord, both Ottaviano's mother and Ignatius do not get stuck in crippling expectation, but accept the existence of enough uncertainty for God to upset their plan and so call the whole matter into question.

The most original point is undoubtedly the insistence on a will which is not ours, but his—his will—and which, insofar as it is "most holy," must choose ways which are not our ways. This means that seeking to have the sense of God's most holy will is never an end in itself. We must "sense" the way in which God acts towards us, in order to be more faithful to what he wishes to manifest to us in this way. Fulfilling God's will is first of all seeking and finding it. What does the clause tell us of this most holy will of God?

In Ignatius's writings the expression "his most holy will" is in no way a stereotyped expression. If the aim of the Spiritual Exercises is "seeking and finding the will of God" [1], they require that the human person offer to God his or her entire will and liberty, so that his Divine Majesty may dispose of them and all they possess according to "his most holy will" [5]. The prayer of the "Exercise of the King" will be precisely to be prompt and diligent to accomplish his most holy will [91]. At the heart of the choice or "election" appears the concern to choose in conformity "with what would be more pleasing to his most holy will" [180]. Even the final prayer of the Exercises [234] is based on the opposition between *toda mi voluntad* and *toda vuestra voluntad*. The presence of this expression in the decisive moments of the Spiritual Exercises transforms the end of the letters into a reminder of Ignatius's fundamental experience. This same expression appears a number of times in the text of the *Constitutions*. Thus it is to be found in the passage which describes how to seek God and love him, him alone *(Const.* 288).

Undoubtedly Ignatius's secretaries were anxious to write, compose or copy rapidly, and did not always have the same devotion to the expression. Juan Polanco sometimes tended to shorten "most holy will" to "holy will." The secretaries also occasionally used the abbreviation "s.ma" and then interpreted it as *suprema voluntad* or *suma/summa voluntad*. No particular attention need be given to the fact that we sometimes find "divine will" or "perfect will." But on the contrary we cannot ignore the *beneplacitum* which substitutes *voluntas* in the letters in Latin.

The *Exercises* already contain the expression *su sanctíssima y beneplácita voluntad* ("his most holy will and one that deigns to be pleased") [180]. Sometimes *beneplácita* accompanies the most holy will, sometimes it replaces the word "will" (e.g., July 3, 1548). Their identification becomes evident if we compare two letters written in the same year: *divina ipsius voluntas* (March 22, 1555) and *divinum suum beneplacitum* (Aug. 28, 1555).

The expression indicates God's *beneplacitum* (good pleasure). In the cultures of recent centuries, which semantically link the word with the prince's "good pleasure," the expression evokes arbitrariness and caprice. In Ignatius's language *placer* still means joy. In a letter from Venice to Teresa Rejadell (Sept. 09, 1536), Ignatius stresses the fact that "God asks only one thing of me, that my soul seek to be conformed with His Divine Majesty; and the soul so conformed makes the body conformed, whether it wish it or not, to the divine will." And he adds: "In this is our greatest battle, and here the good pleasure—*placer*—of the eternal and sovereign goodness." There is question, then, of God's joy, God's pleasure at seeing his plan and his design for us fulfilled. Conforming to God's will implies getting out of a duty-bound world and attaining the joy of the collaborative harmony of God's will and ours. Already on the way to Montserrat Ignatius imagines accomplishing great things to "please God" (*Autob.* 14). Later, struggling with a decision which Ignatius recognizes as God's will, he prefers to abandon his own plan for "the good pleasure of God our Lord" (*Diary*, March 12). His own inclination joyously gives way in favor of "what would be more pleasing to God our Lord" (*ibid.*). Ignatius does not fulfill God's will because of the fittingness and rectitude of his orders, but in order to make God happy. Thus joy and happiness will often be the reflection of this harmony of will.

A final variant, in which the basic structure of the formula undergoes amplifications or clarifications, deserves attention. This occurs less in Ignatius's writing, which preserves the compactness of the formula, than in the letters of his companions, like Francis Xavier, who willingly add embellishments with explanatory variations on the Ignatian theme. Writing to Pietro Contarini (August, 1537), Ignatius, who was preparing for his future task in Vicenza, ends his letter as follows: "May [the Lord] give us all the grace of doing his holy will, which is the sanctification of us all." Walking along the path God has willed for us—for each one of us—is sanctity. In the *Exercises* Ignatius does not exclude either married love or consecrated celibacy, either riches or poverty: in each case what matters, if we are to be holy, is complete union with God's precise and specific will, as manifested in a strictly personal vocation.

Ignatius's prayer, which concludes many of his letters, asks on the one hand to have the sense of God's most holy will and, on the other, to fulfill it. It is Francis Xavier alone who explicitly gives a chronological order to the two verbs. With his usual amplifications he writes (Jan. 27, 1545): to pray to make known to us and let us have the sense of his most holy will and, when we have done so ("once this will has been 'sensed'": (Jan. 29, 1552) to grant us strength and grace to fulfill it in this life with charity. This chronological aspect is absent in Ignatius even if, logically, "to fulfill" never precedes "to sense."

Significance of "Sentir"

It is not easy to translate the verb *sentir*. The Latin translations reduce the verb to knowing (*cognoscere*), understanding (*intelligere*), recognizing (*agnoscere*), and considering (*considerare*) God's will. The letter to the prior of the Carthusian monastery of Cologne (Juna 11, 1547) is interesting: having the sense of God's will is translated in it by the two verbs "to know and to love" (*ad cognoscendam, amandam voluntatem suam*). In the same way that a whole range of meanings underlies the verb to love—from pure love to animal love, from a furtive attachment to an intensive commitment—the verb *sentir* in Spanish embraces the most varied sentiments. In the *Spiritual Exercises* the verb is used to say that one does not feel a desire for food [217], that one does not feel an attachment or a repugnance [157], or that one feels one has greater need for graces [257]. According to a semantic law which applies to verbs in the category of *sentir*, the entire range of uses is preserved when the object of *sentir* does not limit or reduce it. Thus the sentence: John the Baptist "sensed the visit" [263] says more than the fact that the little precursor was aware of the visit or that he perceived the visit. Consequently the *sintamos* which clearly stands out in all the clauses of this category concerns the whole person in his or her docility towards God's most holy will.

Having the sense of the most holy will is so absolute an experience for Ignatius that it needs no qualifications. It is clear in itself. Though the Spanish clauses in the first years of Ignatius's correspondence entirely lack adverbs accompanying *sintamos*, the Latin translations and the letters subsequent to Juan de Polanco's arrival frequently contain the adverb *siempre*, "always." Sometimes we find "eternally" (*perpetuo*) instead of "always." The *quid agendum*, which runs through the *Autobiography*, continues throughout Ignatius's life. For Ignatius "always" does not imply a program determined ahead of time or an inexorable series of arbitrary choices. For him "always" is today's present which alone counts in order to know his most holy will. Using the same basic structure of the formula, Francis Xavier insists a great deal on a *sentir* "throughout the time we are in this exile" (Jan. 15, 1544), or again "in this life" (Jan. 20, 1545), "in this present life" (Jan. 12, 1549). After attributing to *sentir* a clear and precise dimension "in this life" (Jan. 14, 1549), Francis also gives the fulfillment of God's will a precise perspective which is absent in Ignatius's clauses. Thus Francis writes at the end of a letter (June 23, 1549): "to fulfill it [this most holy will] by doing and fulfilling what you would wish to have fulfilled at the hour of your death" (similarly Jan 20, 1545; Jan. 20, 1548).

The verb *sentir* is not qualified only by adverbs of time; though more rarely, it is also qualified by adverbs of place. These serve, first of all, to specify that the *sentir* is "in us," "in our hearts," or else, with Francis Xavier, "within our souls" (Jan. 15, 1544), "inside our souls" (Nov. 10, 1545; Nov. 5, 1549). Since we are considering a correspondence, i.e., a person-to-person relationship, the specification "in all people" is exceptional. Some clauses specify that one should have the sense of God's will "here and everywhere," "in everything," "in all things."

Finally the prayer expressed at the end of the letters is that we may receive the *grace* of "sensing," i.e., an activity of the human person stirred up by God's loving will. In some letters Ignatius substitutes the human person's "sensing" with God's activity that thus works together with that human person. On the very day of his death Ignatius wrote: "May he [God] teach us his most holy will and grant us his grace to fulfill it" (July 31, 1556). This harmony of two wills is evoked in the following conclusion to a letter (April 5, 1554): "May the sovereign and eternal wisdom communicate [to His Highness John III of Portugal] His holy light and clarity, that he may see in all things what is best for the divine glory and the universal good of souls, and that He may make all people have the sense of and always fulfill his holy will."

The fact that we must grow in this *sentir* is presumed not only by the use of "always" as a challenge, as a task to accomplish, but also by the clarification which Father Claude Jay adds to the clause in his correspondence with Ignatius: to have an ever greater sense (*de bene in meglio conoscere*: Sept. 13, 1546; Dec. 4, 1546; Oct. 19, 1546; July 11, 1550; July 21, 1551). However, this growth in the communion between the human person and "his most holy will" remains unreal without the fulfillment of this will. This fulfillment too, is a grace to be asked for.

And Then "To Fulfill"

The verb to fulfill does not pose linguistic problems on the level of words; its difficulty lies in its practice. The Latin translation of Ignatius's letters presents a whole series of verbs to express "putting into practice what the most holy will has made us have a sense of" . . . to realize (*perficere*), to execute (*exsequi*), to obey (*obedire*), to carry out (*impelere*), and far more rarely to accomplish (*complere, adimplere*). The accumulation of *explere, implere, complere et adimplere* aims at a fullness, an integrity in the execution, which is well rendered by the verb "to fulfill." The Spanish text of the correspondence uses the verb *cumplir* (fulfill) with, in Italian, *adempiere*. To accentuate fullness in the carrying out of God's holy will Ignatius uses two adverbs: entirely and perfectly. Writing to his former confessor Emmanuel Miona (Oct.16, 1536), Ignatius measures the perfection of the fulfillment with the grace which each person has received personally: "that [God]. . . may make us fulfill it [his will] perfectly according to the talent entrusted to each of us." The verb "to fulfill" loses a great deal when it is substituted with a simple "to do" (*hacer*), as was the case with the formulation given by Ignatius's secretaries. What is more important is the tendency to recognize that nothing can be done without the divine action. Thus Salmeron wrote to Laínez: "May [God] make us do (*haga hacer*) his holy will" (Oct. 23, 1557). And Polanco often and even more radically says, "May God do (*Dios haga*) in him and in all people his holy will" (Sept. 30, 1564; Sept. 6, 1556; etc.). Claude Jay, who had stressed the need for growth in the *sentir*, does the same in the case of the fulfilment: "to fulfill it more perfectly" (*más perfectamente*: to Ignatius, 03. 07. 1546). To have a sense of, to fulfill: one single prayer and one single grace unites them in the most holy will of God.

The Stable Element: "Grace"

First of all we speak of grace. This gift is one of the most stable elements of the basic structure of the clause: it is very seldom missing. In the cases in which the prayer asks for a knowledge of the most holy will, the intellectual character of the verb used (*agnoscere, cognoscere*) draws forth the expression "the light of his grace" (Mar. 31, 1553), or else simply "light" (Jan. 23, 1548). It is not always a matter only of "his grace," but, in most of the letters, of *su gracia cumplida*. In the *Constitutions* the research student will find many examples to cull the sense of the adjective *cumplida*. The clearest of these is undoubtedly the distinction between those benefactors who have only provided the initial foundation of a college or contributed to its beginning, and those who have been at the origin of a complete and completed college (*Const.* 319: *cumplido*). To fulfill (*cumplir*) the most holy will a "completed" grace is necessary. In some Latin and Italian translations the secretaries use "abundant" (*uber, copiosus*) and speak of an abundant grace. It would be relatively easy to base the difference between "copious" and "completed" on a difference of quantity and quality. However, at least in principle, *cumplida* can have a quantitative sense [cf. 13: the full hour]. By analogy with fulfilling God's most holy will—each one according to his talent—the grace asked for in the Exercise of the King will be to "not be deaf to his call, but prompt and diligent to accomplish his most holy will." Thus the ending of Ignatius's letters of this kind takes up the second preamble of the Exercise of the King [91]: to hear the call/to accomplish). It is the grace "which I desire."

This presentation would be partial and perhaps biased if it did not mention the concrete form given by a certain number of clauses to "your perfect grace." In some Latin and Italian versions the composition *gratia ac spiritus tuus sanctus* appears (Mar. 22, 1555), or "the true light of his Spirit" (Dec. 2, 1553), or again "his Spirit and his grace" (Aug. 2, 1554). Only once does this grace, which is the Spirit, impose itself so strongly in an Italian version that Ignatius writes: *Iddio N.S. ci insegni a tutti un di questa santa discrettione accio con quella ci conformiamo a sua santa volonta* (May God Our Lord teach us all one day this discretion, that with it we may conform to his holy will") (April 20, 1554).

Polanco, writing to Bobadilla, is even more explicit: *a todos renovación de spiritu y gracia pare mejor sentir y cumplir su santísima voluntad* (May all be renewed in spirit and grace the better to have a sense of and fulfill his most holy will) (Dec. 29, 1557). Two years later Polanco identifies "his abundant grace" with "the most Holy Spirit" (May 13, 1559). In fact, we shall have the sense of God's will for us in the light of the Spirit, and shall be able to fulfill it perfectly through the strength of the Spirit. These variants of the clause give the expression "his completed [or perfect] grace" a sense of fullness, the Spirit of the Lord. It is through the Spirit that Ignatius's desire to "be placed with Christ" receives its sense. For does not "being placed with Christ" mean being placed through the Spirit in the situation in which Christ and we ourselves can together look at history? Being placed with the Son is being enabled, through the Spirit, to make the choices Christ made, to make them today in our history.

The "Infinite and Supreme Goodness" of "God"

This clause invites us to ask for such a perfect grace. But to whom is the petition addressed? The prayer is addressed at times to the Holy Trinity, and at times to Christ; but in the greater part of the 992 clauses it is addressed to God or Our Lord. Sometimes the formula is clarified: "God and Father of our Lord Jesus Christ" (June 2, 1546) or "our God Jesus Christ" (Feb. 7, 1550), but in most cases it would be difficult—in fact impossible—to further define or identify "our Lord." Throughout Ignatius's correspondence, some statistics might be able to indicate Christological denominations which give way to theological denominations, probably under the growing influence of Polanco as secretary. However *God our Lord* appears 600 times at the end of the letters of our category, *our Lord* 106 times and *Christ our Lord* 160 times, thus highlighting in any case Ignatius's theocentrism. The prayer is addressed to God, because everything comes from him and everything returns to be accomplished in him. If God our Lord and Christ our Lord often appear as equivalent in Ignatius's writings, this is because for Ignatius a possible alternative between God and his Christ does not exist. He who has seen Christ sees the Father and, outside of God, a Christ without God is nothing but an idol, or at the most a contagious example of a complete human being.

This prayer is generally based on God's infinite and supreme goodness. Under forms of clemency, benevolence, and mercy this goodness of God is sometimes accompanied by God's wisdom. Wisdom and goodness are visibly the attributes which Ignatius prefers. God's wisdom: Ignatius needs this to know Good's will (May 9, 1550); so that eternal Wisdom may teach us all the perfect knowledge of the divine will (Jan. 12, 1552); so that this Wisdom may direct all things towards the glory of God (Aug. 29, 1555); so that the Lord, the Christ and eternal Wisdom, may grant the light always to know (Sept. 9, 1553); so that divine Wisdom may guide us in all things (June 19, 1556); so that divine Wisdom may communicate itself to us in all ways of proceeding (Dec. 24, 1553). But the number of appeals to God's Goodness, which is the source of all that is good, is overwhelming. No human goodness exists which does not come from this source of all goodness. In the face of Him who is essentially the divine and supreme Goodness, Ignatius is nothing but poor in goodness (June, 1532). This confession at the beginning of the clause that all is gift, all is grace [332] immediately situates—as coming from above—the sense of God's most holy will and its fulfillment. "Without me," without him who is goodness, we cannot do anything (Jn. 15:5). This statement is translated into the language of the *Constitutions* as "what is helpful for serving the Divine Goodness better with the help of his divine grace" (*Const.* 79). To receive oneself from the Divine Goodness, to let oneself be seized by God's Goodness so that the author of every grace may make use of all of us, is an Ignatian theme which runs all through the *Constitutions* and the correspondence by means of a repetition characteristic of Ignatius.

Unity and Universality of the Prayer

One and the same grace, one and the same prayer to have the sense of the most holy will and to fulfill it. The clause becomes quite incomprehensible if seen in the perspective of a dualism, i.e., of a space for prayer to have the sense of God's will and a space for action to fulfill it. Without insinuating that work is prayer and that prayer is life—an abuse of language, to say the least—the clause affirms, by means of prayer and by the formulation of this request, that there is one single source for prayer and action. As the same time the fact of having one single purpose—grace as the source, and God's will as the ultimate end—leaves no possible room for a dualist problem. Even though the accomplishment of God's will is not just "any" action, Ignatius exorcises, so to say, certain "anathemas" which an entire tradition has pronounced on action as such. The clause clearly takes for granted the action, far from being dispersive or distancing one from God, can in fact unite one to God on condition that this action is not separated from "sensing" (= having the sense of) God's will.

Very often this prayer at the end of the letters has a universal ring to it. It asks for grace for "us," for "us all, for "all." Without exaggerating the importance of this point, Ignatius gives evidence of his conviction that this clause—a brief compendium of his experience of God—is not anyone's exclusive preserve, but a gift he hopes all people will receive, whatever their condition in life. It would in fact be difficult to prove that the clause is exclusively destined for this or that group in human society.

Conclusion: Survival of the Ignatian Formula?

Finally we must never forget that in Ignatius's correspondence only one letter out of seven ends with the clause of the third category. As always, Ignatius acts with a great freedom which refuses to constrain himself in the conclusion of his letters to one uniform pattern. Polanco undoubtedly liked it very much, even though he gave it a distinctly Christological flavor and abbreviated it down to a minimal basic structure, even to the point of a simple "etc." (June 3, 1559). It is he who ensured the survival of the clause after St. Ignatius's death: the correspondence concerning the election of Father Laínez bears witness to this. Already in Ignatius time some of his companions (e.g., Francis Xavier and Claude Jay) used the clause as an ending to their letters, particularly in their correspondence with their Jesuit brothers. Salmerón used it very faithfully, though he sometimes summarized the complete clause (April 7, 1542); complete: July 10, 1546, etc.). Thus, using another formula he was very fond of, Salmeron wrote to Lainez: *Nuestro Señor a todos nos tenga de su mano y nos haga tracer su santa voluntad* (May our Lord hold us all in his hand and make us accomplish his holy will) (Oct. 23, 1557).

There is only one instance in which another confrere of Ignatius, Master Simon Rodriguez, used the classical clause when writing to Ignatius (June 30, 1546). After this, he preferred to introduce into the concluding works of his letters the term "love" which is lacking in the Ignatian conclusion. Thus he desired that Ignatius would grow in the love of God (June 27, 1547), or that he would look lovingly on all things (*V.R. por amor de Dios miri todo*: July 17, 1551). Even though Polanco often used the Ignatian clause in his correspondence with Bobadilla, Bobadilla himself exclusively used the second category to end his letters. Linguistically speaking, the clause Ignatius loved had little likelihood of survival without a systematic campaign on the part of a secretary like Polanco, who believed in it. It was too long for the growing need of speed in correspondence, too constructed to allow for adaptation to the different personal and objective circumstances of an exchange of letters, too theologically loaded to be worthy of an often banal or ordinary letter. Thus, the clause was to disappear little by little with the memory of him —Ignatius—who had condensed in it the essential and best part of his experience: to have increasingly a sense of the most holy will and of its fulfillment for the greater glory of God.

THIRTEEN

ON THE EFFECTIVENESS OF THE
SPIRITUAL EXERCISES

Among the many qualities that Ignatius sought in a general, one looks in vain for acquired or even infused knowledge of Ignatian spirituality. In any case, even if Ignatian spirituality is not the only way—it is only one *via quaedam* among many others[1]—it has not lost any of its effectiveness or urgency. Without doubt, already in the time of St. Ignatius, the Company never sought jealously to keep the ministry of the Spiritual Exercises for itself. The people of God has the right to expect, from the Society of Jesus and all those who see themselves as inspired by the inheritance of Ignatius, a preferential option and an up-to-date competence in the Exercises. The many gestures of solidarity and complimentary conversations surrounding us during this Ignatian year are also challenges for us, pushing us to respond to a real pastoral need and an apostolic orientation for the Church of Vatican II. This brings us to our theme: the long-range fruit of the Spiritual Exercises, that is, of the "day after" following a retreat.

The particular importance of the Spiritual Exercises is as well recognized in many religious families and in lay associations as it is throughout the Society of Jesus. All these persons constantly make use of them, continuing to discover ever new aspects and usages. Thus they prepare an increasing number of other persons to share this gift which the Lord entrusted to his Church and the Kingdom it announces, through the mediation of Ignatius. In affirming all these points, the Ignatian Year has rendered still more agonizing the problem posed by what might be called the long-term fruit of the Spiritual Exercises. Indeed, how could the People of God at all levels rely on the ministry of the Exercises if these should produce no fruit? Are they not then too often like a talent which, despite its value, its possessor hides in the earth, or like a gold mine that no one ever works?

---

[1] See the following essay.

What is at issue here is not just human weakness, nor yet is it that routine which threatens, little by little, to reduce the most authentic ideal to insignificance. Rather, I am speaking here about the "fruit" most characteristic of the Spiritual Exercises, the actualization of one of the intensive comparatives which give Ignatius's style its special quality: "further," "better," "more." At issue here is the very person of Ignatius, of whom James Laínez testifies that "He always sought to make progress" (Letter of June 16, 1547). So we shall not be astonished to discover in the text of the *Exercises* this well-known semantic field—progress, expressed in the dream of bearing abundant fruit [174]. Ignatius often employs the substantive *provecho* and the verb *aprovechar*, even if drawing profit—*aprovechar*—does not necessarily signify progress in the sense of taking a decisive step. Ignatius thinks, speaks and lives the comparative; he seems to ignore dead-end situations and irreversible destinies, joyously believing that persons find their reason for being when they progress and perfect themselves, when—always *mas*—they renew or reform themselves.

This is the level at which one locates the problem of the fruit of the Spiritual Exercises. On the one hand, the annual retreat may be carried out with fervor; but, on the other hand, one's religious life and apostolic work remain frozen, for better or for worse.[2] In various places, the Spiritual Exercises in daily life have been, for religious life, an undeniably positive experience for personal and community prayer life. But this experience has not always made people more available to move ahead on the path of renewal in their apostolic projects. One need not multiply examples; they are well enough known. However, it would be a mistake to reduce this problem of the fruit of the Exercises to the case of "prayer" and "life" alone, or, in more classic terms, of "contemplation" and "action," simply conceding that they are an eternal and inevitable problem. In referring to the Spiritual Exercises, the late Father Arrupe had already identified the problem with the help of the "three pairs" or the "three persons," comparing certain situations with the second type of persons[3] [154]. Thus, there is the person who prays and works and is

---

[2] Translator's note: Father Kolvenbach seems to be alluding to the state of "no movement" here, in which nothing dynamic is happening, neither consolation nor desolation [Cf. 6: Annotation 6].

[3] *Acta Romana* 17, 570.

involved in the dynamism that the Lord sets in motion, but only in an oblique way, *en algune manera*, without "looking only" [169] to the praise of God our Savior; that is, in such a way that they do not go directly to God, but want God to come "to them" [169]. The Exercises thus lose their effectiveness, yielding no "fruit," if the retreatant remains only "of a certain type" in prayer and action.

Contemplatives in Action

As we travel along this path of reflection, we attempt to clarify how people today are "contemplatives," and in what way they are contemplatives in action. A formidable question, this, immediately confronting us with the problem of prayer in our communities. Even so, twenty-three Jesuits have recently published a testimony to their life in the Spirit. They do not express these in the technical language of spirituality, and the word "contemplation" hardly figures there at all. All these persons are involved in work and, without responding to a questionnaire, describe their ways of being contemplatives in the style proper to their own contexts. In the living out of the Spiritual Exercises, there is a great diversity in the way of being contemplative, based on a most personal manner of finding God in all things. Thus we meet there the *mantra*, repeated in rhythmic breathing, as well as a charismatic type of rosary. Again, there is an appeal to the imagination extended to the level of psychodrama or to great care in maintaining a spiritual diary. One of these persons, convinced that the Lord can take possession of us more easily when we are half asleep or barely awake, takes his morning cup of tea in God's presence.

Longing to let God take possession of us: such is the general impression that emerges from all these testimonies. Beginning with rather traditional expressions like "to abandon oneself to the incomprehensible mystery of God," or dogmatic affirmations such as "to believe in a conscious way," we read more existential observations such as "It is God who prays in me," "to patiently await the gift which God is for me," "to let God love me." Many are aware that there is a progression in their ways of being contemplatives. When we schematize it, this belief presents itself thusl: "At first I was speaking about God, then I spoke to God; after that I listened to God and now I hear for God." That this growth might be something other than the progress which Ignatius wants us to make in the Spiritual Exercises, we can detect in the fear that tries one confrere encountering the claim of Christ, "What more can I still do for Christ?" In the *Suscipe* this is transformed into "What more can I, the Lord, do for you?" Behind all these witnesses there is a way of being contemplative that gives the primacy to God to act in us.

Several publications of the Ignatian Year have underlined, as a characteristic of Ignatian spirituality, the experience of a God who acts. In fact, someone wrote me a note when, while still working on a project, I asked advice on how to distinguish the contemplative religious life, the conventual life and the apostolic life of which Ignatius was clearly the initiator. In that note, he suggested that I take as the point of departure the third point of the Contemplation to Attain Love [236]: "To consider how God labors and works . . . conducting himself as one who labors. . . ." Our God is a very busy God, as a recent issue of *Review for Religious* describes him;[4] and this labor is shared by the friends of the Lord as collaborators in the work of salvation. "Observe and consider that which they are doing, how journeying and suffering so that the Lord can be born. . . ." [116] It is well enough known that, in the mysteries of his life [261 ff.], Christ is present as a person who acts, and who speaks little more than the beatitudes [278], for "love ought to be put into deeds rather than words" [230].

It is precisely because the labor is done in God and that God is at work, that God lets us encounter him in his activity. Ignatius drew from this the conclusion, when writing to Francis Borgia, that our prayer is not the only way to serve God. Spontaneously, persons who bear witness to their life in the Spirit engage in activity with the joy of being taken hold of by a God who is at work. On the one hand, many of them note that their apostolic experiences deeply affect their way of being contemplatives; on the other hand, one person comments that, in an apostolate of research, contemplation helps him to carry out this task with greater detachment and less egoism.

The ideal type of contemplative in action is the Good Samaritan. He is contemplative in the act of seeing his neighbor in the half-dead traveler and responding from the depths of his heart; he devotes his full attention to healing

---

[4] "The Jesuit Heritage Today," 1991, p. 21 ff.

him and, even after he leaves him behind and physically absent, he provides for his care. Without referring directly to the good Samaritan, others of our companions experience compassion as a dimension of their contemplation, whether by looking on Christ who moves them towards the suffering poor, or simply experiencing how poverty and misery enter into their prayer. They feel it as an anguished question put to them by God, who is at work for the salvation of humanity and who would inspire in us a concrete, collaborative engagement to announce the good news to the poor.

Nadal's Famous Formula

However incomplete, the analysis of these testimonies illustrates very clearly the accuracy of Jerome Nadal's lapidary formula, *simul contemplativus in actione*. It is well known that, as the author saw it, the phrase had the same meaning as "finding God in all things," or the grace of familiarity with God in the work of salvation. However, I should add here that, to grasp the distinction between the second and third groups of persons, this contemplative attitude implies seeing both God and the human condition as they really are. If this condition is not fulfilled, we condemn this contemplative approach to futility. The temptation to avoid looking at the whole reality of God and of the human condition, to prefer that God not be a working God, and to fail to let truth and justice be what they truly are, ambush us today under two widely prevalent forms—fundamentalism and ideology.

Everywhere in the world, to some degree, even deep within the Church, indeed at the heart of the Spiritual Exercises, Jesuits encounter the phenomenon of fear in those who feel their faith or their conviction threatened "to the foundations" by sociocultural evolution and by the technological revolution. Thus, they refuse, sometimes in a violent and aggressive manner directed even at their co-religionists, to "reform," to "renew," or to "modernize." If being contemplative in action signifies what we have tried here to emphasize, it will be difficult or even impossible for a fundamentalist or an integrist to grow in Ignatian spirituality.

Recently, an article in *America* recalled the substantial changes that Ignatius dared to introduce into the original project of the Society. He had discovered, in prayer and work carried out contemplatively, the problem in manifesting the glory of God to those in a world undergoing extensive change: there would have to be some reversals that he himself had not foreseen, let alone willed. One thinks here of the apostolic prayer of Paul, inspired, as he said, by the activity and the faith of the first believers in service of the Lord, by the labor of their charity and the constancy of their hope (1 Thes 1:2-3), and by the concrete recollection of personal cases with which he was struggling (Col 4:2). This life of the apostle resembles that prayerful and active solidarity of Ignatius which shares the joys and hopes, the anxieties and sufferings of those to whom the Lord of the vineyard sent him, of those with whom he places himself in solidarity at the very source of his being and by his mission as an apostle of the Lord.   Contemplatives-in-action insert themselves within the paschal activity of the risen Lord, through which a future has already begun, not to be arrested or hardened into a rigid position. This path calls for constantly fresh beginnings, and the contemplative needs the renewed outlook that enables him to traverse this world in perpetual change. Within it we have no lasting abode, since our apostolic vocation is a pilgrimage, guided by Ignatius the pilgrim.

The effectiveness of the Exercises is threatened as well by the ideological approach. One would have to be unconscious or at least naive to believe truly that, in the Spiritual Exercises, one could bring an undistorted viewpoint and a strict objectivity to the reality of God and the human person. All too easily, we present the matter of the Exercises laid out on a grid shaped by our way of seeing, or that of a group with which we share a certain mental outlook. If we fail to be attentive, our way of presenting the Spiritual Exercises can give an opening to a kind of crude sloganism with its stereotypes and clichés. The ideological risk is especially great, as every tradition demonstrates, in the key meditations of the Exercises. A philosophical grid can transform the Principle and Foundation into an abstract affirmation with a stoic quality to it; the military—or perhaps feudal—grid can color the Contemplation of the Kingdom; the Manichean grid easily surfaces in the presentation of the Two Standards. From another angle, significant authors and scholars have presented the Spiritual Exercises as a way of freedom, a guide to integral liberation, and a school of prayer, modeled on the movement of the Covenant and the Exodus.

Ignatian spirituality possesses no specific guarantees that keep it from having its own share of ideology; it is, after all, the work of persons with the power of choice. This makes it all the more indispensable as well as Ignatian to submit it in its entirety to the questioning of the word of God, to examine it in light of the mystery of Christ's life, and to submit it to the challenging breath of the Spirit. The Spiritual Exercises can in fact bear no fruit if they are not moved by such questioning. It is the natural bent of all ideologies to look for assurances and legitimations that suit their own proper ways of thought and conduct. For this reason Ignatius becomes quite unsettled when, during the Exercises, a person remains unchallenged, and thus unable to abandon oneself to the One who examines and chastizes the heart. In ideology, the human person easily disappears behind certain masks which may serve him or her, or of which they may make use. The Spiritual Exercises effect an unveiling which causes masks to fall away and which permits persons to discover themselves in deeper truth. Certainly this is a painful truth, but it is the true path to joy, because the truth will make us free.

The author of the famous formula *simul contemplativus in actione*[5] would perhaps be shocked to see us deal with this original insight as if it were some kind of foreign body or an isolated element. His phrase was the expression of his overall experience with Ignatius, and as he saw it the basic constituent of Ignatian spirituality. In the light of the anthropology of his time, Jerome Nadal wanted to add the phrase "all our activity in Christ," placing it in a cyclical movement. Our activity thus passes from the spirit to the heart, from the heart to practice, and resumes its flow back to the heart and then to the spirit—*spiritu, corde, practice*. Thus there is a coming and going that highlights the *simul* of the formula *simul contemplativus in actione*.

Nadal did not choose one form of prayer to be characteristic of the life of an apostle. All the forms contributing to the Spiritual Exercises can be chosen for personal prayer, but the important quality of Ignatian prayer is the orientation of these forms. In his sensitivity to the need for effectiveness, Nadal is convinced that the fervor of an apostolic life will depend on fidelity to this truly Ignatian orientation. In the Spirit, the call of God and his power are made manifest and received into a heart which recapitulates the whole person. Just as the Spirit cannot bear fruit if not received into the heart, the heart remains on the level of mere speculation and a kind of dreamy velleity

---

[5] Cf. Epp., t. V, Rome, 1962, *Ann. In Exam.*, c. IV, 162-163.

if one fails to see that the integrating factor within the heart is the execution of God's call. Nadal is well aware of contemplatives who do not have the orientation of Ignatian spirituality: "Contemplatives who do not give themselves to an active life—*ad praxim*—are satisfied with good desires. They leave it to others to put everything into action, and assist them with their prayers. As for us, we must add the effective desire—*inclinatio efficax*—to move into practical action.[6]

Still today, the apostolic religious life is represented as a more or less successful compromise between an authentic religious life and an absorption in distracting occupations. But Nadal, appreciating all the possible dangers in both activity and prayer, considered praxis to be an enriching factor which would ordinarily strengthen rather than weaken life in the Spirit. Clearly, Nadal expressed the necessity "of returning often to prayer and of realizing a circular movement passing from prayer to action and from action back to prayer."[7] However, there is a risk of forgetting that the circle is never closed, as something serving its own purposes. This movement is at the service of a "devotion" for contemplatives who are engaged with all their being in the divine plan that looks always to the salvation of the other. Thus, in Nadal's language again, the circle of prayer and action is described: "If you are occupied with your neighbor, and at the service of God in your ministry or in any kind of duty, God will help you towards more effective prayer. This more effective help from God will in its turn help you to serve your neighbor with greater courage and spiritual profit."[8] We progress toward that "grace" by letting God guide us, but, at any given moment, there will be, as in the life of Ignatius, that "habit of working under the effect of that grace and that light which God communicates—*infundit*.[9] The cyclical movement, this Nadalian circle, does not imply two realities, of which the one would detract from the profit of the other. Rather, it is the one divine grace with which we must be always more deeply penetrated so that it might shine with ever greater

---

[6] M. Nicolau, *Jerónimo Nadal, S. J. (1507-1580). Sus obras y doctrinas espirituales*, Madrid, Consejo superior de investigaciones cientificas, 1949, 307.

[7] *Ibid.*, 511.

[8] *Ibid.*, 324-325.

[9] *Ibid.*, 145.

radiance.[10]

Keeping the image of the cycle, one might say that, in the spiritual progression of the apostolic life, the circle ceaselessly contracts until the two components—prayer and action—mutually penetrate in a harmony by which our human activity becomes the activity of God with us. Nadal does not hesitate then to specify this union in an "incarnational" way: "[y]ou wish by his will—that of Christ,— you remember by his memory, so that all your being, your willing and your action are not in yourself, but in Christ."[11] For Nadal, this was the meaning of Ignatius's *in Domino nostro*: "Make every effort to work under the impression of a true and humble sense of God working in you." "And if you do not perceive the action of the Spirit, at least believe that it is acting." (723) So it is one shimmering light that surrounds a person to the very ground of his being and directs all his activity, giving it a divine value and effectiveness.

Thus, there is really only one light, that of the Incarnate One, who, in carrying out his mission from the Father, is not divided between two opposing currents, that of prayer turned towards his Father and that of action turned towards persons. To come together with his Father, Jesus must not forget his own who are in the world, and to go out to persons, Jesus never leaves his Father's side. He has been sent before his Father and before persons; his mission expresses that union. When he presents himself to the Father, it never happens through an impossible abstraction that would artificially separate him from his commission and from the whole world of people. He enters in before his Father in solidarity with all humanity, saints and sinners, and in him, the Father loves all people. The apostolic prayer of the legate, sent in the company of the Son, is a wholehearted consent to be that legate, one who is open to renewal and deepening in that being-in-God. We pray to share in his spirit with all our heart, and, in the practice of mission, with all *his* heart.

To translate the vision of Nadal into our language with a view to a greater effectiveness of the Spiritual Exercises, both in the retreat experience

---

[10] Cf. R. Hostie, "Le cercle de l'action et de l'oraison d'apres le p. J. Nadal", in *Christus*, 6 (1955), 208. Editor's note: This article can be found in English in William J. Young, trans., *Finding God in All Things: Essays in Spirituality Translated from* Christus (Chicago: Henry Regnery) 1958, pp. 153-165.

[11] Epp., t. IV, Madrid, 1905, *Journal*, 697.

and for "the day after," certain aspects of the life in the Spirit should be mentioned. That is, Ignatian spirituality does not limit life in the Spirit to certain specific areas, such as the time of prayer or sacramental life or some particular work of Christian charity. Rather the whole personality of the contemplative, the entire reality of human existence becomes the holy place where the action of God reveals itself, so that we may engage in the work of human salvation. Thus, in contemplating the mysteries of the life of Jesus, we should accept the burden of the presence of persons whom the Lord puts in our path. We should admit into our prayer the professional and ethical demands of our labors, whatever they may be, and accept the deep cares of a heart ceaselessly challenged by present and future events. Finally, there should be solidarity with a consolation drawn from the examen and discernment of signs of the times announcing the coming of the Kingdom. These in turn should combine with the compassion that enables us to deal with injustice and the evil that causes the structures of sin. So the contemplative may even question God about any event experienced, as received from God's hands, and respond to it, as Ignatius said, "in Jesus Christ."

Quite possibly, this prayerful atitude might be acquired through the Spiritual Exercises in daily life, under normal human conditions. One testimonial puts it this way: "This presence of the real that one must always consider helps to make the gospel present, brings to light new depths of the Incarnation and of the Church, and clarifies the criteria for judging the interior movements of the Spirit in us." Thus, the contemplative in action gives to the dialogue with God the whole burden of one's existence.

Conclusion

The activity of the contemplative in action is not just any activity, however. The demands of the contemplative life can in fact help one decide on the compatibility or incompatibility of any given work with one's contemplation. Ignatius, however, knew from experience that all activity can be transformed as a result of the activity of the Spirit. Basically, this is what discernment is about: to be able, through the Spirit, to impress on all activity the characteristics which are those of the Lord, sent by the Father. Ignatius summed up certain distinctive traits of this activity in the phrase "our way of proceeding." He includes here a visible line of behavior in our activity, which the Lord, as contemplated in his activity, could take possession of with us and for us. Ignatius insisted on the freedom which should mark our activity, on the availability which should guide our way, and on the passionate desire to discover the will of his Divine Majesty which should precede all our efforts. He desired us to be conscious of the universal direction—implying always both divine and human truth—which should direct our actions. Ignatius was certainly aware that the action of the contemplative is not dull routine, but is on the contrary so original in the way of proceding that, so to speak, Ignatius has to resort to strange constructions such as the well-known expression *para con los otros*. Through a million details, the correspondence of Ignatius reveals this transformation of action through contemplative meditation. Ignatius is thus found to be an active person totally absorbed in the jungle of business, never tempted to float easily over the demands of reality, or to close himself off in endlessly complicated matters. Being a contemplative in action, Ignatius puts into practice that which he never ceases to call for at the close of his letters: "That we might have the sense of his most holy will and fully carry it out."

FOURTEEN

A CERTAIN PATHWAY TO GOD
("VIA QUAEDAM AD DEUM")

The theme of "the way" recurs twice in the bull *Regimini Militantis Ecclesiae* of September 27, 1540, the Papal document which officially approved the Society of Jesus. Beckoning the companions to keep God first of all before their eyes, Pope Paul III exhorts them to dedicate themselves to "this Institute" whose character is to be "a certain pathway to God" *(via quaedam ad Deum)*. Commentators have highlighted the "relativizing" tone of this text: God is always greater than any path whatsoever that leads to him; and in any case, there is question here of just *one* pathway among many other possible ones. Later on, in the *Constitutions,* Ignatius will say that "the way which leads men to life" is Christ *(Const.* 101: cf. Jn 14:6); only in Christ is the Church, in the words of *Lumen Gentium,* 14 "necessary for salvation." Again, at the end of the papal bull, the companions who will later follow "our plan of life" are called "imitators along this path" *(MI, Const.* I, pp. 26-27 n.3 and p. 30 n.8).[1]

In comparing the Institute of the Society to a pathway, did Ignatius intend to do away with a juridical definition of, or a set plan for, the Society's manner of living and operating? Did he intend to offer the Society no more than some general guidelines of orientation, while leaving the onward course of his companions to chance developments and experimentation? Or would it be right to affirm, rather, that the *Constitutions* are characterised by this image of a path to be traversed in view of "achieving with all his effort the end set before him by God" *(MI, Const.* I, p. 27 n.3)? This would be analogous to the plan of other founders who conceived of their constitutions or rules in terms of service of the divine liturgy, of silence, or of martyrdom. True, and this

---

[1] These very two occurrences of "path" or "pathway" are to be found in the *Five Chapters* of the *First Sketch of the Institute of the Society (MI, Const.* I, p. 16, n. 2 and p. 20, n. 7), and in the 1550 Bull of confirmation of Pope Julius III, *Exposcit Debitum (MI, Const.,* I, p. 376, n. 3 and p. 381, n. 6.

is well known, the buildup of the *Constitutions* describes the path followed by one who seeks admission into the Society. This idea of Ignatius was original: described in this way, the unfolding of the personal history of each companion flows into the growth of the apostolic body of the whole Society.

Yet we must say that the *Constitutions* do not give the impression of being consciously constructed or, at any rate, elucidated in terms of a kind of symbolism of path. If we are to take as witnesses the words which translate the idea of "way, path, journey"—namely, the Spanish *vía* and *camino, or the Latin *via*—we have the impression that the author of the *Constitutions* uses these terms without meaning to focus any particular attention on them. Even today the use of the term "way" or "path" is so firmly rooted in the vocabulary of religious language as to make it difficult to compose any text of some length without in fact employing it. Thus, we are all walking along the good or evil path; we must choose the path we are to follow, find our way and know well the paths of life.

Vía *in the Constitutions*

Thus, for Ignatius, the usage of these words is so broad that "way" can come to signify just one of the means used. Of twenty instances of the use of the Spanish *vía,* nine in fact belong to this category. Speaking of poverty, for instance, Ignatius remarks that it is so important that the devil will try to destroy it "in one way or another" *(por unas o por otras vías) (Const.* 816). And so Ignatius forbids every professed member to take part in altering what pertains to poverty in the *Constitutions* "either in a congregation assembled from the entire Society, or by attempting this himself in any manner *(por vía alguna) (Const.* 554; in the same vein we have *Const.* 117, 130, 610, 692, 696, 707, and 818). Among the other uses of the word *vía,* we have just one instance when the "path" is not further qualified: in *Const.* 308, Ignatius acknowledges "proceeding by another path" which is that of admitting young men—which, in fact, was not what he and his early companions had originally considered.

The other ten uses of the word *vía* are situated frankly on the spiritual level, thanks to a further qualification added to the word. Thus, if Ignatius writes constitutions, it is clearly "to aid us to proceed better . . . along the path of divine service on which we have entered" *(Const.* 134). The expression seems to pick up the idea, proposed by the 1540 papal bull, of the Institute as "a pathway." The same is true of *Const.* 243, where Ignatius spells out the idea of "progressing": "enabling them to make progress, both in spirit and in virtues, along the path of the divine service . . . to labour in the Lord's vineyard." Whether with many spiritual visitations or with fewer, "they should endeavor always to go forward in the path of the divine service" *(Const.* 260). The call to go forward along this path of the divine service leads to "the path of his greater service and praise" *(Const.* 618). Such progress is possible because of the member's leaving the disposition of himself completely to the superior who directs him in the place of Christ our Lord" *(Const.* 618), for, in the last analysis, it is the path of Christ himself. And so the long years of formation give reason for hope that formed Jesuits will be men who are "sufficiently advanced to run in the path of Christ our Lord" *(Const.* 582). On two occasions Ignatius employs the Latin expression *in via Domini* or *in viam Domini:* precisely because the path is not that of Ignatius or even that which I as member of the Society have discovered, but the path of the Lord; it is others different from me—namely, the Vicar of Christ on earth (*Const.* 605) or my superiors (*Const.* 91)—who direct me along the path of him who is the way which leads men to life" *(Const.* 101).

This way, then, is "the path of salvation and perfection" (*Const.* 551), along which the superiors, through great openness to them on the part of their subjects, are "the better able to direct them in everything" *(ibid.).* Ignatius requires of his companion in the Society that, once this path has been discovered, he should remain faithful to it, "proceeding with all humility and obedience to make his way along the same path, which was shown to him by him who knows no change and in whom no change is possible" *(Const.* 116). Ignatius accepts the fact that not everybody, even within the Society, will go forward in this way along the path of the Lord. This is why he desires that the men in formation, for their greater spiritual progress and "while they advance along the path of the spirit . . . should deal only with persons and about matters which help them toward what they were seeking when they entered the Society for the service of God our Lord" (*Const.* 244). If, therefore, they are "worried or disturbed by persons who are not walking in the path of the spirit" (*Const.* 245), they may be moved to another place where they can apply themselves better in the divine service.

"Camino" and "Caminar"

The word *camino* is employed only twice: once, to indicate very clearly the "journey" as different from "remaining in the destination" *(Const.* 610: *estar alla);* the second time, in an apostolic context, when speaking of the manner of dealing with "a diversity of persons throughout such varied regions." Here Ignatius affirms that "although all this can be taught only by the unction of the Holy Spirit and by the prudence which God our Lord communicates to those who trust in his Divine Majesty, nevertheless the way can at least be opened by some suggestions which aid and dispose one for the effect which must be produced by divine grace" (*Const.* 414). Along the path of divine service, the way "which can be opened" is none other than the way of the Lord.

If now, to round off our enquiry, we extend it to the use of *vía* and *camino* in the *Spiritual Exercises*, the overall picture is scarcely modified. In the *Exercises*, too, *vía* signifies "means" [20 and 367], and is even used literally in the sense of a route followed when the *Exercises* speak of the Magi who withdrew to their own country "by another way" [267]. In line with the more frequent use of the word *vía* in the *Constitutions, vía* here is related to the goal of the Exercises: "dispose it (the soul) for the way in which it could better serve God in the future" [15]. As for the word *camino* which, as we have seen, figures only rarely in the *Constitutions,* it occurs fairly frequently in the *Exercises*. This is not strange if we recall St. Ignatius's particular liking for journeys and routes: the way from Nazareth to Bethlehem, for instance, or that from Bethany to Jerusalem [112, 192; cf. 202, 287, 301]. The only other different use of *camino* occurs in the Rules for the Discernment of Spirits: following the counsels of the evil spirit, "we can never find the way to a right decision" [318]. This picture would be incomplete if we passed over the fact that the verb *caminar,* which in the *Constitutions* is combined with the word *vía (Const.* 116 and 244), takes on in the Exercises the very symbolism suggested by bodily exercises: "taking a walk, journeying on foot, and running" [1], or what our Lady and St. Joseph do in "making the journey and laboring *(caminar y trabajar)* that our Lord might be born . . ." [116].

The Characteristic Word: "Discurrir"

All these texts concerning *vía* and *camino* form a harmonious whole, in which we sense the primacy in all of him who is the way and who opens out for us a way along which he will lead us towards salvation—he himself or those who represent him. And so, the concern "first of all to keep before his eyes God as long as he lives," rather than relativising the character or *raison d'etre* of the Society, becomes the indispensable condition for discerning one's path and for opening the way to those whom the Lord puts on one's path. And yet, we do not feel that with all this we have as yet touched the originality of the Ignatian way. In effect, it is not the verb *caminar* but rather *discurrir* which puts us on the right path. As long as the language we have been analyzing remains bound to *a* particular path, a person can only "proceed to make his way along the path" *(Const.* 116) or "advance along the path" *(Const.* 244). Strictly speaking, while the Jesuit can indeed "run in the path" *(Const.* 582), he ought to "discurrir"—that is, "travel through various regions of the world" *(Const.* 82).

It is not by chance that this expression is found in the context of pilgrimages and begging, "thus imitating those earliest members [of the Society]" *(Const.* 82). The expression "to travel about in various regions of the world" recurs once and again as the very grounding for the close relationship between superior and subject in the universal body of the Society *(Const.* 92). And then, "traveling through the various regions of the world" is intimately linked with the very aim and end of the Society *(Const.* 308). The members of the Society are thus described as those who ought to be ready "at any hour to go to some or other parts of the world where they may be sent" *(Const.* 588). Indeed, what is at stake here is "the first characteristic of our Institute, [which is] to travel through some regions and others, remaining for a shorter or longer time" *(Const.* 626). While certainly acknowledging great freedom in this "travelling about wherever [the Jesuit] judges this to be more expedient for the glory of God our Lord" *(Const.* 633), Ignatius does not rule out works of a more stable nature in helping the neighbor. Thus we read: "The Society endeavours to aid its fellow human beings not merely by traveling through diverse regions but also by residing continually in some places" *(Const. 636;* for *discurrir,* cf. also *Const.* 603, 605).

Something strange thus emerges: while the word *camino* is so very concretely literal in the *Spiritual Exercises* and *vía* or *camino* so very spiritual in the *Constitutions,* just the contrary is true of the word *discurrir* which is concretely literal in the *Constitutions,* whereas in the *Exercises* it is used for spiritual efforts and experiences. Thus we note, for example: "to think over the matter more in detail" with the understanding [50, 51]; "ponder upon what presents itself to my mind" [53]; "gone over . . . every aspect of the matter in question" [182]; "diligently *thinks over* and recalls the matter contemplated" [64]; "go over the single hours or periods" [25]; "going over the points" [2]; "going over [the solid foundation of facts] . . . for himself" [2]; "make use of the acts of the intellect *in reasoning*" [3]. . . . One might be content with remarking that for Ignatius the understanding is not intuitive or, of itself, contemplative. But in paging through the Carthusian Ludolph's preface to his *Vita Christi,* which was the convalescent Ignatius's bedside reading, one very quickly discovers that the word *discurrir* is used as much of the person who travels through different parts of the world as of the person who transposes this operation to "passing in review all creatures" [60] or to having "gone over and pondered . . . every aspect of the matter in question" [182]. Thus it is that Ludolph wrote: "Going through *[discurrentes]* the various places with a deep interior spirit let them kiss or embrace the spot where they have learned that the gentle Jesus stood or sat or performed some deed."

The *Spiritual Exercises* present a clear opposition between *discurrir* and *divagar*:" . . . because the intellect, without any digression *(divagar),* diligently thinks over *[discurra]* and recalls the matter contemplated" [64]. This marked concern of the *Exercises* to avoid any "aimless wandering or digression," and to urge rather a diligent "going through" or following the Lord to the fullest extent, is found again in the *Constitutions.* In these latter, while prohibiting all types of random roaming about or spiritual tourism, Ignatius explains that, "to avoid erring in the path of the Lord," the first companions, through their "promise or vow," allowed "His Holiness [to] . . . distribute them for greater glory to God . . . in conformity with their intention to travel *[discurrir]* throughout the world" (*Const. 605*). There is something paradoxical about this text: while explicitly excluding for "the path" the sense of a determined "one-way traffic," it does not exclude the risk of aimless wandering or "erring" in it; on the other hand, traveling throughout the world in every direction by allowing the pope to distribute them all over, is precisely "for greater glory to God." The text implicitly supposes an assembling or coming together—what they call their "plan" or "intention"—but with a view to being scattered to the four corners of the world.

All that Ignatius puts into the *Constitutions* on the theme of "way" or "path," Benedict of Nursia could well have put into his religious Rule; all that Ignatius compassed with his word *discurrir,* Benedict Joseph Labre actually lived out. The originality of the founder of apostolic religious life lies in this harmonious yet paradoxical union that is in effect the Institute of the Society of Jesus.

The *"Pilgrim"*: Autobiography *and* Memoriale

Let us try now to move a step further. We recall that St. Ignatius was pleased to call himself a "pilgrim." While this word is certainly linked with all Ignatius's pilgrimages in Europe and to the Middle East, it also signifies all his availability along "the way in which God had led him from the start of his conversion" (Nadal, *Preface to the Autobiography,* n. 2), or even "the way in which the Lord had been guiding [him] from the start of [his] conversion" *(ibid., n. 3).* According to a letter of Fr. Diego Laínez written at Bologna on June 16, 1547 (*MI, FN I,* 54-145), Ignatius at Alcalá helped some persons "to renounce mortal sin," others to "make progress in the way of God," and still others—it was alleged—"to go on pilgrimage" (n. 24). Pilgrimage, then, appears as a kind of "being more for God" in relationship to "the way." Actually in Ignatius's *Autobiography* the account of what took place in Alcalá has additional connotations. There were, in effect, "many persons who followed the pilgrim;" some of them "had made great spiritual progress," so much so that "though they were noble women, they had gone to the Veronica of Jaen on foot"—that is, some three hundred kilometers to the south of Madrid—in order to venerate there a relic of the Holy Face. This pilgrimage was only a partial fulfillment of their great desires, for "they wanted to go about the world serving the poor in one hospital and then in another" *(Autob.* 61). Those who thus "follow the pilgrim" actually walk, in their deep desires, the same path that Ignatius walked from the house of Loyola on: for "the one thing he wanted to do was to go to Jerusalem" with "a generous spirit, fired with God" *(Autob.* 9). As for what he desired to do after returning from Jerusalem, Ignatius hesitated between "the rule of the Carthusians" and "going about the world" *(Autob.* 12).

In his *Autobiography* Ignatius calls himself a "pilgrim" only after the spiritual experience of Manresa when he has already begun his "pilgrimage" to the Holy Land. The only exception to this is the story of the Moor and the mule *(Autob.* 15). Even after his pilgrimage to the Holy Land, he sticks to this term of "pilgrim" right up to the end: "from Rome the pilgrim went to Monte Cassino to give the Exercises . . ." *(Autob.* 98). In dedicating as much space in his *Autobiography* to the spiritual path followed at Manresa as to his journeying along the routes of the world, Ignatius offers us a hint of the new way that is opening up for him. For Ignatius's pilgrimage possesses certain original traits.

According to the very etymology of the word *peregrinatio,* the pilgrim leaves the sphere of daily life which has been perceived as profane, and moves *per agros* towards a center that is generally situated on the outskirts of this profane sphere of living in a spot perceived as "distant" and, therefore, somehow "sacred." In this spot the pilgrim hopes to have a direct experience of the invisible through the mediation of sacred objects and symbolic actions. Ignatius's journey to Jerusalem corresponds in every detail to this definition of pilgrimage; it reaches a peak in his "great consolation" on Mount Olivet where "there is a stone from which our Lord rose up to heaven, and his footprints are still seen there" *(Autob.* 47). It is significant that this experience coincides with the end of the pilgrimage as far as Ignatius's desires go—"to remain in Jerusalem, continually visiting those holy places" *(Autob.* 45). It corresponds further with the beginning of a new path to which the Lord calls him—"he continually pondered within himself what he ought to do *(quid agendum?)*" *(Autob.* 50). Instead of the pilgrimage to the Holy Land finishing with a clear manifestation of the Lord's will, it gave rise in the end to a new uncertainty within Ignatius, only to incarnate, not in Jerusalem, but "else-where" the "plan he had, in addition to this devotion, to help souls" *(Autob.* 45).

What had Ignatius hoped for from his pilgrimage? First of all, an experience of penance: "He began to think more earnestly about his past life and about the great need he had to do penance for it"; from this sprang the desire "to go to Jerusalem . . . with as much of disciplines and fasts" as possible (*Autob.* 9). Very shortly before his death, Ignatius still imposed as a penance "a pilgrimage of four hundred leagues" (Câmera, *Memoriale* 58). Fr. Jerome Otello, who had criticized the Pope in a homily, saying, "The Pope would do well to take some definite steps," was asked by Ignatius to choose a fitting penance. He then brought to Ignatius a whole list of possible penances among which figured that "of going to Jerusalem on foot . . . indeed, barefoot" (Câmera, *Memoriale* 95). Pilgrimage thus became a sort of "paschal rite" which Ignatius used not only to bring about new life or a conversion. Thus, he prescribed "three months on pilgrimage" for Fr. Arnaud Conchus who had exchanged harsh words with another (Câmera, *Memoriale*, 398) but also to transfer to another way of life, that is, to leave the Society, but "in a spirit of complete friendship" (Câmera, *Memoriale* 61). Again, "pilgrimage without money and even in begging from door to door" would be a novitiate experience or experiment for those who sought admission to the Society (*Const.* 67).

To be sure, it was not just in the form of penance or a sort of "paschal rite" that Ignatius as General sent persons on pilgrimage. Some Fathers were sent on pilgrimage to Loreto "for the healing of Pope Marcellus" (Câmera, *Memoriale*, 336). Actually Ignatius wanted to send many more on pilgrimage to Loreto, but the house doctor opposed this plan because of the great heat at the time. "The doctor's advice seemed good to our father, who then commuted these pilgrimages into stational visits to the *Scala Santa*" (Câmera, *Memoriale* 339). While thus moderating its expressions and always using discretion, Ignatius nonetheless highly valued the pilgrimage: "The reason is that I myself have experienced their usefulness, and that they were sort of congenial to me" (Câmera, *Memoriale* 137).

"Pilgrimage" in the Constitutions

If today there is a certain revival of the practice of pilgrimages, the reason is not their penitential character, nor even the original sense of moving away from a profane sphere of living to a sacred one. Even the tourist business is amply saddled with journeys of all kinds. The sociologist would say that the experience of pilgrimage is also lived as a passage from a given social structure to a charismatic type of fellowship and solidarity which is universal in character. Ignatius's desire "to help souls" is grafted on to the idea of pilgrimage. It is well known that Ignatius abandoned his own social status to take on the condition of a pilgrim; what is less familiar is the new form his social relationships assumed. On the boat from Barcelona to Gaeta some passengers accompanied the pilgrim-beggar Ignatius: "They joined him because they also were begging" (*Autob*. 38); in a way, they would be the first "companions" of Ignatius. In Jerusalem, above all, Ignatius experienced, as a pilgrim, an authentic religious enthusiasm with all the other pilgrims (*Autob*. 45); indeed, throughout the journey, he had experienced so many signs of great hospitality and sincere fraternity among the "companions." Later on, for his second projected pilgrimage to Jerusalem, which will however not take place, the would-be pilgrims became his true "companions." From then on Ignatius cannot no longer imagine a Society of Jesus without the experience of pilgrimage. In his *Constitutions*, "to go on pilgrimage" becomes one of the experiments for the novices. An early project of 1541 even puts it this way: "The one who is not capable of remaining or going on foot for a whole day without eating, and of sleeping in discomfort, does not seem capable of persevering in the Society." The final text of the *Constitutions* is more moderate in its demands, but highlights even more forcefully the grounding principles of pilgrimage in the Society. The requirement of penance is held on to firmly: "to grow accustomed to discomfort in food and sleep" (*Const*. 67). So, too, the change in social status: "without money and even in begging from door to door at appropriate times, for the love of God our Lord" (*Const*. 67). The charismatic element is brought into bold relief: "Through abandoning all the reliance which he could have in money or other created things, [he] may with genuine faith and intense love place his reliance entirely in his Creator and Lord" (*Const*. 67). In this we hear a re-echo of that "great assurance" Ignatius had during his pilgrimage to Jerusalem: "He could not doubt but that he would in fact find a way to go to Jerusalem" (*Autob*. 40). This assurance flowed from his companionship with the Lord "who appeared to him often, giving him great consolation and determination"

(*Autob*. 44). It is in Simón Rodriguez's account of the origin and progress of the Society *(Commentarium:* Lisbon, July 25, 1577) that we should read how the first group of companions "resolved to live the pilgim's way," to use a phrase of Ignatius (*Autob*. 92). The experience of dangers, at times danger of death, but even more the experience of the companionship of the Lord all along the journey, transformed their pilgrimage from Paris to Venice into an experience of a group of "friends in the Lord" who felt "an incredible joy of spirit" (Rodriguez, *Commentarium* 37).

Both in Ignatius's pilgrimage to Jerusalem and in the pilgrimage of the first companions from Paris on to Venice and later to Loreto (Rodriguez, *Commentarium* 25-56), the passage from the social condition of the pilgrims to their fellowship and solidarity entailed also a certain distance-taking in regard to the Church. Being implicitly something of a critique of the style of life characteristic of social status, the reality of pilgrimage contains a potential core of a "counter-culture," and remains even in today's Church a type of expression of the freedom of the children and people of God. Little wonder, then, that pilgrimage tends to provoke reactions of rejection. In Venice the pilgrim Ignatius was the object of a regular persecution: a stranger, one "marginal" to society, has no rights, and "the business went so far that a trial was held" (*Autob*. 93).

This was the seventh trial he faced in the course of his spiritual adventure. And yet Ignatius made every conceivable effort not to be uselessly "strange." In keeping with the orders given him in the name of the Church, he dyed his clothing and wore shoes (*Autob*. 59). But there are limits, to be sure: Ignatius could not allow "that the door be closed for him to help souls" (*Autob*. 63). While he and a companion of his, following orders given them in Alcalá, willingly dressed like students, they did not hesitate to give a gown to "a poor cleric" in need, even if, as a result, they had to look grotesque because they dressed strangely *(Autob*. 66). So, too, on their journey from Paris to Venice, the first companions behaved always like curious strangers: they had to cross countries at war, mountains that were snow-bound, without knowing either the language of the place or the route to follow, passing through regions torn asunder by politics and religion; they were even thought to have "definitely come by way of the sky" (*caelo plane devolasse*: Rodriguez, *Commentarium* 34). The very fact of their being "pilgrims" was given scarce recognition and even roundly despised (Rodriguez,

Commentarium 36). In the 1547 letter of Laínez already mentioned, there is an account of the pilgrimage of these first companions from Paris to Venice: termed "novices in this matter of journeying on foot" (n. 33), the first companions are described as less "marginal" or more fortunate than the pilgrim Ignatius: "People did not believe that we were in need because we were not in rags and because we traveled with sacks containing our books" (n. 38). As in the experience of Ignatius himself, the pilgrimage of the companions tends to take the shape of apostolic journeying, in which "helping souls" becomes the preponderant element, to the point, it would seem, of snuffing out the mystical flame of pilgrimage pure and simple.

And yet, Ignatius remains rooted in his conviction that the way for "giving glory to his Divine Majesty," "traveling through various regions of the world," will not be possible without the heart of a pilgrim who must, "in imitating those earliest members . . . beg from door to door for the love of God our Lord" *(Const.* 82). This is doubtless "contrary to common human opinion." Nevertheless, "without asking for or expecting any reward in this present and transitory life," we ought to be completely "prepared and very much ready for whatever is enjoined upon us in our Lord, and at whatever time" (*Const.* 82). For this reason Ignatius cannot imagine a Society of Jesus in which pilgrimage has no place in the formation of its members.

Far more than in the image of the pilgrim, it is in its reality that the Ignatian paradox is resolved, provided that we do not limit pilgrimage to a mere quest for the Absolute. A certain craze for "the road" or for "a people of God on the march"—and here the story of the disciples on the road to Emmaus would appear to be the Gospel passage most to the point—may well make us forget the requirements for every authentic pilgrimage of which Ignatius never loses sight. He is a pilgrim not because he has no idea of where he is going or because he does not know the way. The pilgrim Ignatius opts for the *Via Domini*: a way, that is, which does not rely on money or human assurances, not on retribution for services rendered along the way, not even on a given orientation predetermined once and for all. The attitude is, rather, one that is always prepared to change course in order to travel to the four corners of the world in the service of the Lord. All this fits in very naturally with the image of the apostle and with the call to mission which the evangelist Luke sums up in some lapidary sentences (Lk 10:1 ff.). To leave all in order to follow the Lord, who calls together disciples not for the purpose of establishing a permanent court around himself, but to send them out and scatter them among other persons.

Apostolic Character of Ignatian Pilgrimage

And so, for Ignatius, *peregrino* is more important than *peregrinación*—"pilgrim" more than "pilgrimage." Though he read in the "Imitation of Christ" (his "little Gerson," according to the *Memoriale* of Câmara: n. 97) a fairly stereotyped criticism of pilgrimages—*los que mucho peregrinan rara vez se santifican*—Ignatius does not see in this an attack against his passionate attachment to the image of the pilgrim. For his "pilgrimage" went well beyond the then current *romeria* (or excursion connected with a religious festival) with its many attendant abuses; Ignatius's "pilgrimage" transformed the penitential and devotional journey to a holy place into an apostolic journey "to help souls." Instead of a knight-errant or an adventurous wanderer, Ignatius saw himself as one of the *caminantes apostolicos* (apostles on foot) for whom going on foot and visiting shrines always went hand in hand with begging, staying in hospitals, serving the sick, and engaging in spiritual conversation with those whom the Lord put on their path. This apostolic context conveys the full meaning to that phrase *el pobre peregrino* with which Ignatius signed off his letter of December 6, 1525, to Inés Pascual. When very much later Ignatius had, so to speak, to define what he meant by "apostolic mission," he forged the link with his image of the pilgrim (true, without excluding a less charismatic form of being sent on mission). Thus, "the first [way of being sent] is apostolic, without money, going as pilgrims and ill clad . . ."[2]

In spelling out the Ignatian understanding of pilgrimage, we have noted its indispensably "apostolic" character. For Ignatius the apostle would stand out as the model and archetype of the pilgrim. Of this Fr. Jerome Nadal was absolutely convinced. The *Autobiography* already bears witness to Ignatius's familiarity with the apostles: it is always Christ with his apostles that inspires Ignatius's way of acting, not only when there is question of receiving orders

---

[2] Letter of early September, 1551, to Fr. Elpidius Ugoletti: *MI, Epis.*, III, 638.

(*Autob.* 75), but also in a little detail like the use of the second person in addressing others, even a captain (*Autob.* 52). The *Spiritual Exercises* text bears the marks of this experience of Ignatius on his journeys, as for instance when he invites us to "imagine Christ our Lord at table with his apostles, and consider how he eats and drinks" so as to transform our meals [214]. This familiarity with the Lord and His apostles gives a value all its own to the phrase *predicando a la apostolica* (preaching in apostolic fashion), which was used to describe the pilgrim Ignatius's activity already in Salamanca *(Autob.* 64).

But Ignatius does not employ the adjective "apostolic" in his *Constitutions*. Apart from terms like "apostolic letters" or "Apostolic See," where we would gladly use the word "apostolate" or "apostolic," Ignatius employs phrases like *ayudara las a las almas* (bring profit to souls). In a letter of June 1, 1551, to Fr. Antonio Brandão, Ignatius wrote: ". . . one of the most efficient means of helping the neighbour *(que más ayudan al projimo)*—for to this the Society is very specially geared—is that of preaching" (6th point). It is, however, in the *Spiritual Diary* that we find the clear indication that the apostles were the model pilgrims for Ignatius in his spiritual experience. On February 10, 1544, he began to go over his elections with the reasons he had put down "for complete poverty" (*Diary* 12). On the following day (February 11), "I received new insights, viz., that the Son first sent his apostles to preach in poverty, and later the Holy Spirit, by granting his spirit and his gift of tongues, confirmed them. Thus, since both Father and Son sent the Holy Spirit, all three Persons confirmed such a mission" (*Diary* 15).

In his deliberation on poverty of the same year, 1544, Ignatius enumerated among his reasons for having no income whatsoever (complete poverty): "Jesus, the Lord of us all, chose this poverty for himself, and this was what he taught them, when he sent his beloved apostles and disciples to preach" (12th reason: *MI, Const.* I, 80). Normally very sparing in his use of adjectives, Ignatius makes an exception for the apostles: "beloved (*queridos*) apostles" is what we have just read in his deliberation on poverty; in the *Spiritual Exercises*, he remarks that "Christ calls his beloved *(amados)* disciples . . ." [281]; and in a letter of June 1532 to his brother Martin Garcia de Oñaz, Ignatius qualified the apostles as *elegidos* (chosen): "We revere, honor and love the chosen apostles more than we do the other saints since they served God our Lord more faithfully and loved Him more perfectly."

This singular devotion to, and preference for, the apostles—*queridos, amados, elegidos*—reaches a climax in the way Ignatius spells out in the mysteries of the life of Our Lord the contemplations of "the call of the apostles" [275] and "how the apostles were sent to preach" [281]. In the third point of this latter contemplation, Ignatius says, "He [the Lord] tells them how they should go *(el modo de ir)."* Quite remarkably we find here all the elements of apostolic journeying: the dangers along the way, the gratuity of service to be rendered on the journey, help to the sick and the proclamation of the Kingdom. If the young Society feels called to make its vocation concrete by sending Jesuits to Ethiopia, Ignatius tells its Negus or Emperor that he is sending the Patriarch and twelve other companions "out of devotion to the number which represented Christ our Lord and his twelve apostles" (Letter of February 23, 1555). This identification with the apostles has not merely to do with their qualities: during the "deliberation of the first fathers" of spring 1539, the companions drew strength from the fact that even the apostles had difficulty in reaching agreement (n. 1: *MI, Const.* I, 2).

Jerome Nadal has literally exploited this theme of the imitation of the life and the journeying of the apostles which is the Institute of the Society of Jesus. The organization of the Society, from the novitiate to final vows, the grades in the Society, but especially its aim and purpose, correspond in everything to the way and path of the apostles (*Mon. Nadal* IV, 719-720; V, 125-127). In the strict sense of the term and founded on pilgrimage, the Society of Jesus is an authentically *apostolic* order drawing on the life-giving springs that flow from the fountainhead of the Lord with his apostles.

A Jesuit: A Man on Mission

Today a Jesuit would probably hesitate to call himself a "pilgrim." While the word "apostle" is certainly used to designate a worker in the Lord's vineyard, one has often to reinforce it to make clear one's meaning by saying something like: "he is a *true* apostle." General Congregation 32 returned unambiguously to the terminology of Ignatius's *Spiritual Diary* when it declared that "a Jesuit . . . is essentially a man on mission: mission which he receives immediately from the Holy Father or from his own religious superiors, but ultimately from Christ himself, the one sent by the Father (Jn

17:18). It is by being sent on mission that a Jesuit becomes a companion of
Jesus" (Decree 2, n. 14). GC 33 only deepened our understanding of the
Jesuit as personally sent in the following of him who was sent on mission,
"that we might hear anew the call of Christ dying and rising in the anguish
and aspirations of men and women" (Decree 1, b. 28; cf. GC 32, Decree 4,
n. 14). This vision and this language coincide with those of Ignatius in the
Constitutions, particularly in their Part VII. This section describes that mission
and that being sent by the one "whom they have in the place of Christ to
direct them as the interpreter of His divine will" (*Const.* 619), "to whatsoever
place [he] thinks it expedient"; for the one sent, it will be "always to accept
his mission joyfully as something from God our Lord" (*Const.* 621). But
where are Jesuits to be sent on mission "in the vineyard of Christ our Lord,
which is so extensive" (*Const.* 622)? St. Ignatius responds: "that part of the
vineyard which has greater need, because of the lack of other workers or
because of the misery and weakness of one's fellow human beings in it and the
danger of their eternal condemnation" (*Const.* 622).

The recent general congregations only translate Ignatius's call into
modern parlance. By radically grounding the being sent on mission in the
Mystery of the Trinity, these congregations give to the apostolic journeying
of the Society of Jesus its character of insertion into the anguish and
aspirations of men and women the world over. The close solidarity of the poor
pilgrim with the poor was of unquestionable evidence to the first companions:
how, indeed, can one claim to be a companion of the Lord without sharing his
preferential love for the poor? The first companions knew well that the poor
pilgrim must become the voice of the voiceless to defend and promote justice,
and they lived accordingly. When sent on pilgrimage, they very naturally and
spontaneously got into regular and frequent contact with the marginalized, the
poor and the wretched of human society.

Suffice it to read the 1547 letter of Fr. Laínez, to which we have
referred earlier, to realize that the first companions were seized by the fact
that they were sent "for the service of the poor" (n. 35) and that they had so
much "to do with and for the poor that we were not able to prepare ourselves
for our first Masses" (n. 41). Sent to preach the good news to the poor, the
first companions never separated what was linked together in the Lord,
namely, the total and universal good of the human person, who is both soul
and body. Thus, at Ferrara, "they preached, heard confessions, and helped the

poor in the hospital" (n. 44).

Evidently the socioeconomic conditions of our day make it impossible for us to employ the same terms or language used by the documents of the early Society; since then, human history has known a Karl Marx and others. But the modern formula coined by the recent general congregations links up admirably in its depths with the original inspiration: the Jesuit companion is sent by his Lord to preach the good news. This is "the service of faith" which includes as an integral part, after the example of the same Lord, "the promotion of justice." In this way GC 32 gives a renewed thrust to the Jesuit companions of today, sending them on mission towards those paths and routes where the joys and the hopes, the griefs and the anxieties of an afflicted humanity are lived out dramatically. The long letter which Fr. John Nuñes Barreto, Patriarch of Ethiopia, received from Ignatius in 1555 demonstrates the importance given to the service of faith and the promotion of justice in Ethiopia: all this should be done gratis and for the love of Christ" (*MI, Epis.* VIII, 680-690). Thus the one sent on mission is always to bear witness of the One who sent him to those to whom he is sent, if he is to accomplish his mission.

It is clear now in what sense the Society of Jesus is a pathway—the pathway of a pilgrim who, after the example of the apostles, is sent on mission "going about the world" (*Autob.* 12, 61, 71). Precisely because it is one "way" among so many others, it is important to highlight the specific traits of this "way" as compared with other possible ways. Since this Ignatian "way" is a peculiar admixture of several elements, it happens—and it has happened in the history of the Society—that one or other specific trait of this "way" is not sufficiently preserved in all its original vigor. Hence the importance of spelling out these traits.

We must first of all say what we mean exactly by the figure of the "pilgrim." Every human being is a *homo viator*, and every Christian is a "stranger and exile in this world" (1 Pet 2:11). It is in this sense that Ignatius has Polanco write on March 26, 1554 to Antonio Enriquez, who as part of the Emperor's retinue had to travel widely, that "we must never lose sight of the fact that we are *pilgrims*" on the road to "our heavenly country" (*MI, Epis. VI,* 523). But it is not the fact of being an "exile" that is the starting point of the Ignatian "way." A whole monastic tradition consisted in voluntarily going "into exile" and, being thus "without homeland," preparing oneself for "the homeland on high." "As long as we are at home in this body we are away from the Lord's home, for we walk by faith . . ." (2 Cor. 5:6-7). So the pilgrim should ceaselessly be "going into exile" with no security and no roof over his head, for "life in this present world is a pilgrimage; our dwelling place is that which is yet to come."[3] The distinct risk of ending up along this way as tramps, vagabonds, and aimless wanderers was already perceived by Benedict. As for Ignatius, he seems to want, on his peculiar "path," to multiply movement from place to place, urging his companions to consider the entire world alone as their "home" (*orbis universus . . . habitatio . . . : Mon. Nadal* V, 773-774). The reason for such movement from place to place is not every Christian's condition of being an exile, but rather the desire to share the Lord's passionate love for those who are in the world. For the Lord prayed to his Father, not that his disciples "be taken out of the world" (Jn 17:15), but "to keep them in Your Name" (Jn. 17:11). It is precisely to "keep" those who are in the world that the pilgrim Ignatius refuses to go into exile or flee the world or walk past the world, marginal to it. The pilgrimage characteristic of Ignatius and his companions places them at the very heart of the world "to help souls."

Seemingly closer to the pilgrim Ignatius is the "wandering saint," the "missionary monk"—despite the judgment passed by history that a monk, by vocation, is not a missionary. But when in 747 Boniface wrote to the effect that "born of the English race, we come here in pilgrimage in virtue of a command of apostolic authority."[4] Could this not be, but for the mention of English extraction, an apt self-description on the part of Ignatius? We must, of course, acknowledge that Boniface stands out as a rather exceptional figure, in whom are summed up the aspects of apostolic preaching, of pilgrimage to go into exile, and especially of martyrdom. For the monk, pilgrimage and preaching both exposed him in the same way to trials and perils as to so many opportunities for "self-conversion." The peak of fulfillment of this "way" was martyrdom, the great dream of all the missionaries of the Middle Ages. Of two of them it is written that they "determined to make themselves exiles" and, while they waited to accomplish their ideal, they preached the Gospel to

---

[3] Hesychius, Migne, *PL* 93, 1081.

[4] Boniface, *Epis.* 74, Tangl. 156.

unbelievers in the hope of receiving martyrdom.[5] The typically Ignatian "way" entails being "accounted as worthless and a fool for Christ, who was first treated as such, rather than esteemed as wise and prudent in this world" (167). It does not aspire, however, to extreme asceticism and martyrdom except in the measure in which "our Lord deigns to choose him" [147] for this, in sharing His love for those who are in the world.

If a recluse cannot be at the same time a pilgrim, pilgrimage does not of itself exclude a certain degree of stability: *stabilitas in peregrinatione*. In this sense even pilgrimage gets institutionalized and becomes "a state of life," while distinguishing itself clearly from "false hermits who wander about as vagabonds."[6] Even Ignatius's accounts seem to invest pilgrims with a sort of juridical status, with the rights of "protected strangers." True, Ignatius strives very clearly not to identify himself with the "official pilgrims," and the relentless effort of his companions to associate with the poor in and around hospitals demonstrates the same preferential love for the poor. However, this tendency of monastic life towards the institutionalization or stabilization of a life of pilgrimage will only be reinforced by the spiritualization of pilgrimage in the Cistercian tradition. If *vagatio* (aimless wandering) is opposed to *quieta stabilitas* (tranquil stability), *peregrinatio* does not exclude stability: the true *peregrinatio in stabilitate,* the authentic exodus, consists in not allowing oneself to be distracted by so much going about the world, in dying to this world by breaking free from one's egoism and one's sin. Such an interiorization of the reality of pilgrimage is undeniably present in the spiritual adventure of Ignatius, but with a difference. It will never set aside or give up the concrete availability for being moved from place to place, and the motivation for such movement will not be distraction in the world but quite definitely the help to be rendered to persons in the world.

This is why it would not be right to present pilgrimage in the Ignatian sense exclusively on the spiritual level. Thus complete ignorance of the ways in which the Lord will lead us to himself and an apathetic indifference towards discovering the path God has traced for us have nothing to do with the Ignatian "way." Quite the contrary: to scrutinize and discern, like a true

---

[5] Venantius Fortunatus, *M.G.H. Auct. Ant.* IV, 2 - 4, p. 34, n. 15.

[6] *Revue Benedictine*, 1958, p. 52 ff.

pilgrim, the *Via Domini* is typically Ignatian. But such contemplation of the will of God in regard to the world and to ourselves in carrying out the salvific work of his Son is never to remain shut up in a sealed interior world, but always to open up to possible movement and displacement. "Traveling through the world" is never to be excluded. Such a pilgrim spirit necessarily entails, then, both a universal contemplation—with the gaze of the Holy Trinity (102: cf. GC 32, Decree 4, n. 14)—and an election or choice which excludes neither movement from place to place nor residence in one place, for all is to be in accord with God's will. For this reason, the Ignatian "way" has experienced, and still experiences, a passion for both inculturation *and* the international apostolate. It has known, and still knows, a profound desire to serve the Lord here and now in this particular part of his vineyard and, at the same time, to make itself available to go wherever in the world the Lord has willed to need its services. The Ignatian "way" bespeaks a dynamism which seeks to discover the Lord's designs, and which can transform this unjust world into the city of *Emmanuel,* God-with-us. If the movement of interiorization within monastic life gave rise to a paradoxical harmonization between pilgrimage and stability, the Ignatian "way" reaches this particular harmonization by keeping alive, within the clear perspective of every manner of "helping souls," the concrete need of traveling about this wide world after the example of the apostles.

The "Russian Pilgrim" and Ignatian Pilgrimage

This comparative study cannot pass over in silence the "Way of the Pilgrim"—the Russian Pilgrim.[7] He has at least this in common with Ignatius: his accounts, like the account of Ignatius in his *Autobiography,* are still being regularly published and republished. Having lost his house and his home at the age of thirty, this young Russian pilgrim enters a church one Sunday and hears there the word: "Pray without ceasing" (1 Thess 5:17). Thereupon he travels through the whole Russian territory in search of the fulfillment of this word in his life. On the way he encounters a *starets* who indicates the path by

---

[7] Father Kolvenbach refers to the celebrated (and anonymous) figure in eastern Christian spirituality, a wandering hermit or holy person—the *starets*.

communicating to him his "way," which is the *philokalia* (the love of beauty) enclosed in the Jesus Prayer. This life of journeying of the Russian pilgrim is essentially an experience of the pilgrim condition of all human beings, but lived out as a praying experience. "I was heading towards St. Innocent of Irkoutsk thinking that along the plains and through the forests of Siberia I would find more silence and so be able to give myself more easily to reading and prayer." The Russian pilgrim is spurred on by "a hunger for prayer . . . and a driving need to let it burst forth from within. . . ." Without ceasing to move and march onward on its journey, the pilgrim's body is "enraptured." "When a violently cold wave gets hold of me, I recite the [Jesus] prayer with greater attention and soon I feel warm all over. If hunger becomes too acute, I invoke more frequently the name of Jesus Christ and I forget that I was even hungry. If I feel sick, and my back or my legs ache, I concentrate on the prayer and I no longer feel the pain. My spirit has become utterly simple . . . God knows what is taking place within me." If the entire pilgrimage of this Russian is shot through with his apprenticeship in, and in-depth learning of, the Jesus Prayer, Ignatius's pilgrimage has by no means any such concentration of theme or purpose. While prescinding from Ignatius's manner of praying and even setting aside momentarily his overriding concern "to help souls"—"besides his seven hours of prayer, he busied himself helping certain souls" (*Autob.* 26)—the difference between the two pilgrims appears to lie in their characteristic experience of the Lord.

The Russian pilgrim has no apparitions of the Lord: all his experience is *in the Lord* with whom he unites himself by means of the Jesus Prayer. Ignatius, on the other hand, never ceases, all along his path, to have apparitions of the Lord who reveals himself as a *companion on the journey*. On the way to Venice the other pilgrims abandon him and, while all alone in a large field, Ignatius is much comforted by the company of Christ who appears to him *(Autob.* 41). The same happens in Jerusalem when that "belted" Christian leads him away by force to the other pilgrims: "it seemed to him that he saw Christ over him continually" *(Autob.* 48). Before arriving in Rome, when Ignatius was at prayer in a church, "he saw . . . clearly that God the Father placed him with Christ his Son" (*Autob.* 96). To live with Christ: *this* is the "way." In the last analysis there is only one way: the Russian pilgrim seems to incarnate the Pauline words: "I live, now not I, but Christ lives in me" (Gal 2:20), so that in this way he can pray without ceasing. Ignatius rather situates himself in the companionship which the Lord established when He called twelve "to be with him and to send them out to preach" (Mk 3:14). This companionship, which was confirmed at La Storta, is what Ignatius is called to continue as a way and path of life. Words are, perhaps, too weak to distinguish the paths of the two pilgrims. Yet there is a mystical "way" of union which the Russian pilgrim proposes; and there is a mystical "way" of companionship, or companionship for service on mission, which the pilgrim Ignatius has delineated, through his experience of the Exercises, in the *Constitutions* of the Society of Jesus.

PART THREE

CONTEMPLATION IN ACTION:

PRAXIS

FIFTEEN

ST. IGNATIUS'S NORMS ON SCRUPLES

During the past ten years, Jesuits and colleagues interested in Ignatian spirituality have breathed new life into sections of the *Spiritual Exercises* which had been less well known or even totally neglected. The task will not be completed, however, until we have turned our attention to the notes which Ignatius developed in order to aid us "in recognizing and understanding scruples and the suggestions of our enemy" [345-351]. The text itself is forgotten or neglected—maybe rightly. To take one example: in his outstanding translation of *Spiritual Exercises* into modern American English, Fr. David Fleming just gives up when he comes to the notes on scruples. Fr. Fleming writes that the text is so outdated that "there seemed to be less purpose in rendering them in a more contemporary style."[1]

However, Master Ignatius had himself experienced the torment of scruples at Manresa. He made no secret of it, and recounted his experience in a few simple observations which are in no way intended to provide a *treatise* on dealing with scruples in spiritual direction. It is clear from twenty or so of his surviving letters,[2] as well as from five passages in the Constitutions, that the problem of scruples continued to command his attention.

In the *Constitutions,* Master Ignatius pointed to the fact that we should always be very clear in asking what we have to ask for so that there will be no doubts and no room for scruples. What were the scruples of the Jesuit in the sixteenth century? Some examples of what scruples can be come from the problems they had with the strict poverty of the Society. The normal house of the Society had nothing like what we would call a regular income; the colleges, however (or what we might call high schools) had income (*Const.*

---

[1] David L. Fleming, S.J. The Spiritual Exercises of St. Ignatius: *A Literal Translation and a Contemporary Reading* (St. Louis, Institute of Jesuit Sources, 1978, 231; and Anand, India: Gujarat Sahitya Prakash, 1978), 275 Revised as *Draw Me into Your Friendship: A Literal Translation and a Contemporary Reading of the* Spiritual Exercises (St. Louis: Institute of Jesuit Sources, 1996.

[2] See Appended Note for references to these letters.

555-565). This was the beginning of scruples.

A professed Jesuit comes through a city and there is no other Jesuit house, only a college. Can he take a meal with the Jesuits of the college, he asks Master Ignatius in a letter, thereby taking advantage of the fixed income of the college?[3] Take one other letter: in a certain city one of the fathers is sick and he needs to walk in a garden. The professed house, which has no income, has no garden, either; the college, however, has both income and a beautiful garden. Can he go to that garden and walk a little bit?[4] These instances show that this was not a merely theoretical matter but a very practical one. To all such queries, Ignatius answers emphatically *yes*, there should be no scruple about any of this. Master Ignatius knew that these were small details; but that is exactly what the term *scruple* means.

What Is a Scruple?

What exactly is meant by the term *scruple?* The Latin word *scrupulum* is a noun indicating a tiny pebble. If a pebble gets into your shoe while you are walking, and is sharp, it can cause great pain. *Scrupulum* also came to name a tiny weight used on scales. The more sensitive the balance of a scale, the more easily it can be tipped by the tiny weight of a pebble. This sense was subsequently transposed to the level of a delicate conscience: the more delicate a conscience, the more it will be agitated by an inconsequential thought and excessively disturbed by some trifling matter. And this can cause great pain.

If we look in the libraries today, we will see that scruples have disappeared from treatises on the spiritual life. On the other hand, if we look at a dictionary on psychology or on psychotherapy, we always find scruples there. Why has our time no *religious* scruples? Well, it could be said that in our time everything is possible, everything is allowed, everything is relative, so there is no more room for scruples. Our modern conscience is not overdel-

---

[3] Letter to Luis Conçalves da Câmara, January 15, 1556, *S. Ignatii de Loyola Epistolae et Instructiones,* vol. X, 505-511. *Monumenta Ignatiana, Monumenta Historica Societatis Jesu,* vol. 39 (Rome, 1910). (Hereafter *Epp.Ign. MI* with volume number.)

[4] Letter to Giovanni Battista Viola, 10 March 1554, *EppIgnMI* VI, 447-450.

icate. But it has to be noted that an overdelicate conscience is not itself an adequate explanation for scruples. We can discover this fact in the spirituality of the first monks of the desert. When we read St. Anthony, St. Macarius or St. Pachomius, we see that all these monks certainly had a very delicate conscience; yet they did not have scruples. Why? Probably it was because they were very open with the spiritual guide or the spiritual father they had. They told him everything, and if everything is open, there is no space for scruples. In light of all this, the first question we must ask is whether we should still speak about scruples. Or should we just forget these two pages of *Spiritual Exercises?*

Scruples, Grace, and Neurosis

A case of scruples exemplifies how the healthy sense of sin, nourished by the meditations of the First Week of the Exercises, can degenerate into an unhealthy sense of guilt, a morbid preoccupation with sin, a pathology. Scruples are one among a variety of pathological symptoms such as phobias, morbid anxieties, and obsessional neuroses. But does this mean that we should simply refer all scrupulous persons to psychotherapists and ignore the counsels of St. Ignatius, who was unaware of the discoveries of depth psychology?

Master Ignatius, we know, could not draw upon Freudian insights; but we should also realize that he had no need to do so. St. Ignatius's observations concern only a particular category of scrupulous persons: those who suffer from scruples "for a certain length of time," and indeed those who "are giving themselves to spiritual exercises." [348] Even among those making the Exercises, in the view of the earliest commentators on the Spiritual Exercises, not all would be tormented by scruples; so there was no need to explain the rules to everyone.[5] In this context, the phenomenon being considered is occasional and transitory.

Two letters of Francisco de Vitoria written while Ignatius was alive

---

[5] *Exercitia Spiritualia S. Ignatii de Loyola et Eorum Directoria, nova editio. Monumenta Historica Societatis Iesu,* vol. 75 (Roma, 1955), 326, 457-458, 743.

(November 13, 1526, and August 12, 1546) indicate that the spiritual fathers of that period were quite capable of distinguishing between scrupulosity which "is of no slight benefit" [348] and a permanent morbid scrupulosity which leads to madness, wears down the patience of any spiritual director, and indeed produces no benefit whatever.[6] The latter class of persons, in a permanent pathological state, if they are to be cured, must be referred to a specialist equipped to get at the emotional roots of their scruples. Even in cases such as these, however, a spiritual director—while not encroaching on the terrain of the medical specialist—can and should assist the one suffering from genuine scruples in his constant doubt, his perpetual uncertainty, in the fear and remorse from which nothing, it seems, will ever be able to free him. This labor of accompaniment, which to a spiritual director seems at first glance so vexatious and so useless, is an opportunity to fulfill the Lord's words: "I was sick and you visited me" (Matt. 25:36).[7]

The Spiritual Problem

The distinction between a situational crisis of scruples and a scrupulous condition that is pathological raises the difficult question of the source and cause of scruples. On this subject Master Ignatius had definite ideas: "A person in desolation should consider how the Lord has left him to his natural powers in order to test him, so that he will resist the various agitations and temptations of the enemy; for he can do so with God's help, even if he does not clearly feel this" [320]. We may not say that God is the cause of the person's scrupulous state; rather, that God *allows* it, "in order greatly to purify and cleanse the soul" [348]. Ignatius's mode of expression is somewhat unfortunate in the sense that it conveys the impression of an abandonment by God, but the context makes it quite clear that the person will never be without "strength in our Creator and Lord" to resist the enemy and "obtain eternal life" [324, 320].

---

[6] Cf. Santiago Arzubialde, *Ejercicios Espirituales de S. Ignacio* (Bilbao: Mensajero and Sal Terrae, 1991), 791.

[7] Cf. J.-F. Catalan, *Dictionnaire de Spiritualité,* s.v. *scrupule.*

Still, when God withdraws "his great fervor, his strong love, and his intense grace" [320] from us, this is a serious loss for us. In the case of scruples, moreover, we are faced not simply with the absence of a good, of a consolation, but with the power of an obsession capable of plunging us into despair or even of provoking the desire to commit suicide, as it did in Ignatius at Manresa. Even more serious and painful is the fact noted by Ignatius that scrupulosity afflicts a conscience that is already meticulous: "If it is delicate, the enemy strives to push it to the extreme of delicacy, the more to trouble and undo it" [439]. In modern terms, this means that a permissive, loose, and dissolute moral conscience will be shielded from the torture of scruples, while a person striving "to go forward in the spiritual life" [350], instead of receiving in his exertions consolation from God, will be tried by obsessive worries, anxieties, and phobias.

If the Lord is accustomed to treat in this seemingly quite unfair manner persons who love him and seek him, then we can join the great St. Teresa in not being surprised that so few people serve him. However, we need to ask ourselves whether we have correctly read and understood what Master Ignatius says. Is it true that God gives free rein—even though it may doubtless be for our good—to Satan, the enemy of human nature, the tempter who attacks us "from outside" [351]?

Saint Ignatius's Struggle with Scruples

Since what Ignatius wishes to impart to us through these general remarks is his own lived experience, let us go back to that section in the *Autobiography* where he recounts his crisis of scruples to see whether we can find greater clarity on this difficult question of their cause.

From March 25, 1522, to February 17, 1523, Ignatius stayed in a little Catalonian town called Manresa. He was then about thirty, recently converted at Loyola after having been wounded in the leg at the siege of Pamplona. His state of soul corresponded exactly to the description in the fourth note on scruples: "a soul [that] does not allow within itself any mortal sin, venial sin, or appearance of deliberate sin" [349]. This is therefore a saint, a perfect man who "in order to be agreeable to God and to please him" (*Autob.* 14), aspired to outdo the saints in heroic exploits. Then came an attack of scruples, which

Ignatius described for us in order to help us avoid the destructive aberrations which can quite easily beset us when we have an intense experience of the First and Second Weeks.

The First Week

Let us begin with the First Week. A specialist in psychology has rightly remarked that it is the paradox of Christianity that, in the very process of presenting liberation from sin, it renders the sense of sin more acute. When the xercises of the First Week propose that I consider, with sorrow and shame, the foulness of my actions, and when they stress death, judgment, and hell as the consequences of sin, they are disposing us to develop a "crushed and broken heart" (Ps. 51:19); but they also expose us to the danger of a morbid sense of guilt, an obsessional neurosis.[8]

In his own experience, Ignatius's advice to "call to my memory all the sins of my life, examining them from year to year" [56], was turned into an attack against himself. While he was at Manresa he went to confession every Sunday, but "in doing so he came to be much troubled by scruples" (*Autob.* 22). Even though his general confession at Montserrat had been made "with great care and entirely written out," Ignatius still felt that he was not living in the truth and that an unacknowledged sin was at the root of his living a lie. He considered himself more and more as "a wound and a sore from which issued so many sins and evil deeds" [58].

He began seeking spiritual directors to help rid him of his scrupulosity. He finally found an ideal spiritual father: a confessor, doctor, preacher in the cathedral, a deeply spiritual man. The latter ordered him to write down whatever he could remember. "And after he made his confession the scruples kept recurring, the matters becoming increasingly more minute, so that he found himself in great distress" (*Autob.* 22). Ignatius thus shows us the inability of even the best of confessors to cure scrupulosity. Yet Ignatius himself was partly responsible for the confessor's failure: he lacked courage to suggest that his spiritual father command him not to go back over the past

---

[8] Cf. A. Vergote, *Dette et désir*, 1978, 64.

or the details of the present.

The aim of the scruples became apparent: to lead Ignatius to extreme disgust, to suicide, or at least to the point where he would have to renounce a style of life which had come to a dead end and no longer had any meaning. This dramatic turn of events left Ignatius in a morbid universe of sin. He declared himself culpable of trifles; he examined and accused himself incessantly. Nothing helped; Ignatius was constantly guilty of something more, something else, that he had been unable to confess.

The Prison of Narcissism. He was the prisoner, not of a God ever ready to condemn and to damn, but of himself. His was a narcissistic posture evident to a linguist in the grammatically reflexive expressions he used to depict his state: telling himself, analyzing himself, accusing himself, examining himself. Psychoanalysts know that scrupulous persons can cling to their condition with a secret complacency. Through a refusal of effort—both wishing and not wishing for a real cure—a sort of strange complicity holds the person fast in an unhealthy sense of guilt.

It is important to say here that the scrupulous person must be brought to the realization that an accurate account of sins will never do. Rather, one must confess one's *truth,* which is a different matter altogether. The scrupulous have to be content with a global admission of their own failures, leaving further judgment to the Lord. There is no savior but Jesus and all other crutches should either be thrown away as false gods—or else accepted as temporary gifts from God's kind hands. When the scrupulous finally believe that their guilt is perfectly known—known by One who still loves them anyway and demands no account whatsoever—the compulsive need to keep telling their sins will disappear.

The Way to Peace. To escape the prison of his scruples and escape from himself, Ignatius, enriched by his own painful experience, proposed a colloquy of mercy" [61]. It begins here:

> In the case of an unhealthy feeling of guilt, one is faced with a debt which can never be paid because it is unlimited and undefinable. The repentant sinner comes to realize that for him "this debt is not payable" precisely because what he has received from the One who

pardons him is the gift of a *gratuitous* love, a love which can be responded to only with an equally disinterested love, the gift of his entire self in thanksgiving.[9]

I must go out of myself radically in order "to converse with God our Lord and thank him for granting me life until now, and to propose, with God's grace, amendment for the future" [61]. Actively to accept life—my life—is to experience salvation from a fundamental despair, together with the grace of seeing open up before me a future in which the memories of a painful or inglorious past, old emotional wounds and traumas long repressed in the unconscious,[10] will no longer trouble the psyche, thanks to a reconciliation with self brought about by this heartfelt faith in God's mercy—"so as to arrive at complete peace" [350].

The first purpose of the notes on scruples, then, is to say that things can go wrong in the First Week and we can feel too guilty. They give us to understand that even if we feel like the most guilty person in the world, we will never, in any way, be able to pay for this guilt because the Lord forgives, and forgives without any limit or any reserve.

The Second Week

Scrupulosity, therefore, revealed to Master Ignatius the aberrations that were possible in the First Week, but not only then. His tormented experience at Manresa is relevant to the Second Week also. Faithful to the call of Christ our Lord, "eternal King and universal Lord," Ignatius longed most of all to give his heart to this call ever more completely and "to distinguish himself in total service" [95, 97]. At Manresa Ignatius began his new life with a desire to outdo the heroic exploits of the saints. These exploits were for him the point of reference for his own stance before God.

---

[9] F. Catalan, *Expérience spirituelle et psychologies* (Paris: Desclée de Brouwer, 1991), 91.

[10] Catalan, "The Healing of Memories," *Expérience spirituelle*, 100.

See the self being seen. Ignatius presents a certain image of himself in this regard, as one being seen. This comes back many times in the *Spiritual Exercises*, it may be noted: to be seen like a little servant at the Nativity, to be seen also as a knight who is guilty, and so on. There had of course been a true upheaval in his existence: the worldly man was changed into an ascetic, his elegant courtier's attire was exchanged for the rough garb of a beggar, his sensational military feats became scourgings and mortifications. Yet he was still concerned with exploits, with signalizing himself in order to be seen. But by whom did he desire to be seen? Was it "Christ our Lord, the eternal king"? Or was it after all still by his own eyes, in his own self-beholding?

He saw himself being seen in a narcissistic experience in which, no matter whose the eyes are before which one wishes to signalize oneself, they are never really the eyes of the other, for in them and in their beholding one still sees oneself as being seen. On his sickbed at Loyola Ignatius was already picturing the feats he might perform in the future (*Autob.* 7). In these imaginings Ignatius remained centered upon himself. At Manresa this heroic identification with idealistic models actually impelled him to go beyond them. His abstinence in matters of food surpassed in rigor what St. Francis had prescribed in his rule (*Autob.* 14, 19). There is an element here of putting on a performance: Ignatius makes a show of himself; he not only beholds himself but does so on the basis of others' real or imagined beholding of him. In this realm of fantasy, the desire to be perfect becomes an obsession—to be even more perfect than the heroic models of his reveries.

Radical perfectionism. But this kind of determination is at the mercy of the power which, "if a conscience is delicate, strives to push it to the extreme of delicacy, the more to trouble and undo it" [349], to the point where it ends in a complete rejection of whatever in the person is not perfect, a denial of all that fails to correspond to the ideal image he has made for himself, a desire—probably unconscious—of becoming purely spiritual.

Ignatius does not go into details on this crisis of scrupulosity, which locks him into a diabolic cycle of obligations and constraints where one "imagines a sin where there is no sin, for example in some trifling word or thought" [349]. It is not at all surprising that Ignatius then experienced "certain feelings of disgust for the life he was leading, as well as impulses to give it up" (*Autob.* 25). According to the testimony of Diego Laínez, Ignatius heard himself saying in his weakness and exhaustion, "You wretch! Are you going to go on for fifty years living like this?"[11] But since in his perfectionism (or "perfection-itis") he was morbidly and obsessively captive of his determination to be perfect, the only way out of this neurotic state seemed to be suicide: "He had many extremely vehement temptations to throw himself into a deep hole in his room near the spot where he prayed" (*Autob.* 24).

The Gift of Spiritual Freedom

"Thereupon the Lord willed that he should awake as from a dream. . . . And from that day onward he was free of the scruples, with certainty that our Lord had willed to deliver him through his mercy" (*Autob.* 26). He awoke as from a dream: he thus recognized that this entire obsession stemmed from an imaginary power which had attempted to keep him enslaved. His scruples had been so many manifestations of the spirit of lies, the work of the one who was a liar from the beginning. From now on Ignatius strove to place himself in the Truth, where "God treated him just as a schoolmaster does a child, instructing him" (*Autob.* 27). He experienced himself as a new man, no longer tortured by the idols which his models of holiness had become but guided by the heart of a God who wished to save and heal him and who was disposing him to "aid souls."[12]

False mirror of perfectionitis. The scruples had tried to close Ignatius in upon himself, standing before a beautiful mirror in which he could contemplate his own perfection under the fatal aspect of a perfection without fault and without fail. Delivered from scruples, Ignatius began a movement towards him who is Son of the invisible Father and who invites persons to follow him on paths which he has chosen and which are not always our own. The model of holiness is just *a way,* and *The Way* is Jesus Christ.

This step reverses every detail of Ignatius's style of life. No more

---

[11] Diego Laínez, letter of 16 June 1547, *Fontes Narrativi I, Monumenta Historica Societatis Jesu* vol. 66 (Roma, 1943), 78.

[12] This well known expression of St. Ignatius appears in the letter of Diego Laínez of 16 June 1547, just cited, 84: *ayudar . . . almas.*

predetermined projects, no more static models of perfection, no more turning in upon himself, no more trying to achieve spiritual success through his own efforts; rather, simply, "to be with the Son," a commitment to follow him towards a still-unknown future, even while aware of his own hopes and weaknesses. What do his inevitable shortcomings matter now? What is the point of using a magnifying glass to detect the slightest fault, as the father of lies had tried to make him do through his scruples? Letting go of all morbid and destructive narcissism, all backward-looking and guilt-inducing self-reflection, Ignatius lets himself be drawn forward by Christ: the path of the pilgrim is the path of Christ.

The Continuing Pertinence
of the Ignatian Norms

When he described for us his own spiritual experience of scruples, Ignatius clearly could not use the data of modern psychology and psychoanalysis. Today we have concepts available such as superego, moral conscience, neurosis, obsession, psychotherapy, and countless others to describe and treat a crisis of scrupulosity. Ignatius remains within the bounds of what he himself experienced spiritually at Manresa, as seen in the light of the temptation of Adam, a temptation of all times and of every human creature.

Two different cases. The tempter will not assail someone whose moral conscience is already far from God the Creator and Savior. Why tempt such a person to become like God or to despair of God when "his law is the satisfaction of his lusts"?[13] A person who longs to live for God, on the other hand, will be tempted to close in upon himself, and this to an extreme, in a sense of guilt that leads to despair. Under the influence of scruples, that person will believe that it is impossible that he has not sinned [349]. Or else it will take the infernal form, again carried to extremes, of closing oneself up in an utter inability to continue in God's service, because this is based on a compulsive model of perfection where the ego has chosen "self" as the image

---

[13] See the *Rule* of St. Benedict ch.1 no.8; cf. the *Spiritual Exercises* [349].

which the individual has made for its God.

Despair nourished by scrupulosity is capable of leading to suicide—as in Ignatius's own experience—but it can also lead to a colloquy of divine mercy, and to a colloquy in which there is no longer any desire except to follow Christ, not in accord with one's own will but entirely as God wills. If scruples can "greatly purify and cleanse the soul" [348], it is precisely in order to keep us from trying to make "God come where [we] desire" instead of abandoning everything, including ourselves and our own ideals of perfection, "in order to go where God is" [154].

In his account of the events at Manresa, Ignatius makes it clear that it was God who deigned to bring him out of the diabolical realm of his scruples. He records the exceptional qualities of his confessors, he repeats how he strictly bound himself to a planned program of prayers and mortifications (*Autob.* 21-25, esp. *perseverar*, 27), inspired by the model of monasticism. In the end he had to cry out, "Help me, Lord, for I find no remedy in men nor in any creature" (*Autob.* 23). Abruptly and unexpectedly [330: "consolation without previous cause"], the Lord suddenly intervened and awoke him as from a dream. God had now seized the initiative, and Ignatius began discernment in order to know God's choices in all things. As he went back over this experience, Ignatius formulated a further remark which it would be dangerous to take out of context.

Correctly naming the extremes. According to this remark, to live in the Spirit is for Ignatius to progress, to go forward—and not just for a time but *always* [350]. The direction to be followed can be clearly known, thanks to the fact that it will always be the opposite of that taken by the enemy. In Ignatius's own language, a coarse soul needs to become delicate. Yet Master Ignatius does not say that an overly delicate soul needs to become coarse. The opposite of excessive delicacy is "a correct mean" [350].

The two extremes to be avoided are thus a conscience that is without God or awareness of sin and a conscience which sets itself up, by its exaggerated delicacy, as lord and master of what is good and evil, eventually reaching the point where, in sheer despair, it turns into evil what is actually good. The goal should be that the conscience "establish itself firmly in a correct mean and thus arrive at complete peace" [350]. Here is not the place for the *agere contra* of the call of the temporal king—for doing battle against whatever in a person might be all too human, with the simultaneous risk of battling against what is simply human [cf. 97]. At least in the context of scruples, Ignatius was in no sense an advocate of such an inhuman battle. He was aware—without being able to give it its Freudian name—of the many drives that characterize human nature. To serve the Lord as he wishes to be served means, among other things, to make good use of all the tendencies, all the dynamisms of the human psychic constitution without repressing them.

Peace and the Proper Mean. How can one mobilize all of these drives so as to respond freely to the Lord's call? To give free rein to the drives of unrestrained or of excessive perfection would be to play into the enemy's hands. Knowing how to manage the drives in such a way that they leave us—positively or negatively—open to the call of God as he wishes to be served by us is something that supposes "peace in a proper mean" [350].

When Master Ignatius in the *Spiritual Exercises* speaks of peace, he often couples it with war, as in the contemplation on the Incarnation: "some at peace and others at war" [106]. To understand the meaning of peace in our context we must turn to the first prelude of the meditation on the "Three Classes of Persons." There we find persons who have acquired a fortune and are so attached to it that it has become a weight and a hindrance in serving the Lord, since no one can serve two masters [150; cf. 143]. In order to have peace, the person must get rid of the burden and hindrance constituted by this attachment, whether he keeps the thing itself or gets rid of it, whichever should be God's will [150, 155].

In this context, the *proper mean* is not some sort of compromise or state of tranquillity; it is to refrain from inclining in one direction or the other and to keep poised in the middle like the needle of a balance, allowing "the creator to deal immediately with the creature and the creature with the creator" [15]. Ignatius explicitly defines "being in the middle" as being "like the pointer of a balance, in order to be ready to follow that which I shall perceive to be more to the glory and praise of God and the salvation of my soul" [179].

Reaching the proper mean in this sense does not at all signify that I have obtained what I seek; hence this peace is not something to be sought as an end in itself. The proper mean will rather be the disposition which allows God to let me "perceive" *(sentir)* how he wishes to be served [179]. Thus, beginning at Manresa, it was on the basis of this proper mean that Ignatius decided when to sleep, what to eat, how to dress, and so on (*Autob.* 26 ff.).

Conclusion: The Divine Use of Authority

The road leading to escape from and healing of the narcissism in a crisis of scruples proceeds by way of recourse to the Other who is God, along with seeking the help of those others who are associated with God, such as confessors or spiritual directors. In a final remark Ignatius reminds us that the other can also be ecclesiastical or religious authority in one of its many forms. The voice of the Church or of a superior can deliver the scrupulous person from the burden of scruples.

At Manresa Ignatius realized that this deliverance was available, but he lacked the courage to pursue it. He wrote, "Sometimes he thought it would cure him if his confessor ordered him in the name of Jesus Christ not to confess anything of the past; he wanted his confessor to order him thus, but he did not dare say this to his confessor" (*Autob,* 22). This trust in the mercy of the Absolutely Other, and in the authority imparted by him to other persons, is the sole path of deliverance for the scrupulous person.[14]

It is therefore not surprising that the tempter exerts here his perverse and disorienting influence through our sensitive faculties by way of affective disturbances. After a person has been called to ecclesial service—a situation that appears often in Master Ignatius's letters—it is quite possible that the effect of the First Week, wrongly understood, will make itself felt in his abandoning this service out of a conviction of his unworthiness. Likewise, the

---

[14] Ignatius offered this remedy for scruples to one of the early Jesuits:
"So there, Master Marin, make up your mind to keep these two points fixed in your memory: (1) not to make any judgment, or determine by yourself that something is sinful when it is not clearly evident that it is and others do not think so; (2) when you fear that there is sin, you should refer the matter to the judgment of your superior . . . and believe what he says . . . who holds the place of Christ our Lord . . . . [H]umble yourself and trust that Divine Providence will rule and guide you by means of your superior. And believe me, if you have true humility and submissiveness, your scruples will not cause you so much trouble. A kind of pride is the fuel they feed on, and it is pride which places more reliance on one's own judgment and less on the judgment of others whom we trust." Letter to Fr. Valentine Marin, 24 June 1556. *Epp.Ig. MI* XII, 30-31. Cited from *Letters of St. Ignatius of Loyola,* selected and tr. William J. Young, S.J. (Chicago: Loyola University Press, 1959), 430-31.

effect of the Second Week wrongly understood can paralyze a person for greater service of the Church, when, for instance, success or prestige are equated with vainglory. In many letters to Ignatius, a bishop or even a superior writes that he has scruples being a bishop or a superior because he is not worthy and how can he go on in this way? Yet another extreme: a person is no longer willing to give a homily because he cannot live out to the letter the holiness he preaches.

In these situations, it is service to others in the name of the Other who is the Eternal King which must be the criterion for the greater glory of God. Ignatius here draws upon St. Bernard, about whom he had read a story in the *Flos Sanctorum.* Bernard was preparing to preach a sermon. The tempter suggested to him that, as he would preach magnificently and be sure to win honor and esteem, would it not be vainglory that Bernard was pursuing under the pretext of the greater glory of God? Bernard realized that the Lord wished to make use of his brilliant preaching ability, and he routed his diabolical adversary with the terse reply: "I did not begin because of you and I will not desist because of you" [351].

SIXTEEN

SOCIAL JUSTICE AND THE SPIRITUAL EXERCISES OF IGNATIUS LOYOLA

"We deeply feel the anguish of persons who, despite their continual striving, cannot escape the growing poverty traps of our country," the Canadian bishops declared a few years ago. "We proclaim the Gospel message that exalts the lowly and fills the hungry with good things." Interventions like these, especially by conferences of bishops, occur quite regularly in many countries. To proclaim the Gospel includes the duty to denounce practices of injustice and discrimination that clearly contravene the values of the Gospel. So we have the Church everywhere making declarations on situations of misery and poverty, on the market economy and neo-liberalism, on unemployment and immigration, on the environment and the need for peace. These positions provoke reactions. The episcopal statements rarely offer practical solutions; they appeal to conscience but cannot, on the basis of the Gospel, resolve the concrete technical problems involved.

It is therefore easy to dismiss the statements as unrealistic or utopian and criticize the bishops for exceeding their competence. Still the churches are convinced that appropriate governmental or political bodies, banks or corporations, science or technology, are capable of finding solutions to the ills of society. Missing is the will to become aware and act in solidarity with a suffering humanity. By default and as humanity's conscience, the churches have the moral obligation to intervene in the name of our Creator and Savior.

Surely we must be committed to the poor. But social activism is a consequence of religious faith, not a substitute for it. Nor does talk about the preferential option help the poor one bit, not without more professional knowledge and skills than most priests or religious possess.

A different reaction comes from within the churches themselves. Since their primary responsibility is to promote a spiritual, supernatural salvation that is not of this world, do the churches not stray beyond their true vocation when showing interest in worldly social problems? Should we not be wary of any such socio-political involvement? Does the Church not unwittingly shift her sphere of activity from heaven, because interest for the things of heaven is diminishing? As if the only way to catch the media's attention and reach people is to focus on the dramatic sufferings of refugees and the marginalized and their struggles for justice. But does a focus on such issues not risk denying the true mission of the Church which, while present in the world, is neither merely nor finally of this world?

Justice and Faith

Here we touch the heart of the question: is the social dimension essential to our faith, an integral element of it, or simply additional, optional and, in fact, superfluous? The prayer we most often say together seems to orient us above all towards a Father who dwells in heaven and to urge that his name be glorified, that his kingdom come, and that his will be done on earth as surely as it is fulfilled in heaven. In this marvelous prayer, Jesus teaches us how to pray personally as a son and daughter appealing to their father. The Good News is above all the revelation of this filial relationship with a God who reveals himself through his own son Jesus as Father, our Father. Seek first the kingdom of God and all the rest will follow. Is this not why Jesus—doubtless always surrounded by the poor, and the suffering—finally seems to speak out less than the prophets and without their typical Old Testament stridency on the social issues of his time? Yet the spirituality of Jesus is always incarnate: it is really in this concrete humanity that Jesus desires the hallowing of God's name, it is really among us that his kingdom should arrive, and it is really in the reality of our world that the vision of God for the good of our world might come true. It is our desire too that a happier history, which from the beginning God has always willed to write among us, be written.

In revelation, God himself has unveiled a project to be realized in close alliance with us on earth, as it is in heaven. The history of revelation we read in the Bible speaks of nothing if not the total and tireless fidelity of God to humanity in its world, even when humanity proves unfaithful. For a better world God struggles for us and with us and even, when necessary, against us to the point that, in his Son, he allows himself to be overcome, for his great love is without end. In Jesus, he becomes more than ever Emmanuel, God with us. Impossible therefore to separate what in all freedom God has united, while respecting the autonomy of humanity and of our world which still exist only in dependence on their Creator and Savior. Precisely because humanity has been entrusted with responsibility for the world and for the effective management of its history, men and women, with their capacity to deviate and repudiate God's vision of the world, have unfortunately taken advantage of it, but never to the point of destroying the covenant with the Creator and Savior who takes every occasion and makes every gesture to continue loving us, our world and our history.

In this unrelenting fidelity, the believer discovers why there is no right to become disinterested or take distance from this world so strongly marked by sin, or to take refuge in a disincarnate spirituality and to flee from the world under the pretext of pursuing a higher, purer spirituality. For the link with the world made by the hand of God is a constitutive dimension of every believer's profession of faith in God as our Father, Creator and Savior. In this vision of faith Ignatius encourages us to find God in everything: in all things and not in spite of all earthly things as if these were unfortunately unavoidable obstacles which would prevent us from seeking and finding God; in all things and not solely with their help, as if the world were purely transitory and, once having lifted us up to a celestial orbit, exhausted of meaning. Even when taking seriously the discouraging bad news that the papers and television convey, if we talk positively and optimistically about our world—and rightly so—this is because God in his fidelity never ceases to love this world wherein he can be sought and be found.

Social Involvement

But does God's covenant with people justify the Church's social and political involvement, the social action of the clergy, the strident positions of Christian groups, the demonstrations to defend human rights and the vigorous protests against injustices? Has Jesus inducted us into concerted action against misery and discrimination? Did he not die on a cross? How can we gaze at the Crucified One on our walls—very much the sign of impotence and resignation in the face of injustice—and still believe in the struggle for justice? Does faith extolling a Lamb crushed on earth and now upright in heaven allow us to believe in victory over injustice in this world, or does not faith rather gently insist that final victory will occur not in the world but beyond?

By taking on the human condition in all things, Jesus also assumed the political conflicts and social injustices of his milieu. Recently the press caused something of a sensation by suggesting that Jesus belonged not to the poor stratum of society but rather to the middle class: a craftsman, he was well enough connected to possibly be a rabbi, and his rich friends gladly invited him to dine at home. At that time, belonging to the middle class meant a certain well-being, though of course exposed to the many common vicissitudes. All the more remarkable then that Jesus, though belonging to this class, unambiguously took up the cause of all those who suffer. We must never forget that material well-being was commonly considered a divine blessing, the reward for a holy and righteous life, while upon every misfortune hung the question: has this one sinned, or was it his parents? In word and deed Jesus takes his place in the line of the prophets and, without hesitation, claims straightaway that their words are now being fulfilled in himself. Thus his proclamation in favor of the poor and the oppressed, the widows and the orphans, the marginalized and the sick, even if coming to their aid means decrying the law in force. More important still, Jesus pursues the prophetic vein in condemning as scandalous any invocation of the Divine Name or worship used as a pretext for refusing justice or violating minimal human rights. Jesus does not behave like an agitator or revolutionary but, defending the vision of his Father for the salvation of the world, he does not hesitate to challenge the religious establishment and the political power. In his indictments we do not sense the visceral reactions of someone angry at an unjust society, but instead we see expression of his ardent love for his Father and of a just vision for a more just world. Comparing his maledictions with the denunciations of the prophets, the accent seems less radically on overturning structures. Jesus takes straight aim at injustice but, having come to save the unjust, he also aims at the conversion of their hearts.

There is something disconcerting, we must admit, in this image of Jesus. Though nothing of the social agitator, even to this day his Sermon on the Mount calls our best intentions into question; containing nothing of political revolution, nevertheless his Good News would turn the Roman Empire upside down and so too many others. Jesus does not even give the impression of wanting to reform Palestine pacifically or to re-organize the Chosen People socially and politically. Above all, he is neither an ideologue nor a utopian in an area which perforce has produced many.

Ideology, Faith and Justice

In our century, the strongest social ideology has been the Marxist-Leninist one which, far from dead, still finds fertile ground in the grinding injustice of so many poverty-ridden countries. This ideology wedges itself between the two halves of the Great Commandment: in the name of justice for the poor, it advocates the rejection of God. We ourselves have seen how ideology serves to invigorate social action and make it dynamic, especially by reducing the many complexities and complications of social reality into sweeping judgments and ringing slogans. The same temptation exists in Christian contexts, for the effort to consider reality in all its aspects with so many possible pluses and minuses, threatens to weaken or paralyze social action. "Ideology," according to one author, is a triple exemption or dispensation: from the intellectual, from the practical, and from the moral.

Ideology is an *intellectual* exemption as it retains only those facts which support its key ideas: for example, limiting poverty to the socio-economic field as if we lived by daily bread alone, or of seeing everything in terms of class struggle alone as if no other conflict existed than those of poor against rich, while overlooking the oppression done to women, to native people, to people of color, or to immigrants. Ideology also dispenses from the *practical* by paying attention only to success, registering every success, systematically ignoring any failure, and thus giving a totally false picture of the circumstances it claims to uphold. And ideology is finally *moral* exemption whereby the end justifies all the means, and hatred becomes indispensable for the social transformation of the world. A country without hatred, they would say, is unworthy of its independence. In the eyes of every ideology, Jesus' social message seems weak and indecisive, but the Gospel which embraces the whole reality of earth and of heaven, of poor and of rich, rejects the triple dispensation of ideology.

How is the Gospel anti-ideological, according to this view? The Gospel holds out no *intellectual* exemption, even at the risk of weakening a radical involvement on behalf of the poor. Jesus is not afraid (because this is the whole truth) of presenting the paradox of poverty: poverty as a non-value to be eliminated at all costs and, all the same, poverty as a value essential for living the kingdom of his Father. The beatitudes encompass all reality: blessed are those who struggle for justice and even suffer martyrdom in order to destroy all injustice which is the source of misery and poverty in the world. However, this has to be done with the heart of the poor: if not, the oppressed will become oppressors. An ideologue does not accept this paradox but sees poverty as the only real affliction and reduces the struggle to a total eradication of misery. The ideologue would claim that since this misery is all-urgent, now is not the time to quibble or get lost in fine points. Yet experience shows that, in such an approach, the formerly poor and oppressed risk becoming neo-powerful oppressors who in turn commit new injustices.

The examples are many and disappointing, for the histories of the Soviet Union or a Central American republic are unfortunately eloquent in this regard. The Gospel declaring "blessed are the poor" can be used ideologically to legitimize the structural injustices that produce the Lazaruses of this world only by conveniently forgetting that the Gospel, which aims at all truth, does not bless the poor without equally blessing those who struggle for that justice of which Lazarus should be the first beneficiary. Conversely, if the Kingdom in our time is exclusively and so ideologically identified with the mere struggle for justice while forgetting that the Lord Jesus also blesses poverty, we risk ending up with a new totalitarianism and missing out on the kingdom of God where, thanks to the poor of heart, the Lord is served as he desires in the poor and the starving, in the sick and the imprisoned. Instead of opting ideologically either for spiritual poverty without a concrete struggle for justice, or for the contemporary struggle for justice pursued without a poor and disinterested heart, Jesus dares to bless equally both the struggle for justice which strives to eliminate the insulting penury of the poorest and the poor of heart who, without self-interest, truly serve others. In the ideological or political order, those two beatitudes appear incompatible, but in Jesus both are essential for the kingdom of God. A struggle for justice, an engagement for the poor, is senseless without a poor and disinterested heart. That is why the poor are blessed, not at all because of their poverty and misery, but because those who follow Christ will struggle for them with a poor and disinterested heart of Christ.

Having touched on the intellectual, gospel values allow no *practical* dispensation either. Ideology recognizes only success, but Jesus speaks of persecution, for he knows what human beings are made of. Nearly fifty years ago, my predecessor Father Jean-Baptiste Janssens articulated this fundamental minimum: our Jesuit social praxis should "aim at procuring for as many . . . as possible or rather, in so far as conditions permit, for all . . . an abundance of both temporal and spiritual goods even in the natural order, or at least that sufficiency which man of his very nature needs so that he may not feel depressed or looked down upon." This is justice, justice among people: to give and ensure what each one as a human person should have.

Is Justice Enough?

No doubt our contemporary world has awakened to a sense of justice. But does justice by itself suffice in practice? Experience through the ages leads to the summary conclusion that any right pushed to the nth degree becomes the peak of injustice: *summum jus, summa injuria.* Pope John Paul II has written: "It is clear that sometimes, in the name of presumed justice, a neighbor is annihilated, killed, deprived of freedom, stripped of the most basic human rights." An ideologue may be content with justice sufficient to itself, but John Paul II retorts: "Past experience and our own times show that justice is not sufficient to itself and can even lead to its own negation and its own ruin, if one does not allow that deeper force which is love to shape human life in its various dimensions." The Good Samaritan powerfully illustrates the insufficiency of justice alone. The story, about someone "outside the law," begins with a priest and a levite who do observe the law. The two are journeying toward Jerusalem, and were they to touch a half-dead body, they would become legally unfit to perform their liturgical duties according to the law. Jesus does not condemn the two clerics; they are simply doing what the law requires. But he does point out that it is the Samaritan, this "outlaw," who has grasped the heart of the law. Jesus confronts us with the fact that fulfilling the justice of the law may be perfectly correct but also cruelly insufficient. This is what Father Arrupe once wrote:

No, justice is not enough: the world needs a more powerful remedy,
a better witness and more effective works, the witness and works of

charity. When we read the headlines in the newspapers and reflect a
little on what might be the real cause for such abysmal levels in
human relations—in family, government, labor, the economy or
personal relations—it becomes obvious that answers in terms of
justice and injustice are inadequate. Never have we talked so much
about justice, and never has contempt for it been so flagrant.

Jesus does not dispense humanity, pervaded by egocentrism and self-
interest, by violence, and by hatred, from responsibility for effective action,
for real praxis. Faced with the need for a remedy to every inhuman situation,
Jesus profers no other form of response than a disinterested élan which goes
out in compassion and sharing, an élan by which we believe in the love which
God has for us, an *élan* which we recognize in many of our brothers and
sisters. Such love neither seeks suffering and the cross nor recoils from giving
one's life so that others may live. While the masters of suspicion push our
contemporaries to take up with Karl Marx, to revolt with Nietzsche, or to
pursue self-knowledge with Freud, Jesus encourages us to give ourselves in
the practice of Christian life so that the world may be more just and discover
true life to the full.

There is dispensation neither from the intellectual nor from the practical,
and no *moral* exemption either. Ideologies naturally tend to debar each other.
Totalitarian ideologies, in order to simplify the process towards a socially
ideal society, eliminate whoever opposes them. If certain obstacles seem to be
blocking the road, the ideology claims the right to eliminate them even by
force of violence. An extreme example was the ideology of Pol Pot.
Convinced that a population who had once tasted freedom could never be up
to building a new Marxist society, Pol Pot wiped out entire cities in order to
start afresh. A people's commissar once declared, "If nature seeking its
balance causes thousands of victims through natural catastrophes, why hesitate
to kill thousands of men and women in order to accomplish as important a
project as the construction of a new just society?" Even though the ideologies
in the realm of "-ism's," i.e., liberalism, capitalism, socialism, sexism do not
go to such extremes, they do tend to devour everything around them and to
devalue whatever contradicts their idealistic schemes, to reread the past
according to their criteria of interpretation, and to demonize whoever opposes
them, no matter what Christian or human morality might require. Compared

with these, the Gospel's social message again seems fragile and precarious.

Decades ago Pope Paul VI stated that the difference between the Church's social involvement and totalitarian ideologies of the right or left can be found in the life of a single child. The Gospel never permits even one child to be sacrificed in order to contribute towards the establishment of a more just society. In the spirit of Jesus, a Christian struggling for social justice will refuse to pay the price of violence against men, women and children, eliminating entire groups, in order ultimately to attain a better human society. Whereas, for an ideology the enemy is finally someone to be beaten and destroyed, for the Gospel the adversary remains a human person with a capacity and openness to salvation, someone to be loved and for whom one may even lay down one's life. With a certain logic, then, thinking of so many poor countries of Christian tradition, it is not surprising if some people blame the commandment of love for the fact that social conditions do not change or improve, given the blanket refusal to use force to put an end to injustice once and for all. This last observation does not take into account the radicality of Christian love that underlies all the social teaching of the Gospel. In the words of the Canadian bishops a year ago, "Like the Gospel, the social teaching of the Church insists that love or charity be both the basis and summit of individual and community life. It also insists that justice be an essential demand of this love."

While justice may be satisfied with giving only this or that, Christian love of neighbor demands the whole person. In a similar vein Father Arrupe noted that "The promotion of justice is indispensable because it constitutes the very beginning of all charity." Insisting on justice seems revolutionary at times, and demands appear subversive. Yet what one asks for, is so little: much more is needed. We must go beyond justice in order to fulfill it with charity. Justice is necessary but it is not sufficient. Charity adds to justice its transcendent and interior dimension. Just as justice has its limits, and stops where right also comes to an end, love runs into no frontier because it reproduces on our human scale the infinity of the divine essence and causes each human person, our neighbor, to be the object of an unlimited service on our part. Where ideology excludes and marginalizes, the Gospel always opens up in an encounter with others, especially in compassion for the poor and all who suffer, for the design of God is to gather and not to separate. Thus it is impossible to forge justice without love, impossible to put oneself off from love and harbor hatred in order to resist injustice. The universality of love is a commandment to which Jesus admits no exception, even if for us it remains an always new commandment because we believe in it so little.

In our time too there are some famous people and also some quite unknown ones who live the justice of the Gospel, the social dimension of our faith in its fullness—still, are these not rather the exception? After twenty centuries of Christianity, can we consider the social teaching of the Gospel to be effective, or are we utterly in utopia, that is, literally nowhere? Since Sir Thomas More invented his ideal paradise, the utopian model has stimulated the human spirit to dream of a better and more just world without injustice or discrimination. Authors who speak of the Christian utopia: are they not right since Jesus asks us to turn the other cheek, to let others take our shirt, to love our enemies? A philosopher replies: "Utopia, Plato taught from the beginning, is the fire we must play with, for it is the only way we have to get out of what we are. False interpretations of utopia must be critiqued, but the easy out offered by realism is fatal." No doubt, utopias can be completely unreal dreams or a refuge in an imaginary world, a sort of science fiction transposed to the social domain. All the same, utopias have the ability to shed critical light on miserable social conditions in the present and open up new, better, happier possibilities unknown or unhoped for until now. In this way utopia may offer light in the desperate night to those who in their long-term struggle for justice know only failure and frustration. But is this a real light or a mirage? Utopia which draws us away from the real tragedy of our existence, which lets us cruise well above the unjust sufferings of humanity today, is just another aspirin or soporific. But the Christian utopia, which Jesus willingly makes use of because he believes in it, prevents us from getting confused, paralyzed, resigned, skeptical or cynical about the struggle for justice. He invites us to keep on being the salt of the earth, not only in personal witness and communal action, but also in the whole social dynamic.

Conclusion

The recent general congregation of the Jesuits expressed our vision in the following words:

That the social project, in its present form, is seriously flawed, no one doubts; that we are more skeptical now than we were even thirty years ago is true; that there have been massive dislocations and inequalities is clear to all; that the totalitarian experiments of this century have been brutal and almost demonic in intensity, none will dispute; that it seems sometimes to resemble the Babel and Babylon of the Bible is all too evident. But our aim is the confused but inescapable attempt to cooperate in the creation of that community which, according to the Book of Revelation, God will bring about—and God will bring it about in the form of the holy city, the radiant New Jerusalem.[1]

Listening to this visionary affirmation, this divine utopia, we understand that social involvement, the option for the poor and the struggle for justice can only be an integral part of faith and a constant challenge addressed to faith.

And so here we are in the Christian utopia, with our faith drawing its strength to struggle for justice from the very action of Jesus who teaches and prays, who nourishes with the bread of life and with daily bread, who heals people and sets them upright, who shows compassion and solidarity with the poor. In him, with him and through him our faithful social involvement declares: "Arise! Get up! Your faith has saved you!"

---

[1] This citation can be found in slightly different translation in *Documents of the Thirty-Fourth General Congregation of the Society of Jesus* (St. Louis: Institute of Jesuit Sources, 1995), pp. 61-62 (Ed.).

SEVENTEEN

THE SPIRITUAL EXERCISES
AND PREFERENTIAL LOVE FOR THE POOR

Introduction

Clearly, the preferential love for the poor is contained in the Spiritual
Exercises. We ought to love the poor with a love of predilection, and traces
of this can be found in the book of the *Exercises*. For example, in the
"Mysteries of the Life of Christ Our Lord," a text in which the personal
comments of Ignatius seem to be rare and thus are all the more significant, the
preferential love for the poor is expressed in the choice of apostles "of humble
condition" [275]. Likewise, the only discourse which is offered for contemplation among the Mysteries of the Lord is the Sermon on the Mount with the
beatitude concerning the poor [278]. On the other hand, while Jesus
overturned the tables and scattered the money of the wealthy money-changers,
"to the poor vendors of doves he spoke kindly" [277], asking them to respect
the prayer of the temple, the house of hls Father. But these references show
as yet merely an implicit connection.

"Rules for the Distribution of Alms": A Misconstrued Text

We find in the Exercises, however, a connection between the spiritual
urge to follow the Lord and help offered to the poor. The classic means of
helping the poor is by alms. And here is found the link between the Spiritual
Exercises and love for the poor in a much forgotten section of the book of the
Spiritual Exercises: the "Rules for the Distribution of Alms" [337-344].

Why have we generally left this text hidden in the shadows? Above all
because it is too particular. The document in fact is in the first place addressed
to almsgivers, to those who by their office looked after the poor, to the clerics
who practiced charity as a function. The text is very clerical, very priestly,
but despite the heavy emphasis on institutionalism in the text—many references

to ministry, condition, office, function—Ignatius points to Christ the high priest as the one who should inspire all charitable activity. This particular reference to Christ the priest [344] transforms the clerical character of this document, making every Christian a sharer in the ministry of the Lord through the exercise of almsgiving. In fact Ignatius, who in this document justifies the existence of the official "almsgivers"—in that way implicitly recognizing that not all Christians are directly called to such a task in regard to the poor—exhorts them not to be content with working as functionaries, but to be inspired by the ministry of Christ on behalf of the poor. Such an attitude is the concern of all Chrlstians without exception, each according to his or her vocation and state of life. Ignatius, then, clearly intends this document only for a certain group; at the same time, however, he lets it be understood that all Christians ought to have this link with the poor.

The second reason why this document is mostly overlooked is the fact that in our day almsgiving certainly does not have the same significance that this preeminent exercise of charity had in the time of Ignatius. In the old economic order it was by means of alms that the good will of the rich helped to correct excessive social inequality, though of course in a very imperfect way. Saint Francis, the poor man of Assisi, had people pray every day so that thanks to the rich we could continue to be poor. But moderns, even if poor, no longer wish to be under guardianship: from the state they expect the means of livelihood as a right, not as something subject to arbitrary distribution, or to some "good will" of the "good rich"—the very contrary, then, to what takes place in the practice of almsgiving. On the other hand, modern society's growing esteem for work tends to bring almsgiving into disfavor, not only because it is seen as an affront to human dignity, but also because it could encourage idleness and sloth.

Ignatius and Help Given to the Poor

Ignatius in his day faced this problem. When in 1535, having just finished his studies in Paris, he was resting in his native air of Azpeitia, he could not resist involving himself in the spiritual renewal of his fellowtownsmen, and reform of the charitable work in the area could not but form part of it. For Ignatius there was a clear link between the two. On the one hand, Ignatius did not want to see poor people obliged to beg (the same would be true of him in Rome at a later date): all must be helped. On the other hand, all are encouraged to give alms to the official "almsgivers," whether of the township, of the clergy, or of the laity.[1] So, to avoid abuses, the poor ought not to seek alms or beg. On the contrary, the almsgivers should receive alms on behalf of the poor and distribute them, not in their own name, but "for the love of God.""[2]

There is a third reason favoring this text of the *Exercises*. It consists in the fact that for Ignatius himself alms had gradually taken on various forms and purposes. The pilgrim who in 1523 wandered the alleyways of Venice was a solitary mendicant living exclusively off alms; but the companion who, in 1537, lodged in a Venetian hospice for the poor, wished "to preach in poverty," seeking alms so as to be able "to help the poor." He no longer sought alms for himself, but in order to help others.

From 1540 on, Ignatius courageously established two coexisting regimes of community poverty, without ever confusing them, either in theory (a relatively easy matter) or in practice (always a more delicate affair). The formed Fathers would continue to live off alms, while the colleges would have stable and secure incomes to be able to respond better to what the Church wanted of them. Only in case of extreme necessity would alms be the last resort, and all the companions, without exception, were to be ready to beg from door to door. And this is still true today.

Material Poverty and Spiritual Poverty

Once the "Roman" and "German" colleges had been started in 1550, Ignatius did all in his power to secure alms or, what we might call in economic language, to establish funds. Nobody was willing freely to give money: neither the princes nor the civic authorities nor the bishops. Already in those times such money was squandered on wars for which religion was

---

[1] Cf. *MI Fontes Docum.*: Mon. 88: *De Azpeitiae pauperibus sublevandis:* 1535-1542, *MI Epp I*, 161-165: "To the Townspeople of Azpeitia."

[2] *MI, Epp. XII*, 656: Instruction of November, 1554.

given as a pretext. And Ignatius wrote, "After spending so much on material arms to support religion in Germany, it would not be too great a burden if the emperor spared something for spiritual arms which could more effectively gain what is intended."[3] Considerable sums were being sought—and here one sees the development of the Ignatian concept of poverty—not any longer for those who were economically poor, but for the formation of future priests, called to assist those who were spiritually poor.

Ignatius himself, who in 1522 had dreamed of living off alms like the Egyptian hermit Onophrius, thirty years later discovered "God in all things," even in "Egypt." This is an Ignatian expression meaning "the business dealings" that were necessary to meet the Church's needs, through almsgiving. In his spiritual adventure Ignatius learned to take seriously the admonition of the Lord: "He who does not gather with me, scatters" (Luke 11:23). And alms for him meant gathering with the Lord for his brothers and sisters, the poor. No wonder, then, that the *Spiritual Exercises* include these rules for the distribution of alms, in which a whole rich spiritual doctrine is applied to the practical and material need of helping those who are suffering, through almsgiving and the giving of one's very self.

The Spiritual Exercises *and Alms for the Poor*

The mere presence of this document in the book of the *Spiritual Exercises* witnesses to the fact that the Spiritual Exercises are geared to "the salvation of souls," but souls which may experience either material poverty—hence the rules for the distribution of alms—or spiritual poverty—hence the rules concerning scruples (345-351). But the presence of these rules also shows that the Society of Jesus was already involved, in the Rome of that time, in helping the poor. Already during the winter of 1538-39 the Jesuit house sheltered 400 poor people. Although completely absorbed in the government of the young Society, and continuing to give the Exercises, Ignatius himself did all he could for the poor of Rome. If the Good News is not proclaimed in a practical way to the poor, the message of the Spiritual Exercises is vain and lacking in

---

[3] Sept. 14, 1555, to Francis Borgia: *MI, Epp. IX,* 614.

authenticity.

We have yet another document to bear this out, namely, a letter from Ignatius to the Patriarch of Ethiopia. In the context of Ethiopian asceticism with its innumerable penitential practices, Ignatius asked the Jesuits to work towards lessening people's esteem for excessive corporal penance so as to draw their attention to working for the poor. In a nation where social concern was lacking, Ignatius wanted to found hospitals, to give alms to the poor or urge such almsgiving both privately and in public, to ransom prisoners, to educate the abandoned, and to help young men and the unwanted girls settle down in marriage. "Thus," he wrote, "the Ethiopians will see in a palpable way that there are better works than their own fasts and suchlike."[4] It is the problem of the Orthodox Church.

Alms "for the Love of God"

Finally, the presence of these rules in the book of the *Spiritual Exercises* is explained by a simple formula: "for the love of God." Jesuits, and all who seek alms, do so "for the love of God." Alms give concrete expression to that beatitude so lovingly addressed to the poor person. Such norms, then, appearing as they do in the body of the *Spiritual Exercises*, can guide the process of discernment towards this concrete expression of the love of God. Recent commentaries on the *Exercises* generally judge severely those retreats which are exclusively centered on such an experience of prayer as tends to turn exercitants in on themselves in narcissistic fashion. The expression *solus cum solo* does not mean an isolated person with some solitary God, but a "self" that has received everything from others and is called to be a person for others, with a God who reveals himself as "God with us." Despite the very frequent use of first person pronouns in the text of the *Exercises*—a testimony to one's personal responsibility—all these commentaries stress the profoundly communitarian character of the Exercises. This is clearly evident right from the "principle and foundation": a person's authentic search for God necessarily entails insertion into the human community, and reciprocally there is no

---

[4] *MI, Epp. VIII,* 680-690.

perfect engagement towards people that is not the fruit of the discovery of the love of God.

The First Rule for the Distribution of Alms

a) The love that comes from above

After having reflected on the historical and spiritual contexts of the rules for the distribution of alms, let us now consider the first of these rules [338]. It situates the gift of alms right away within the *agapé*, "the love that descends from above" [184]. In no way is this to be seen as a kind of psychological preparation or some sort of religious motivation for charitable activity. Nor is it even a nice exhortation to generosity or a way of spiritualizing the basic human instinct of solidarity. We should also avoid interpreting this first rule as a mere invitation to purity of intention.

Taking up once again an Augustinian inspiration, already used in the first rule for making a good choice [184], this norm for distributing alms, while not in any way excluding *philia* (affection for relatives and friends), urges its being caught up and transformed by *agapé*. The expression "from above" recalls the fourth point of the Contemplation to Attain Love [237]. God, "this infinite treasure of all good," is in his Trinitarian mystery both gift and gift giver [237]. If almsgiving is to be divine and therefore true and authentic, it must find its place in this mutual interchange of gifts, within the loving movement of gifts "which descend from above" [237].

In this matter we have a great many examples in Ignatian literature. Ignatius kept this vision of the love from above alive even in the midst of the most complicated affairs. Thus, for example, he exchanged some ten letters with a certain Bernardino Taro from Naples, who offered to sell his house in a complex deal involving some suspicious price fluctuations. A charitable work was involved, the payment was difficult, the Society sought a discount and the benefactor got irritated. Even while dealing all the time with prices and money, Ignatius placed the whole financial transaction within the loving movement coming from above: "Let us pray that the Divine Goodness may grant us all the grace to be sensitive to his most holy will."[5]

Is it perhaps by chance that Ignatius, in writing to the royal treasurer of the Kingdom of Aragon who acted as generous intermediary between the Jesuits of Spain and of Rome, speaks about the love from above? Ignatius wrote on September 16, 1553: "May God our Lord, whose love should be the foundation and norm of all love, repay you by increasing his love in your soul to such an extent. . . . For just as there is nothing good without this love, so nothing is lacking where it is present."[6]

The criterion, then, for the distribution of alms is not per se human solidarity and not even just philanthropy, but the *agapé* of God which takes flesh in our capacity to give and to forgive. The effort in the Spiritual Exercises "to rid oneself of all inordinate attachments" [1] is aimed at allowing the divine *agapé* to take possession of our capacity to love. These rules for the distribution of alms have no other purpose than to put into effect what John says in his first letter: the one who does not love his brother most surely cannot be said to love God; on the other hand, one does not truly love his brother unless it be with the love of the One who first loved us (I Jn: 4:19-21). In this Ignatian conception, the principal criterion to judge our preferential love for the poor is decidedly its coming "from above," and not the simple fact of helping one's poor brother and sister; in other words, its value is judged in the measure in which philanthropy has been seized and won over by the divine *agapé*. Service of the poor, to be sure, but before all else service "in my name" if it is to be true and authentic.

b) *The Love from Above for the Poor*

In reality, then, the first rule for the distribution of alms brings together *philia* and *agapé* face to face with each other. "To give to people to whom one is attached by relationship or friendship" is not "ordered towards the love of God that comes from above," except in so far as the gift reflects preferential love for the poor. We can find an application of the first rule in a letter from Ignatius to the archdeacon of Barcelona, Jaime Cassador

---

[5] May 17, 1556: *MI, Epp, V,* 411.

[6] *MI, Epp, V,* 488-489.

(February 12, 1536): "I mean, it would be better to give to the poor when relatives are not so poor as those who are not relatives. But, other things being equal, I have more obligations to my relatives than to others who are not relatives."[7] In this way, attachment to relatives and friends is caught up into the divine agapé: the poor are to be preferred to relatives who are not poor.

c) The Love from Above for All the Poor

This collection of Ignatian texts cited with regard to the first rule for the distribution of alms raises a delicate issue. The preferential love for the materially poor is quite clearly a revelation or "epiphany" of the love that comes from above, beyond any philanthropy or friendship for one's own relatives and friends. The well-ordered practice of such divine love makes possible many social initiatives in the service of the economically poor.

The fact that this love is not to be directed exclusively to the socially poor springs from the Ignatian conviction that almsgiving is not meant in the last analysis to create persons who are economically rich, but those who are rich in God's eyes according to the expression of Luke. The free response of the love of God makes us deeply sympathetic towards the hopes of poor people under every form and at every level of human choice, but not in the pursuit of any and every messianic dream or of any and every political or social option. If in the text of the *Spiritual Exercises* the use of the word "poor" is quite rare, it is only at the end of the election documents and in the rules for the distribution of alms that the poor appear in a social and economic sense [344, as an application of 189]. There is no doubt at all that, following the example of the Gospel, the primary concern of the Spiritual Exercises is the conversion of the heart to the love from above. Without this all social activity, even the most generous, would already be condemned, since its aim is not "man taken as a whole."

Why was there, already in the Old Testament, an obligation to help a poor person? It was not to make him rich, but because a person without money—in this sense poor—is not a "complete person" in the image of the

---

[7] *MI, Epp, I*, 93-99.

love of God. A social revolution without the love of *agapé* means, and cannot but mean, death and hatred. As is well known, the Old Testament prophets and finally John the Baptist expressed themselves on social and economic matters in radical, violent and realistic fashion. On this point, compared to the invectives of the prophets, Christ's message seems like a climb down. And yet, the new commandment, which should, according to Ignatius [338], be the root cause of that human love which finds its expression in the distribution of alms, possesses a radicality and a newness without precedent that are capable of transforming humanity. In other words, Ignatius affirms in the *Exercises* that man's search for God is not authentic if it does not express itself in a loving commitment to the world of the poor. Reciprocally, there is no perfect commitment to the cause of man and concretely of poor human beings, unless it be the fruit of a discovery of the love of God that comes from above.

d) The Love from Above Opposed to All Poverty

The critique of the theology of social justice, of the theology of liberation, does not call into question the urgency of the political, social and economic concerns that inspire it. But the whole of divine revelation to the world cannot ever be restricted to a political, social, and economic liberation, nor even to the general idea of liberty. This theology rightly presents one aspect of theology taken as a whole; in practice it requires and demands that the Church strive to reform the world, under every aspect, according to the spirit of Christ. The option for the poor is not, then, to jeopardize the offer of salvation to all persons, the offer of that liberation which is a gratuitous gift of God proffered to all. In his fight for liberation and justice, the Christian is called not to curse those who have possessions, but to encourage them towards conversion to Christ. Just so is it in the Exercises, which do not limit themselves to one single apostolic objective—say for example, speaking of the time of Ignatius, the struggle against nascent Protestantism, or the evangelization of the European masses, or the reform of corrupt clergy, or the missions. So true is this that, in our day, the Exercises should not be used just to arouse zeal for the social betterment of the oppressed or of peoples who live in subhuman conditions. The Exercises urge one to a radical gift of self and through this gift the Lord calls each person "by name." This is the overall vision that Ignatius had: like the Lord, he had an evident preference for the poor, but he saw them rather as "persons" than just "poor people." Hence the absence of any kind of paternalistic pity—a subtle but real form of domination. Without this regard for persons, one has no right to approach the poor.

The Second Rule

I will only make a few brief comments on the other rules. The second rule to be observed in the distribution of alms [339] draws its inspiration from the second rule for making a good choice [185]. It is necessary here to abstract as it were from one's own individuality, to consider oneself as some unknown person whom one meets for the first time, but a person one esteems and for whom one desires all perfection in his office or state of life.

The rules to be observed in the distribution of alms contain a positive and rich outlook on other persons, on our neighbor. The perfection that we desire for another person, in distributing alms and in our preferential love for the poor, consists really in wanting him to be another Christ. While people can make life hell for their neighbors, they can also be a source of living hope. All Ignatius's love for poverty was really a love for the poor Christ [cf. 167]. He longed to be poor because Christ was poor. He longed to be poor as Jesus was poor. Jesus is the one who must inspire me in the way I go about distributing alms and serving the poor; or rather, I need to enter into Jesus' preferential love for the poor.

At this point the distinction between poverty and riches in the *Spiritual Exercises* is very important. Poverty in the *Exercises* readily takes on the form of gratuitousness as opposed to greed. Gratuity of ministries contrasts, and is intended to contrast, with a sort of business market in ministries, benefices, and alms. The powerful or rich man, who has others at his beck and call, does not expect anything from them except a calculated response and reaction. The Lord in the Gospel is poor. His service is freely given. To remove almsgiving, then, from every area of interestedness, to decline gifts automatically calling for gifts from others, rather to give freely to those who count for little in the world of interests—this is to be poor with and for the Lord who is poor. Gratuitousness is a sign of the radical change in human society which can be created only by the love from above. Already in the Old Testament, the paschal mystery of the Exodus gives evidence of human incapacity to change society on its own resources, of the impossibility of converting Phaoroh and of being satisfied with a social teaching that is aimed at bettering the lot of human beings. Only God with his gratuitous gifts can create the new humanity, a humanity "without poor people" (Acts 4:34), where the poor of the Exodus live the new commandment of God's free self-giving.

The Third and Fourth Rules

The third [340] and fourth [341] rules present another characteristic of the Lord who is poor. If one considers himself in the light of eternity, he realizes that of all his riches nothing belongs to him, that he is forever receiving in order then to be able, in keeping with the judgment of the Trinitarian God, to give himself to others with and through his gifts. This "eternal judgment" is the Lord of the cross who died stripped of all, with a poverty not just of one who dies without leaving any possession, but of one who dies as a complete failure. Here then is another characteristic of the divine *agapé*: giving to another evokes the giving of one's own life. It is at this point in the Spiritual Exercises that Ignatius increasingly uses the words "humble," "humility," "humiliation." One could love in a possessive or domineering way; a preferential love for the poor could be ideological, partisan, partial, paternalistic. A passage in the "Treatise on the Election" (1541) by Pedro Ortiz explains that Ignatian humility is the divine way of loving: the love of God, revealed in Christ, consists in the humble offering of self to men that they may live. It is in this sense that the rules to be observed in the distribution of alms urge a person to "imitate as closely as he can our great High Priest, model, and guide, Christ our Lord" [344].

The preferential love for the poor will move, through inevitable humiliations, towards a love that refuses to be condescending or domineering, refuses to impose itself by domination or violence. The desire of humble love, of humiliation in the Ignatian sense, is then the prayer to incarnate the paschal mystery so as to reach a radical poverty with Christ poor. This must be my desire—whether it relates just to the desire to give oneself as the Lord wants or its realization—to give myself to the poor to whom the Lord sends me.

The Last Rules

The final rules to be observed in the distribution of alms explain more clearly the practice of almsgiving, which already for John Chrysostom was the expression of God's compassion in human beings. Ignatius encourages a generous distribution that calls for a simplification in the standard of living of the almsgiver [344]. The rules for the distribution of alms do not admit of a spiritualizing or abstract definition of poverty. That person is not poor who shuns the thought of death and ensures his own security by amassing goods; it is rather the person who opts for the insecurity of gratuitous giving, offering his own goods to others and giving himself in them. To be poor is not just to give what is superfluous, but to keep ceaselessly calling into question, both at the personal and community level, habits in the matter of food, dress, living quarters, and entertainment, not simply for the sake of thrift but in order to give to others, to the poor.

Finally Ignatius gives the classic triple division: to give to the poor, to give to the service of the temple, and lastly to provide "for the support of themselves and their household" [344]. This order of priority shows clearly his preferential love for the poor. It is not the same in other documents with a different type of spirituality. For example, we find this order: in the first place to provide for divine worship, then for the support of the monks, and, finally, to distribute alms to the poor. Ignatius demonstrates his preferential love for the poor by putting them in the first place.

Conclusion

In a letter to Father Lorenzo of Modena (May 16, 1556) Ignatius writes: "You must understand that our Society, in its practice of a universal charity towards all nations and classes of men, does not approve cultivating particular affection for one people or for any individual person, except in the measure that well ordered love requires."[8] Guided by such well-ordered love—"the

---

[8] *MI, Epp, XI*, 408-409.

spiritual works which are more important" *(Const.* 650), because the goal is the whole human person—one dedicates oneself to the corporal works of mercy, among which commitment to the poor takes pride of place. And so in one single movement of love Ignatius is both attached and detached: a humble love, as we might today translate "the love from above."

The Exercises, school of Christian freedom, give to "philanthropy," to the preferential love for the poor, for all the poor, its true Christian dimension: the free response to the love for the poor which God from on high reveals in the poor Christ, who is rich in the Spirit.

EIGHTEEN

THE VOCATION AND MISSION OF
THE BROTHER IN THE SOCIETY OF JESUS

It was on June 5, 1546, that the Holy Father, in his brief *Exponi Nobis,* first permitted the Society to have brothers. Thanks, though, to our historians, we know that there were already brothers, hard at work, prior to the papal approval.

It is right and just to give thanks to the Lord of the Vineyard for all the brothers who have given their very best for the service of the Lord in the Society of his Son Jesus. This is true not only for the more than fifty brothers who are saints and blessed, not only for the brothers we have known and who have confirmed us in our vocations, but for that whole cloud of brothers who are unknown to us, but whom the Lord knows well.

When the first Jesuits met together in 1539, they stated: Since the Lord had deigned in his clemency and paternal goodness to bring us together in a group, unworthy men born in very different countries with very different customs, we thought we should not break the unity of this group but rather continue to bolster and strengthen it more and more to form a unique body.

In this beautiful text, we read that it is first of all the Lord who gathers us together. In this way, the saying of Jesus that we cannot call ourselves to his service but rather that he, the Lord, calls and gathers us, is fulfilled. Speaking concretely, these first Jesuits were aware that they were neither a family nor a tribe, and that they had not come together in the same way that people come together to form a social club, an athletic association or a political party. Nothing else but the love of the Lord, as well as each one's passion for the service of the Kingdom, disposed them to come together. Even if today we "promote" vocations, we do not regard people as would a commercial business or an industrial corporation offering them a great deal of work to be done. It is the Lord who chooses.

Thus it was not St. Ignatius who recruited brothers for practical purposes. It is the Lord, as our story tells us, who sends people to share, each in his own way, the early Society's single-hearted passion for helping people to encounter him who is their true Life. If the body of the Society wants simply to be an instrument to serve the Lord, which the Lord can use to give his life to the world in abundance, then each Jesuit is sent by the Lord to be incorporated into it by *helping* the entire body of the order *(Const.* 547). In his talk of October 31, 1976, Father Pedro Arrupe drew two conclusions from the fact that everything that happens in the Society comes from the initiative of the Lord who calls and chooses, who sends and who gathers together.[1]

The first conclusion is that everything must be seen in the perspective of a Society at the service of Jesus. Of course, this has to do with a vision, a point of view "illumined by faith, for without faith none of this makes sense." Indeed, it may well be that in our times, with the advantages founded on democracy and human rights, the first thing that we can say about the Society as a group of men may is something socio-political, but this can only be an introductory word. The last word will always be that of our faith, with everything that it implies of renunciation and utopian thinking.

Without this perspective of faith, we can never experience companionship in Jesus as brotherhood, for we know from the Gospel that this perspective implies a gift ever renewed, a forgiveness ever repeated. Law and legal structures can help us to protect the most essential rights and responsibilities; but law can never have the last word, which must always go to the loving spirit of faith. To say it as St. Ignatius would, the last word must go to the loving humility which founds our way of praying, our way of living and our way of working together as brothers. When we abandon this mystical perspective—a mysticism of service—then nothing can save the apostolic body of the Society, neither the claiming of rights, nor psychological techniques, nor political shrewdness.

A recent study in the United States highlighted the importance for a group of having a purpose, a plan or direction. The Society has no other ideal than that of St. Ignatius: to serve Christ by continuing his work throughout the world. To take on this ideal no doubt means to renounce this or that particular

---

[1] *AR*, 1976, 391-403.

perspective, but it is the Lord who calls us to choose the same direction together, in the expression of one of the first Jesuits, to choose the direction, the "sense" (*sens*), of the Lord. This perspective of faith does not keep us from talking about both the good and the bad of our experience, from expressing our sorrows and our grievances, or from frankly formulating our ideas and our desires; rather, it means that we do so always in the perspective of faith, always with hope, because the heart of God is larger than ours, and knowing that in the heart of God even what is humanly impossible becomes possible. And all this, finally, is done with a heart that has found its love in the Society and which because of that love understands all, knows how to be patient, and knows how to move forward with an openness that refuses to close in on itself or to close up in obsession.

It would not be Ignatian to use the perspective of faith to justify the suffering and injustices that can break into our community life. But it also would not be Ignatian to believe that we can truly be "friends in the Lord" without sometimes renouncing even what could be a human right, without the sacrificial gift of one's self.

The second conclusion drawn by Father Arrupe from the fact that it is the Lord who unites us and who sends us, is the conviction that "the services and ministries done by Jesuits all have the same evangelical value. In the Society there is only service; or better yet, there are only servants who work for the Kingdom." Any aspiration in a Jesuit which does not aim for a greater service in order to resemble more and more closely the crucified and risen Lord [167], is foreign to Ignatian spirituality. So too is any socio-political evaluation which, in concession to a local culture, divides up service—or rather work—into higher and lower, into noble and worthy on the one hand and servile and contemptible on the other, into spiritual and material. Any service of the Lord, accepted and accomplished as a mission of the body of the Society, is neither higher nor lower, but alongside and with the One who serves all at his table so that all might live by his life.

The Lord beseeches us explicitly not to ignore his Gospel: that is, we must not want to be the biggest or the best, or to disparage the little and the least, or to introduce the quest for power so typical in national and political life. We are never to abandon the beatitude of the poor by measuring everything on the basis of the apparent effectiveness of work. Despite the powerful pressure of the context in which we live and work, as "friends in the

Lord" we must avoid judging and acting according to the scale of values of acceptability in our modern society. Instead we must even "act against"—*agere contra*—such tendencies so that "the feelings that were those of Jesus" might mark our way of proceeding and might constitute a prophetic witness. Such a union of true brothers in the Lord is never a given, never to be taken for granted; rather, it is always to be built up again and again. The Society is not perfect, and never will be perfect. What is important, even fundamental, is that, urged on by the Spirit, the apostolic body of the Society renew itself again and again.

The Spirit of the Text of 1539

Let us return to the text edited by the first Jesuits during the year 1539. Their astonishment was due, not just to the discovery that the Lord had brought them together, but that he had managed to bring together men so different—in nationality, in character, in lifestyle. When Ignatius describes the world in the Contemplation on the Incarnation, he draws our attention to "those on the face of the earth, in such great diversity in dress and in manner of acting" [106]. Since Ignatius's model of a companion of Jesus is the apostle, the apostolic body of the Society is modeled, like that of the apostles, on union in diversity. Meditating on the vocation of the apostles, Ignatius underlines their "special call," not clearly delineated in the Gospel [275]. Each of the apostles is a person whom Jesus calls by name. Like the group of apostles, the Society should be a free association of persons who have in no way abdicated their personalities. But, far from being solitary individuals, they bring to realization with their entire personality, transformed in the service of the Lord, a "diversity . . . united by the bond of charity" (*Const.* 624).

All of us are different, to which Ignatius would say, "Thank God!" It is he after all, who, from the outset of creation, chose to differentiate day and night, man and woman, and thousands of species of animals and plants so that each one in its diversity might reflect something of the inexhaustible richness of God. If people wanted to impose on themselves one language only, the Lord wants to call each by name, speaking as one person to another. So he confuses languages and disperses everyone, refusing uniformity so as to ensure diversity.

It is at Pentecost that each one, in the diversity of his own language, welcomes the marvels of God to proclaim them to all people. Inspired by this same Spirit, Ignatius hopes that, in the Spiritual Exercises, the retreatant will be moved by different spirits [6] so that from this solitary encounter with God there will emerge not a single human model but a personalized vocation and mission.

Should it astonish us then, to see that St. Ignatius rejoiced in the diversity he found in the Society? It is a diversity of nationalities—of "natures" as he says—which impels the Society toward missions in all parts of the world, as well as diversity in the graces and gifts received by each one of us. Respecting this diversity of graces, St. Ignatius invites us to discover them and to exploit them for the glory of God, and to serve the Lord according to the graces and vocation of each one. Given his belief in this diversity, Ignatius did not hesitate to stimulate it in the Society.

We are not bound to any one model of ministry—for example, parishes only or schools only. We are not limited to one continent or one country. Ignatius wanted us to learn various languages and above all—and this is our problem—he multiplied the possible ways of being a Jesuit to the point of passing from diversity to complexity. At the time of Ignatius, there was in religious communities a difference between those who were being formed and those already formed, between priests and lay members. Ignatius had no wish to complicate things uselessly, but he had no choice. The Lord of the Harvest was calling to the Society young men who had to be prepared to roam the continents in the name of the Holy Father, with a mobility which cannot but stun us. But at the same time those men had to be completely available to assure the stability of new institutions, and to hear the call to cooperate together, using their gifts to make possible the work of the Society. In creating priests professed of four or three vows, and coadjutors who were priests and non-priests, Ignatius was intent only on uniting all these men in the apostolic body of the Society while respecting diversity of graces, and on integrating in one and the same vocation and mission the different responses to different calls of the Lord. He had to wait more than a year to obtain, finally, on June 5, 1546, the approbation of the Church whose laws he had to obey.

This is the inspiration which gave birth to "grades" in the Society. Ignatius was convinced that he had thus respected the diversity of gifts of God, at the service of his greater glory, in the Society of Jesus. Do we think the same? Do we discern in the vocation and mission of the brother today, the original inspiration of Ignatius, or do we have to confess that his religious ideal is no longer valid for the twentieth century?

Ignatius himself, in his own time, was very aware of the difficulty of living together while respecting one another's gifts: the difficulty of living out diversity in one body. Remembering the Roman College, he wrote in 1555: "It seemed to everyone that there had to be a miracle, to see men of such different nationalities and temperaments maintaining such harmony . . . such unanimity of will in Christ" (*Ep. Ign.* 10, 422 n. 6064). Why a miracle? Because our own experience makes clear to us that, instead of recognizing in diversity the grace of God, we easily use the slightest difference to despise and detest others, and even to make war against others with modern arms. On the other hand, a diversity which does not wish to be integrated into the unity of an apostolic body inevitably changes into an exaggerated individualism.

Such social impenetrability, which unfortunately is daily bread in men's lives, is even more difficult to accept in a religious family where, of all places, one might expect to avoid such situations. More than a few Jesuits have suffered not only for the sake of the Society, but also from the Society and from their companions. A wise observer of the human nature of his time, and of all times, Ignatius wanted the professed, by reason of their solemn vows, to equally obey missions given by the Holy Father, be they considered of lofty nobility or of humble lowliness, like teaching catechism to children. In the *Constitutions* Ignatius notes the real danger, for those with studies behind them, of beginning to undervalue an apostolate with simple people or with children, just because works of this kind are not at all flashy (*MI Const.* 1, 28-29). Elsewhere he asks that any sign of honor which would be distinctive of the professed be suppressed (*Epist. Ign.* 10, 594, n. 6146).

To safeguard this diversity in the Spirit of the Lord, Ignatius rejected the idea of assigning all brothers to the same task. Various brothers of his time had been soldiers, artists, judges, or students; they had come not to be servants but to serve and, as in the apostolic Church, they took on themselves work which liberated their brother priests for work which was typically sacerdotal. But still, in the time of Ignatius as again in our times, all shared all kinds of work according to need and according to each one's capacity. And so, just as today, brothers were involved in the domain of the pastoral. According to Ignatius, since our Lord confides to each person the care for his

neighbor, brothers have to exert themselves by way of spiritual conversations—which will sometimes be an occasion for preaching or
catechizing—to work with the Lord for the spiritual progress of whomever he
puts in their paths *(MI, Const.* II, 90-99). At the same time a professed father
like Polanco, Ignatius's secretary, moved between confessional and the
kitchen, and a professed father like Peter Canisius declared himself perfectly
happy to undertake any job in the college of Messina, whether that meant
being cook, gardener, porter, student, or professor. These examples, not a bit
exceptional in the time of Ignatius, show how the feeling of participating in
one and the same mission brings with it a sharing of all apostolic works.

But if Ignatius did not lock brothers into a determined work, he did insist
always on being content with one's vocation. In order that brothers or non-
brothers can give the best of themselves, it is indispensable that they be
content with having received from the Lord their "grade" in the apostolic
body of the Society *(MI, Const.* II, 13). To be convinced of having received
this from the hand of God, for the service which he asks of us, is what makes
us satisfied, free, and joyful, even when such service costs us dearly.

In Ignatius's time, the desire to study theology meant, in practice, seeking
ordination, that is, seeking a change of grade. In the correspondence of
Ignatius, we find letters which show how he entered into discernment with a
brother who wanted "to study," just as today, after having discerned the will
of the Lord, a scholastic discovers his vocation as brother, or a brother his
vocation as priest. The difference of grades is always subject to the
movements of the Spirit of the Lord, whether in being content with one's
grade or in being available for any other work for the glory of God.

We shouldn't wonder that this difference of grade is influenced by the
organization of our world and of our Church. Ignatius ate, spoke and prayed
with brothers like a true companion; but, in accord with the customs of the
times, he thought it strange that one would go shopping with a long cassock,
and so he asked the brother who frequented the markets and the stalls to wear
a cassock "more or less one hand shorter."

There is no doubt that the new weight given to the lay state in the
Church, as well as what our world honors or despises in various cultures,
always condition our judgments and our way of living the differences of
grades in the apostolic body of the Society. The scale of values of the cultural
world in which we live and work can make us fall into the trap of counting

injustices or provoke arguments over the way we live out our differences of grades. But human society's criteria for honoring or despising this or that level or class of work may well have been worked out in view of gaining prestige or importance, or winning a name, instead of being inspired by the Gospel of a Lord who simply smashed the system in which one sought the limelight and an ever more dazzling career. The Lord gave us an example of a life simple, authentic and free, actually seeking the last place in order to serve his brothers for the glory of his Father. It is not public opinion, but the Gospel, the following of Jesus, which ought to be considered when together we try to purify and correct, to evaluate and improve our life as Jesuits in that mutual respect and total reciprocity implied by the different gifts and graces which the Lord has given us, for the building up of his kingdom.

Here we have to come to grips with certain needs of our times. While this spirituality of diversity in one apostolic body is not at all a disembodied spirituality, it does reflect, at least in what concerns St. Ignatius, the sixteenth century, which is not ours. Today's society sees democracy and equality as the ideal; it aspires toward all men and women having the same rights and the same responsibilities. But despite such a widespread, irreversible yearning, our world is still far from being egalitarian and democratic. The Church of Vatican II, for its part, is moving slowly but surely, with many stops and starts, toward a more authentic brotherhood in Christ, and a truer communion in the Spirit. The whole of religious life is an effort to translate this movement into concrete terms, and the Church monitors progress toward a more evangelical life of "brothers and sisters together," at times pushing and at other times applying brakes.

The Church urges evangelical simplicity in the heart of a religious family, where all discrimination should be renounced. Every distinction not stemming from the sacrament of Orders should be suppressed, and the greatest possible participation in government should be fostered. But on the other hand, the Church slows down every change which would not respect the diversity based on Orders, or would radically alter the original inspiration of the founder, or would be premature and so run the risk of disturbing peace. Thus, the Church has encouraged us in moving toward assuring the participation of brothers in province congregations. On the strength of this, the Society hopes to suppress the limit on the number of brothers present at a province congregation and to promote an active presence of brothers at the general congregation. But the

Church has always discouraged every attempt in the past to separate the fourth vow from the sacrament of Orders and, just recently, the attempt to separate the solemn character of the three vows of chastity, poverty, and obedience from the fourth vow. To respect the original idea of St. Ignatius, and not to alter a centuries-old tradition of the Society, the Holy See does not want to see the fourth vow, solemn profession, and the sacrament of Orders separated.

In contrast, the Church urges us to give the vows of chastity, poverty and obedience of the coadjutors, both priests and brothers, the same effects as the vows of the professed. As you know, in the unfortunate situation of a Jesuit's wishing or having to leave the Society, there is a difference between the professed father and the coadjutor, whether brother or priest. For the moment, the Society can itself authorize a brother or priest coadjutor to leave, but only the Holy See, not the Society itself, can authorize a professed father to leave. This juridical difference, when it is applied, has at times given the impression to some coadjutors—brothers and priests—that they are not so thoroughly Jesuits as the professed are, and that they have a less secure bond to the Society. The Church is encouraging the general congregation to suppress this difference in treatment. It cannot be denied that here there is a difficulty to overcome. But if the Society, in its desires and its requests to the Holy See, remains faithful to the Spirit which is at its origins, any eventual conflict will not last, since as Ignatius writes in the *Spiritual Exercises*, it is the same Spirit which speaks in his Church, the Church of the Lord. So, avoiding all disagreement, it is with an attitude of fidelity to the Spirit that we ought to discuss these problems among ourselves for the good of the Society and of the Church of Christ.

Let us return one final time to the text of the first Jesuits:

> Since the Lord has deigned in his clemency and paternal
> goodness to bring us together in a group—unworthy men born
> in very different countries, with very different customs—we
> thought we should not break the unity of this group, but
> rather continue to bolster and strengthen it to form one body.

"To form one body": besides having spoken to you with regard to our diversity, it will be good, by way of conclusion, to underline this belonging to one body. Do we run into a problem here?

In a letter dated October 30, 1959, Father Janssens wrote very frankly that the difficulties experienced with regard to the brothers should be attributed not so much to the particularities of their vocation as to the manner of acting of far too many fathers. Based on this, what is required is a conversion, a change of mentality, in order to live diversity of grades in an authentic complementarity.

GC 31 returned to this remark of Fr. Janssens. In the same spirit, the congregation did not want to reserve only to brothers either humility, or the hidden life of Nazareth, or the religious life in its pure state. Brought together in one body, living the same Ignatian spirit and the same apostolic vocation, consecrated to the same Lord Jesus in view of the same missionary task, all Jesuits are called to be apostles at the service of the Church according to the gifts and graces received from the Lord, and in respect to the personal vocation given to each one, including or excluding priesthood (GC 31, d. 7).

Consequently, the general congregation set in motion a dynamic in accord with which the brothers, "to help the Society" *(Const.* 1148), are integrated into all the apostolic work of the Society, including "administrative duties" (n. 3). And they are incorporated into the social and liturgical life of communities "as befits companions who live the religious life in the same family" (n. 5). As a further consequence, the congregation opted for a formation (n. 7) which makes possible: the elimination of "every social distinction in community life" (cf. *Const.* 250), "the sharing of all in common domestic tasks"; access of brothers to consultations and congregations (n.6).

With his proverbial love for the brothers, Father Arrupe did everything possible to make effective this full integration into the one body of the Society of all Jesuits, brothers and fathers. On October 31, 1978, he confessed that:

> . . . the disappearance of the grade of brother would be an irreparable loss, a mutilation with very serious consequences for the body of the Society and for its apostolate, because it is impossible to replace what the brothers bring both to the internal life of the community and to the apostolic work of the Society. (*AR*, XVII (1978), 368)

Even more recently, GC 33 reaffirmed once again its faith in one apostolic body:

Being all members of the same body, we complete and enrich one another so that we can imitate the way of life offered by the Son of God to the disciples who followed him. This is why the congregation considers that the absence of brothers is a serious defect. (D.1, n. 17)

The congregation confessed openly: ". . . we must change our attitudes so that our behavior toward one another in the Society is not ruled by human standards proper to the world, but by the example of Christ who came not to be served, but to serve (D. 1, n. 19). Once again the word "service": an observer of religious life has written:

The religious priest is doubtless one who serves, but he is always stalked by clerical power, the religious woman is doubtless one who serves, but she seems to do so spontaneously, unless stalked by the vindicating drive of feminism. Only the religious brother is a continual challenge to a Christianity all taken up with power and prestige. It is the brother who reminds us that Christ is Lord in that he was a Servant.

There is still much to say. Our hope is that the brothers and their "co-brothers" (*con-freres*), the fathers, can live fully and integrally their companionship in the Lord Jesus, who continues to serve the world so that it may attain true life, and who makes use of our humble service.

NINETEEN

LAYMEN AND LAYWOMEN
IN THE CHURCH OF THE MILLENNIUM

Introduction

Many laypersons now collaborate in works of the Company of Jesus, and many are nourished by Ignatian spirituality. We have linking us a profound common bond, for we are all moved by the same spirit. The purpose of this essay is to create further openness for questions and points of view, so that there can be ongoing dialogue among ourselves which can deepen the common spirit that unites us.

The Change Experienced by the Church

We are at the threshold of a change in millennium. The beginning of our epoch was instigated by changes that have come more and more rapidly. Through them, the old forms have been shattered, time-honored paradigms have been rendered obsolete, and we have found ourselves forced to travel along new paths if we care to live creatively in a new world.

More than thirty years ago now—years illuminated by the Spirit—the Church in the Second Vatican Council called attention to the fact that Christ is carrying out his mission in the world not only through the bishops and priests, but also through the laity who constitute most of the People of God. And from the conference of the bishops of Latin America in Santo Domingo in 1992 there came a kind of motto for Latin America, "The New Evangelization: Human Advancement and Christian Culture." It demanded more leadership on the part of the laity.

There are many indications that the Church of the third millennium will be a Church of the laity. Why do we say this? Because the laity, both men and women, are continually taking on more responsibilities in the life of the Church, in parishes, diocesan structures, schools, theological centers and works of charity and justice. Moreover, through the laity the Church can be the evangelical leaven for the world of the third millennium. Certainly we Jesuits felt this in 1994 as we were preparing our general congregation: the laity have something to say; they feel themselves an integral part of the mission of the Company; they are waiting for the fulfillment of many expectations in their lives and in their mission in the Church and in the world. Jesuits all over the world wanted the Company to take its stance toward the laity, and they asked the Thirty-Fourth General Congregation to take action on that more frequently than on anything else.

Reasons Justifying Lay Leadership in the Church

The first explanation, a simplistic one, is pragmatic in character: confronted with continually scarcer manpower for the enormous work of evangelizing the world, bishops, priests—and in the present case, we Jesuits—have all felt obliged to recruit the laity. But even though this has happened, to accept this as an adequate explanation is to ignore the deeper reality of the Church and the roots of the Ignatian mystical vision.

The Church solemnly proclaimed in the Second Vatican Council the fundamental equality of all of its members—bishops, priests, religious, laity—in words that are freighted with meaning:

> The heritage of this people is the dignity and freedom of the
> children of God, in whose hearts the Holy Spirit dwells as in
> its temple. Its law is the new commandment to love as Christ loved
> us (Jn. 13:34). Its goal is the kingdom of God, which has been
> begun by God Himself on earth (LG, 9).[1]

This is equally true for bishops, religious, clergy, and laity. It is not surprising that this same Vatican Council dedicated a long chapter to the truth that

---

[1] The reference is to Vatican Council II, *Lumen Gentium (Dogmatic Constitution on the Church)*.

all of us in the Church are called to the holiness appropriate to our state in life (*LG,* 39).

St. Ignatius of Loyola conveys this through his penetrating grasp of the gospel. In the second week of the Exercises, he presents the Call of the Eternal King. In it, one experiences the call given by Christ the eternal King in each person's heart, to commit one's life freely to the King's own task, to hear and to respond with one's whole life for the building of his reign here on earth. Even though some respond to this call as priests or consecrated women and others as lay men or women, nevertheless, the sincerity and the surrender in our response has to be the same for all of us. For what is involved here is that each one be faithful to the call, to the will of God that is the following of Christ in our lives.

In this response, there are no higher or lower ranks. For the issue here is above all the response of each heart to the project God has for every one of us—a project which will vary in the forms that it takes, but not in the fundamental and ultimate content: the call to be sons and daughters of God in Christ.

St. Ignatius, it must be added, did not content himself with a following of Christ which entailed merely offering part of oneself to the work of the reign of God on earth. He says that "those who wish to give greater proof of their love" might make an offering of their life itself, once they are free of inordinate attachments. The *magis,* the Ignatian "more," characteristic of his spirituality, keeps us mindful of the need for people who give themselves totally. Like St. Ignatius, their life will be an ongoing pilgrimage in search of the greater glory of God—no half measures, no mediocre reactions, because mediocrity does not fit into the Ignatian worldview.

Men and women who find that the meaning of their lives is to join Christ in bringing about the Reign of God, choose from among those approved by the Church a way of life that will help them in the service of God [177]. They choose to be lay men or lay women. Being lay ought not be a state of life that results from not making a choice; rather, it is a concrete possibility that one chooses in order to realize the will of God and to commit oneself to God's reign. This is why the pontiffs keep emphasizing the vocation of the laity to be missionaries. John Paul II has said very clearly that it is not just a matter "of apostolic impact, but rather of a duty/right

founded in baptismal dignity through which the lay faithful share in their
own way in the triple office—priestly, prophetic, and kingly—of Jesus
Christ" *(Redemptoris Missio* 71). Getting down to particulars, the pope
recalls that the characteristic mission of the laity is to "seek the kingdom of
God by engaging in temporal affairs and by ordering them according to the
plan of God" *(LG* 31).

Jesuits and Laity Face the Company's Mission Challenges

While he was still in the lay state, St. Ignatius of Loyola was a man
who boldly served the mission of Christ. He was jailed by the Inquisition in
Alcalá, Salamanca, Paris and Venice because even though he had not studied
theology he nonetheless "was engaged in giving Spiritual Exercises and
explaining Christian doctrine" *(Autob.* 571). He could not stifle the Spirit
that he had in him. Many years later, driven by this same Spirit and as a
sign that it was this same Spirit that drives the Church, he put the Company
of Jesus at the service of the papacy.

In this same Spirit, the Company of Jesus today wants to act "by
offering ourselves in service to the full realization of this mission of the
laity, and to that end by cooperating with them in their mission" (GC 34 d.
13, n. 1). The last general congregation of the Jesuits gave expression in its
decree on the laity to the most common concern among Jesuits worldwide:
collaboration with the laity. And in a way that surprised everyone, the
Company became the first religious order to dedicate a special decree to
women and their situation in Church and society.

But this really ought not surprise us, who interpret the lay vocation as
the free response to a special call from God. Do we not have the definitive
example of Mary's unconditional response to her call from God? As she did
then, many women now have made a radical commitment and live the
Ignatian *magis* far beyond mediocre postures and with a strength that only
the Spirit can instill. The time has come to listen to women and to recognize
their role both in society and in the Church.

Regrettably, we have proclaimed Christian truths from a thoroughly
masculine viewpoint, lacking the humility to listen carefully to the same
truths from the feminine viewpoint. Women have made many contributions

and continue making many in fields that are enormously varied. The general congregation singled out one in particular, their contribution to the Spiritual Exercises, this field of "helping souls" where the woman has already given much and has much still to give, having innate qualities that favor it.

We Jesuits cannot rest with just a public admission of our complicity in the marginalization of women. We have to take positive action if we are to honor what the congregation proclaimed. Here, too, we will have to implement one of the attributes that Fr. Pedro Arrupe used to say characterize the work of Jesuits: apostolic aggressiveness.

I am deeply satisfied that I have witnessed in Venezuela the important roles that women play in many of the Company's works. They are in posts of great responsibility, in both primary education and the catechizing of children, but just as much at the university level and in the management of our most representative publications.

Concrete Cases in the Province of Venezuela

I come now to a concrete situation—that of Venezuela. After exploring the ideal proposed by our last general congregation, I would like to catalog the channels of Jesuit-lay collaboration that thrive in Venezuela. This might be one of the richest themes for our dialogue: Do you find the work of the Company open to your initiatives and collaboration? Are we living up to what we proclaimed so solemnly? Here is what the general congregation said:

> The Society of Jesus places itself at the service of the mission of the laity by offering what we are and have received: our spiritual and apostolic inheritance, our educational resources, and our friendship. We offer Ignatian spirituality as a specific gift to animate the ministry of the laity. . . . We join with them . . . learning from and responding to one another's concerns and initiatives, dialoging with one another on apostolic objectives (GC 34, d. 13, n. 7).

As early as 1993, when preparing for the Thirty-Fourth General Congregation, the Province of Venezuela organized the Asamblea de Jesuitas-Laicos. Its purpose was to know one another better, to identify with the same spirituality, and share in the same works.

[Fr. Kolvenbach then lists those works, which show how amply lay men and women share with Jesuits. These include Huellas (a youth movement); CVX in the major cities; Fe y Alegría, forty years old now; parishes and colleges; the Centro Gumilla with its research and publication, directed by Dra. Mercedes Pulido; and the ministry of Exercises in weekend retreats and EVO, retreats in daily life.]

All of this sharing through the years culminated in 1996 in the Comision Jesuitas-Laicas-Laicos. This began a process of apostolic deliberation in which all together desire to find what God wants of the Province of Venezuela in the next years. It is nothing less than inviting the laity to search for what God wants of the Company of Jesus in Venezuela in the third millennium. Doing this means choosing a long and difficult journey: that of communitarian discernment, that of the shared search for the will of God. Indeed, this entails an invitation into the heart of the Company of Jesus, into the great secret of the Jesuits—actually, the only secret!

More recently, there has been another fine initiative, that of the Ignatian Volunteers. It began at the Catholic University with a few students. Now it is open to all laity who will make a two-year commitment, including young professionals disposed to offer their services in the Company's works, wherever there is greater need—which means that they are exercizing Ignatian availability. In certain special cases, there is even a search for juridical formulas to express a tighter and more permanent commitment with the Company, while guarding the integrity of the lay vocation.

At the same time, there is no lack of works which embody a collaboration in the opposite direction: not only laity collaborating in Jesuit works, but Jesuits collaborating in lay works. The experience is illustrated in Merida in FUNDIMMA, (Fundación Cristiana para la liberación popular), the organization which reaches into poor areas to encourage the inhabitants' citizenship.

In this great new historical process, where does the greater need lie? What is the indispensable condition for the growth of the lay vocation and for a more extensive collaboration in its mission? How will it be possible for us to search together for the will of God in our service, talking the same language and understanding the same things?

The answer is this: share in the same Ignatian spirit and set out on the same journey of continuing formation of our Christian life. To this great need, SIGNACE (Servicio Ignaciano de Acompañamiento) responds. In this work, we choose to collaborate together in the development and transmission of Ignatian spirituality and of its instrument, the Spiritual Exercises. This instrument has been sufficiently well tested and proven in the history of the Church to be trusted to contribute now to the formation of the Church's apostles of the twenty-first century.

For the Company of Jesus, it is clear that the Spirit of Jesus "is calling us, as "men for and with others," to share with lay men and women what we believe, who we are, and what we have, in creative companionship, for "the help of souls and the greater glory of God" (GC 34, d. 13, n. 26).

TWENTY

CONTEMPORARY EDUCATION
IN THE SPIRIT OF ST. IGNATIUS

Introduction

For more than four centuries now there has been a network of universities, higher institutes, lyceums, colleges and high schools that operate along the lines of a certain educational plan of the Society of Jesus. In more contemporary terminology, these institutions, with all their disconcerting diversity, share a common inspiration derived from Ignatian education. Today one could easily find more than two thousand such foundations that would recognize themselves within this plan, described as Ignatian rather than Jesuit. This distinction indicates that an institution can freely adopt these Ignatian orientations, without their necessarily having the physical presence of Jesuits.

This reference to St. Ignatius does not designate a system, such as the Montessori or Faure genre, but looks back to a heritage born of a certain secular experience and a vision of the future. That is, they rely on a cohesive ensemble of directives and counsels which arise, sometimes from simple good sense, from a conviction drawn from the Christian faith, from long teaching experience, or from a projection of future needs. Many traits within this Ignatian group are not original, and they can often be located simply within certain respected pedagogical systems. But the combination of all these educational aspects preserves something specific, so much the more as it has proven itself since 1548, and has left its mark within a great number of cultures and civilizations.

Ignatius and the Spiritual Exercises

The impressive inspiration at the origin of this educational system arises, not from a theoretical genius, a visionary creator or an experienced educator, but rather, from the spiritual adventure of the Basque, Ignatius of Loyola, beginning back in the sixteenth century. By his personal account, he let God educate him and in this way experienced a great desire to share that education; it was essentially a spiritual and not at all a scholarly one, offered to others who might share his quest for a personal encounter with God. It was to facilitate this sharing, in which the educator is God himself, that Ignatius committed the *Spiritual Exercises* to a little work of about a hundred pages in sixteen folio format. This small book has enjoyed an overwhelming success that has never been gainsaid. Today there are approximately 4500 editions in dozens of languages.

The work has another special characteristic in so much as it offers no consistent interpretation. There is nothing of the pedagogical manual or didactic treatise about it. It is intended as a functional piece, a working collection constituted by a series of documents belonging to three different literary genres. Yet all of them have as their precise purpose to set forth a concrete path which will lead those who make these Spiritual Exercises to allow the Lord to educate them. They will thus be able to search and discern the direction of their lives and their personal present destiny in light of the eternal, and to live out the consequences of their discoveries through the choices and decisions indicated.

All along this road, educators have not been lacking, beginnning with Ignatius himself, who, with sobriety and brevity, makes his personal experience of God available. He is well aware that this experience is not simply to be copied, but that all men and women must appropriate it in a way that fits their personalities. Then there is the one who is called director: neither judge nor guru, he or she utilizes in a unique way the material furnished by Ignatius and adapts it to the needs of the one who makes the Spiritual Exercises, playing the role of an intermediary in the educational process. Such a director must in effect both initiate and motivate, taking the back seat to the one who in the final analysis will be the true educator, namely, God himself. To put it as one expert has it, the director teaches the one who open-mindedly makes the Exercises to begin a sentence in a way that enables God to complete it as a process of education.

It is clear then that this little book of the *Spiritual Exercises* inevitably contains a number of important elements, which are so many stones for the construction of an educational experience. The work itself carries the life breath which makes it into an educative project. So Ignatius and his first companions, who dreamed of missions to the four corners of the world and even refused scholarly or academic occupations as opposed to their vision, were nonetheless quickened by an educational life energy. Already relatively old—thirty-three years—Ignatius himself was aware, through his many encounters on the highways of Europe and the Middle-East, that the simple sharing of an experience of God would bear no fruit in a complex and sophisticated age. He knew that to help others he still needed a certain amount of professionalism and educational competence. The educator cannot give what he has not willingly received.

The Jesuit Turn to Education

If, without much enthusiasm, Ignatius picked up a master of arts at the University of Paris, it was to enable him to make use of the vast area of what we call today informal education. The desire to give Christian formation to persons whom the Lord placed on his path did not give any hint at all of those colleges[1] which would render the Jesuits legendary for secondary education. But this role in fact reached such a point that still today there are people who cannot imagine a Jesuit as living outside a college, his so-called natural environment.

Nevertheless, we have to look at the evidence: these ardent pilgrims did not envision themselves as absolutely immobilized behind the teacher's desk. Rather than from an an educational fervor, it was for very pragmatic, not to say interested, reasons that the first Jesuits decided to found their colleges around 1548. Not finding in the university world the convictions that he was looking for, Ignatius was virtually cornered into assuming the responsibility for the formation of many youths who wanted to join the ranks of the young Society of Jesus. First created for "Ours,"[2] the college would soon open out to all those who wanted a quality education. When Ignatius died in 1556, the colleges already counted in scores, and more important, the Society came to

---

[1] "College" here refers to the broader, European usage, including what would be called a high school in the United States.

[2] This use of the pronoun is a Jesuit "in-house" way of referring to all Jesuits.

recognize in them an instrument of the first order for the evangelization and humanistic culture of youth called to face the Reformation and the Renaissance. In 1773, when the Society was suppressed for nearly a half-century, there were more than nine hundred colleges to be closed. Today, in spite of every kind of difficulty, the network of colleges is still growing, especially in Africa and Eastern Europe.

In all these establishments, the individual Jesuit, as well as the individual non-Jesuit, is impregnated with the educational dynamism of the Spiritual Exercises, practiced annually in our times. So it is not surprising if, in a manner more spontaneous and intuitive than systematic and deliberate, the broad lines of the pedagogy of Ignatius's small opus should have begun to shape the system of education set forth in the colleges. In the beginning, the Jesuits entrusted themselves to the system that the first companions had known in Paris, the *modus parisiensis*. But gradually, from their experiences on different continents, through dealing with successes and setbacks, they elaborated a veritable manifesto of a "reformed" pedagogy, the *Ratio studiorum* of 1586 and 1591, with a final version appearing in 1599.

The Ratio Studiorum

Growing out of an analysis of school practices of the century, the *Ratio* elaborates the principles and the practices of a structure of studies strongly influenced by the pedagogy of the Spiritual Exercises. There was an attempt in 1832 to publish the 1599 text, but this revised *ratio* never enjoyed great success in the restored Society. Practically speaking, one must turn to December, 1986 to retrieve, in the famous *Characteristics of Jesuit Education*,[3] the successor to the *Ratio*, the principal pedagogical directions of the beginnings. These principles have been renewed in the light of contemporary educational needs, marked by an academic instruction strongly subject to certain rules and regulations, and widely inspired by many different cultures and ideologies.

Once more today, it is interesting to see how the *Ratio* constantly calls for

---

[3] Published by Jesuit Secondary Educational Association, Washington, D.C., 1986.

an anthropology unwilling to grant that a human being can reach the status of an adult in any area of growth, without the interventions of persons who have already arrived there. Simply speaking, no one matures or grows without the help of others. This axiom applies equally to teaching, understood as the transmission of knowledge, and to the training in practical knowledge and the rudiments of good manners. The *Ratio* of 1599, not yet familiar with the problems of educators, gave the absolute priority to teaching. This resulted in an almost total absence of free time for a process of initiation, that is, for the introduction of enduring and meaningful symbolic dimensions of life. Nonetheless, it is impossible to separate teaching, as transmission of knowledge, from that initiation into life that comprises all education.

In fact, every educator who enters an instructional establishment will agree that it is not in his power to initiate another into life as long as he himself is unable to come face to face with it. Can we possibly fail to be closely involved with the younger generation, who cannot pass through the period of initiation without encountering a good education? But then, how far can or should the educator go without going too far? Today especially, it is impossible to teach material in an antiseptic surrounding: that is, all course materials and all disciplines either attest to or contest the values that dominate modern society. Justice and injustice, solidarity and compassion, protection of the environment and the acceptance of those who are different: all these are so many values that the educator will never be able to avoid, if he wishes to examine the profound and the less superficial. It is impossible to be aloof or impartial; everything constitutes a problem. Can an instructor be satisfied to communicate any kind of knowledge in abstraction from the values which that knowledge always includes? Is there a message without a messenger, or more, can there be a messenger without a message? That this challenge goes well beyond the personal qualities of an educator is without question: attention and devotion will leave their positive traces in a student's education, but finally they will not touch the issue—that of initiating persons into life through teaching and experiment.

When asked what he expected from adults, one elder in the town of Purpan responded:

What I expect from adults, I would be tempted to say, is that they must be wise. I mean this: that they retain a certain kind of knowledge or skill and pass it on with good effect, that they be good examples, models of the kind of credible life that one would desire to follow. They would allow me to form myself by passing on to me their knowledge and experience, and helping me to acquire a general culture. But this is not all. I also expect from them a humane formation and that they be realistic incarnations of it. I don't remember now who it was who said, "Dear God, how good his religion must be to make him so good!"

That reaction corresponds exactly to the insights of "Characteristics of Ignatian Education" on the manner of being an educator at the close of the twentieth century. The *Spiritual Exercises* and the *Ratio* take as their point of departure that the maturation and the development of life are not exclusively within the order of knowledge, but count on experience. This experience, even as lived within family or society, remains emphatically personal. It is impossible to remake it or to repeat it as such: it will always be unique and new. With this position as a starting point, the Spiritual Exercises are offered above all as practice in the Spirit, and, in academic institutions, Ignatian education aims by preference at apprenticeship by means of active methods. In the spirit of the *Ratio*, the instructor does not prepare his magisterial course or his *lectio*, but rather, in a *prae-lectio*, prepares the students with exercises to be done. It is quite striking to ascertain how, in the Spiritual Exercises, the director must be satisfied to give a few indications to allow the retreatant to pray for herself the mysteries of the life of Christ. It is likewise interesting that, according to the *Ratio*, the master must content himself with what is essential to stimulate the personal activity of the student. This priority given to the exercise seeks to arouse in students the spirit of initiative, creativity, and responsibility for their own education. Normally, that activity should nourish in them the taste for study, for discovering and developing their capacities, and the desire to mature and to make progress. A celebrated phrase in the *Ratio* expresses this desire in a lapidary and pragmatic way: "It is not enough that the students become knowledgeable in their work. They should also be led to want to work and to want to be knowledgeable."

All this Ignatian pedagogy is penetrated by a dynamism based on an optimism, sustained in its turn by a faith in the work of the Creator and Savior, at work in every human being and in all of creation. It is that optimism, imbibed in the conviction that education accomplishes its important task in synergy with the design of God, who manifests himself in the passion for progress that the *Ratio* typifies. The human person will never be humane enough, human society will always have need to be more just, and, no matter what the system or how good the education, will experience the need for adjustment or reform. As with the book of the *Spiritual Exercises*, the *Ratio* abounds with intensive comparatives along with its appeals for progress: further, better, more, and especially the famous *magis* ("more," "further"). These adverbs mark so much of the discourse of Ignatian education that they risk becoming no more than slogans, like war cries traditionally flung out to enkindle failing courage.

Still, the true sense of the *magis* is first of all to exclude all passive acquisition, all complacency with any system of education, if there is such a thing, that favors inertia and sloth. Satisfaction with mechanical memorization and restriction to mnemotechnical procedures alone are attitudes incompatible with the *magis*, since they so easily impede the mobilization of the whole person. Such a whole person may no doubt have more work to do, but in the final analysis will be better educated. This does not mean that cleverness or erudition have no place in the dynamism of Ignatian education, but that they are part of a vital force that integrates imagination and physical powers, emotions and intuitions, understanding and memory.

This insistence on the *magis* has sometimes given the impression that the *Ratio* is elitist. In Ignatius's era, instruction, which was not yet obligatory, could be free of charge and addressed to those who had the capacity for it. In the colleges, members of the new strata of society could receive a competence that enabled them to contribute to their world. The purpose of research was indeed to form an elite, but only to render them able to serve the Church and the nation. In such a perspective, Ignatian education today will not be elitist, but will rather look to quality or, rather, to excellence, an excellence that may too quickly be identified with the highest levels of the academic establishment, and attested by brilliant examination scores. Without putting aside the search for scholarly success, excellence in furthering the *magis* means first the maximum development of the gifts and capacities with which each person is endowed. None of this is intended for egoistic profit, but for the deployment of gifts in the best possible service of others.

Education of the whole person, chosen for excellence: always it is the person, and the person as he truly is, with whom we must be concerned. Just as the Spiritual Exercises endeavor to touch human beings in their authenticity so that their encounter with the Lord might be genuine, the *Ratio* likewise envisages the student, not as one might wish him to be, in theory or in some idealistic dream, but for what he is here and now. The freedom that reigned in the colleges of the past enabled them to avoid instructing students beyond their strengths, and left open the possiblity of prolonging the studies of one student while another might leap forward from one new stage to another.

Highly sensitive to the needs of each one, Ignatian pedagogy considered the diversity of gifts as an enrichment and no way as grounds for unjust discrimination. In the Spiritual Exercises, Ignatius willingly accepted that thirty days might be too little for one person, and that two days of meditation might be excessive for another. In the same way, the *Ratio* of 1599 does not seem to recognize expelled or retarded students. Each could develop to the utmost his aptitudes and talents; once having reached the highest achievement, the student would move on, regardless of how many years had been foreseen for a complete *cursus*.

The Value of the Person

The practical impossibility of maintaining this respect for each one's rhythm within a highly personalized environment calls for a few observations. If the particular does not stand out now as it used to, the collective is all the more prominent. Modern society brings to educators a generation strongly exercised by acquisition of technology in all areas, by the mass media, anguished by an uncertain future, and disturbed by the loss of so many values and ideals. It would be an illusion to want this generation to be anything else: in the spirit of the *Ratio*, we must accept it for what it is at this moment, as something that inevitably challenges the habitual pedagogical approach.

On the other hand, the ease with which the *Ratio* welcomes diversity in education does not seem to be the dominant characteristic of our contemporary culture. Officially, the difference in relation to that which is considered normal should permit integration according to a structure of peaceful coexistence based on the ideal of reciprocity and the idea of tolerance. In fact, to some degree everywhere and in nearly all education, there is something like a refusal to tolerate that which departs from the norm and a rejection of differences, to which all the "-ism" words bear witness, racism being forever the most ignominious. Nevertheless, the realm of socio-political life is becoming increasingly planetary, and we are preparing the younger generations to live in countries that will be highly dependent on one another, to the point of becoming a global village. The *Ratio* tries to respect and to foster difference and to integrate it positively into a harmonious human community, without doubt in the image and likeness of the Trinity. On the other hand, it rejects the idea that everything which seems to be unconformed to fashion or good taste, everything that is strange or foreign, should encounter the discrimination or exclusion that cannot tolerate the least anomaly.

Each time we have highlighted the traits of Ignatian pedagogy, we have experienced the attention given to the person. In fact, throughout the centuries *cura personalis*—care for the person or the personality—has been the great attraction of Ignatian education. I say care for the person, and not for the individual, who hardly has any need of it, given the ascendancy of the individualism around us. At first sight, the Spiritual Exercises could give the impression of an individualistic spirituality: they urge the person to place himself before God, alone with the alone. More, they envelope the person within the "I": Christ was born for me, was crucified for me, and here I am with my life to live. In fact, Ignatius cast his lot with the belief that no one can take the place of another in the other's freedom, and that God, who calls each person by name, awaits a free personal response to his personal gift as Creator and Savior. But far from shutting the self up in splendid isolation, Ignatius is calling on us to take account of our personal responsibility in the history of good and evil. Ignatius lays bare the sad fact that, through all kinds of compromises and connivances, we participate in a death-dealing history. At the same time he also opens up the perspective of our active and personal solidarity with that other history which God, through Christ and in the Spirit, is in the process of writing with us in hope for the Kingdom.

If the Spiritual Exercises are at the root of the educational vision of the Jesuits, it is clear that this discovery of personhood and responsibility for solidarity with one's brothers and sisters, has had consequences in the educational institutions. Evident here is an allergy to mass education or group formation, in the conviction that personal growth will result from a personal relationship, experienced first between educator and student, then among the students themselves, at the very heart of the educational community. In these perspectives, one can be an educator only through personally interesting oneself, with all requisite respect and discretion, in the questions posed by each man and woman in their authentic personal development.

If *cura personalis* can be carried on in various cultural ways, it always supposes the conviction that the other needs freely given help to motivate him in passing from childhood to free and communal personhood. The Jesuits believed deeply in this *cura personalis*, sometimes to the point of abandoning preaching to crowds for the sake of person-to-person spiritual conversation. In the same way, the retreat intended for a large group has had to make room today for the kind made with personal accompaniment, even with the significant amount of animators that this demands. In the greater number of educational institutions, it is rather rare that there is sufficient personnel to measure up to this *cura personalis*, not to speak of constraints imposed by rules and schedules. But the *Ratio* was already calling on students to participate actively in their own education. "Children understand more easily that which is explained to them by their peers than by their professors." In stating this, it gives another way of taking up, in an active and responsible manner, a way of education difficult to travers without a *"cura personalis"* guaranteed by human and ultimately divine solidarity.

The Growth of Lay Collaboration

Here and there in the rules of the first colleges we find an allusion to cooperation of laypersons in *cura personalis*, one example being the old statues of the German College in Rome. But in general this role is reserved to the Jesuits, and facilitated by an almost obligatory boarding-school context. So today there are some who believe that the *Ratio* has had its day, since we cannot count on the physical presence of a Jesuit in each class, and since the students no longer live day after day within a Jesuit ambiance, merely assisted by the laity. Within such a perspective, the diminishment of Jesuit personnel and the corresponding increase of laypersons seems to be an unavoidable worst-case scenario. It has taken a certain amount of time for the Society of Jesus to discover that this assumption of authority—not of power—in Jesuit institutions is following the dictates of the Spirit at Vatican II. This optimism gets its life from the positive experience of Jesuits in many places around the world, namely, that of a growing kind of partnership. The establishments that had begun with the Jesuits and had been organized, developed and maintained mostly by them, now increasingly owe their dynamism, their oversight and their management to the participation of the laity. Should they so desire, these persons, engaged in an ever-growing number in making up the education community, can exercise their own proper vocation according to the characteristics of Jesuit education.

General Congregation 34 succinctly sums up the task of Jesuits in the near future: first, there is the service to be rendered by the Society to laypersons in order to facilitate their educative work. Secondly, there is the formation of a genuine partnership, which will give to laity and Jesuits together a way of mutual support in preparing for the future. Concretely, the Society's engagement in this promising adventure puts at the disposal of the partnership both what it is and what it has received: Ignatian spirituality, which respects the spirituality proper to each person and adapts itself to present needs, and the pedagogical wisdom acquired over four centuries of apostolic experience. More and more the ideal is being realized by which men and women engaged in a common work exercise genuine co-responsibility. The general congregation concludes its position statement in this way: collaboration with the laity is at once a constitutive element of our way of proceeding and a grace calling for personal, communitarian, and institutional renewal. It invites us to the service of the ministry of the laity, to a partnership with them in mission, and to an openness to creative forms of collaboration in the future. The Spirit appeals to us as "men for and with others" to share with laymen and laywomen what we believe, what we are, and what we have, in a creative companionship for "the help of souls and for the greater glory of God."

I would like here to express my deep gratitude for everything that has already been realized from these perspectives in the establishments that all of our teachers represent. With all the suspicions and criticisms around the role that an educator must play, in spite of the rather unpleasant decline in its social status, its credibility, and sometimes even its usefulness, it remains true that, as a sixteenth-century Jesuit affirmed, *puerilis institutio est mundi renovatio*: the education of youth means the reconstruction of the world. And no one can snatch that privilege from you.

Educating for the Future

To this point, we have explored rather the pedagogical style in its capacity (however old its origins), to challenge us today. This style has given birth to a whole series of practices which look to the past, the present and the future of the pedagogical adventure.

Ignatian pedagogy integrates the past by the practice of evaluation, well known in the Spiritual Exercises and retrieved for the Ignatian educational project. Rather than abstracting from history and condemning to oblivion experiences already undergone, Ignatius proposes rather a permanent kind of recapture, a continuous rereading of the road already traveled. The rapid rate of progress in the world creates the clear risk of leaping from one novelty to another, from one recycling session to another, with the secret desire to make a *tabula rasa* of the past and thus start out at ground zero.

As a matter of fact, the classic examen proposed by Ignatius in the Spiritual Exercises looks to the future as well. For, in drawing profit from rereading and reviewing their experiences as educators, persons may discover themselves ready for a new departure seen in a new light, for capturing anew their responsibilities by correcting a trajectory, changing a direction, or abandoning a dead-end street. Every educational institution recognizes that evaluation is an indispensable factor in making progress. The *Ratio*, which has never forgotten the personal dimension of the educational enterprise, defends the importance of regular self-evaluation. This is not to establish a rigid routine or to favor a narcissistic contentment, but rather to help an institution from time to time to undergo a sifting process. By this process it might escape routine illusions that can easily dehumanize an educational practice so that it no longer confronts reality or sustains future shock.

In relation to the present, Ignatian pedagogy believes in the value of repetition. But, in spite of Ignatius's invitation in the Spiritual Exercises to practice repetitions, it would be inaccurate to call his pedagogy repetitive, certainly not the pedagogy of repetition in the modern sense of the term. Educators are not encouraged to repeat themselves, but—according to the etymology of the word—to go searching anew with students for that which should be appropriated. They should strip off the accidental, leading students to discover in a new light many other aspects of the same reality and thus to extract the kernel lying within the husk. In this way, repetition gives access to *multum* in the course of passing through *multa*, by continuous examination, varied clarifications, and different explanations. For Ignatius says that it is not the acquisition of encyclopedic knowledge of many things that will replenish and satisfy the person, but rather the deep interior feeling for and relishing of things. It is by returning in a vital and dynamic way to the material that there takes place a sort of progressive decantation of the essentials, thus permitting one to make them one's own and to draw enrichment and humane growth from them. It is true that the use of instruments like the calculator and the micrometer during one's apprenticeship will diminish the possible recourse to memory and thus a weakening of it. It is up to teachers to decide whether or not to multiply exercises that reinforce the memory. But this problem, real as it is, does not affect the importance accorded by Ignatian pedagogy to this direct return to the present matter so that the person might make it his own.

Finally, the Spiritual Exercises and the *Ratio* enable advancement according to a pedagogy that progresses methodically through an ordered and coherent study process. This was the secret of the sixteenth-century colleges. For if the university at that time already had a tried and true organization, the secondary cycle had become fossilized. The Jesuit college introduced into it an articulate system looking to a Christian humanism, first of all literary, but quickly opening out to the sciences as well.

However, this perspective on the future penetrates with a certain tension into the very heart of Ignatian pedagogy. On the one hand, in a concern for effectiveness, everything is done to shun the vague and the hazy, and there is a constant striving for a sense of direction. There is a fastening onto precise and progressive objectives, a painstaking marking out of the route to follow by means of programs and schedules, and yet a desire to avoid imposing a yoke on creativity. But along with this, Ignatian pedagogy believes profoundly in the exercise of freedom, especially in discerning what is to be done. This supposes openness rather than certitude, a groping in the unknown, rather than the execution of a program with assured results.

This tension is evident already in the Spiritual Exercises, where the same Ignatius who opens out vast perspectives of the future calls for detailed attention to minutiae that borders on obsession. As a prolongation of the master, Jesuit tradition maintains this tension in education between a vision of the future and the daily management so indispensable to an educational institution. It has been fittingly said,

Besides the appeal to the broad picture, there must also be a certain rigor for daily order and respect for details. We cannot help to form a person by beautiful words, but without such discourse he will not gain the desire to make himself human. He will not be formed by discipline alone, but without discipline all he can do is dream.

All education demands, therefore, the perspective of vast horizons as well as detailed prescriptions.

Conclusion

At the beginning of the seventeenth century, an anonymous Jesuit was so amazed at this tension that he saw in it a participation in the mystery of the Incarnation, in which the One who is always greater descends into our shabby and banal daily order to accomplish our complete education. "To be open to the widest horizons, but to keep oneself on the exact course, this is something divine." Such is the meaning of education in the spirit of Ignatius.